D0469265

Global Giant

WITHDRAWN
UTSA Libraries

WITHDRAWN
UTSA Libraries

GLOBAL GIANT

IS CHINA CHANGING THE RULES OF THE GAME?

Edited by
EVA PAUS, PENELOPE B. PRIME,
AND JON WESTERN

GLOBAL GIANT

Copyright © Eva Paus, Penelope B. Prime, and Jon Western, 2009.

All rights reserved.

First published in 2009 by
PALGRAVE MACMILLAN®
in the United States—a division of St. Martin's Press LLC,
175 Fifth Avenue, New York, NY 10010.

Where this book is distributed in the UK, Europe and the rest of the
world, this is by Palgrave Macmillan, a division of Macmillan Publishers
Limited, registered in England, company number 785998, of Houndmills,
Basingstoke, Hampshire RG21 6XS.

Palgrave Macmillan is the global academic imprint of the above companies
and has companies and representatives throughout the world.

Palgrave® and Macmillan® are registered trademarks in the United States,
the United Kingdom, Europe and other countries.

ISBN: 978–0–230–61589–2 (paperback)
ISBN: 978–0–230–61588–5 (hardcover)

Library of Congress Cataloging-in-Publication Data

Global giants : is China changing the rules of the game? /
edited by Eva Paus, Jon Western, Penelope Prime.
  p. cm.
Includes bibliographical references and index.
ISBN 978–0–230–61588–5—ISBN 978–0–230–61589–2
  1. China—Economic conditions—2000– 2. China—Foreign economic
relations. 3. Globalization—China. I. Paus, Eva. II. Western, Jon W., 1963–
III. Prime, Penelope B.

HC427.95.G555 2009
330.951—dc22   2008050925

A catalogue record of the book is available from the British Library.

Design by Newgen Imaging Systems (P) Ltd., Chennai, India.

First edition: June 2009

10 9 8 7 6 5 4 3 2 1

Printed in the United States of America.

Library
University of Texas
at San Antonio

Contents

Figures

Tables

Acknowledgments

In editing this book we have incurred many debts, foremost to the contributors for their cooperation and willingness to revise their manuscripts whenever needed. Many of the contributions are based on presentations at the conference "The Rise of China," at Mount Holyoke College in March 2008. The conference was hosted by the Dorothy R. and Norman E. McCulloch Center for Global Initiatives. Our thanks go to the New York Times Knowledge Network for cosponsoring the conference. We are particularly indebted to Mary E. Tuttle, '37, whose endowed Mary E. Tuttle Colloquium Fund provided important financial support for the conference.

Jean Costello's superb assistance in copyediting this book was indispensable, and Jennifer Medina provided valuable assistance throughout the whole process.

Eva Paus, Penelope B. Prime, Jon Western
South Hadley, November 2008

Contributors

Sheena Chestnut is a doctoral candidate in the Government Department at Harvard University.

Barbara Hogenboom is Associate Professor of Political Science at the Center for Latin American Research and Documentation, Amsterdam, Netherlands.

Alastair Iain Johnston is the Governor James Albert Noe and Linda Noe Laine Professor of China in World Affairs, Government Department at Harvard University.

Raphael Kaplinsky is Professor of International Development at the Open University, United Kingdom.

Michael T. Klare is Five College Professor of Peace and World Security Studies at Hampshire College.

Cheng Li is a Senior Fellow, Brookings Institution, and William R. Kenan Professor of Government at Hamilton College.

Jonathan Lipman is the Felicia Gressitt Bock Professor of Asian Studies and Professor of History at Mount Holyoke College.

Eva Paus is Professor of Economics and the Carol Hoffmann Collins Director of the Dorothy R. and Norman E. McCulloch Center for Global Initiatives at Mount Holyoke College.

Penelope B. Prime is Professor of Economics, Stetson School of Business and Economics at Mercer University and Director of the China Research Center, Atlanta.

Zhang Ruizhuang is a Professor of International Relations and Dean of the Institute of International Relations at Nankai University, China.

Susan L. Shirk is Ho Miu Lam Professor of China and Pacific Relations at the School of International Relations and Pacific Studies and Director of the University of California Institute on Global Conflict and Cooperation at the University of California, San Diego.

Kelly Sims Gallagher is Director of the Energy Technology Innovation Policy research group, Belfer Center for Science and International Affairs, at Harvard University.

Jon Western is Five College Associate Professor of International Relations at Mount Holyoke College.

Christine Wong is a Senior Research Fellow in Contemporary China Studies and Chair of China Departmental Committee, School of Interdisciplinary Area Studies and Said Business School at Oxford University, United Kingdom.

Shahid Yusuf is an Economic Advisor, Development Economics Research Group at the World Bank.

Part 1

Context and Connections

Chapter 1

China Rising: A Global Transformation?

Eva Paus, Penelope B. Prime, and Jon Western

China is rising. There seems to be little disagreement about this. With economic growth rates hovering around 10 percent per year for the past 30 years, an enormous demand for global resources, and an increasingly assertive foreign policy, China seems poised to become a major power in the twenty-first century. It is now common to hear politicians, pundits, and academics proclaiming that China will eventually become a peer rival to the United States. But how do we make sense of China's rise—what does it really mean for China and for the world? Will China emerge within the existing global order, will it play by the existing rules and succeed? Or will China lead an "irresistible shift of global power to the east?" (Mahbubani 2008a) Does China's rise reflect an impending "great transformation" that will lead to the articulation of alternative development and global governance models?

This book brings together about a dozen scholars and practitioners from multiple academic disciplines and policy perspectives to address these questions and to explore the internal and global implications of China's dramatic economic expansion. It is divided into three sections that explore the following issues: (1) how China's rapid growth has engendered growing social, environmental, and political challenges in China; (2) how the depth and breadth of China's economic competitiveness is challenging the possibilities for economic and political advancement for the rest of the developing world; and (3) how China's international reemergence is likely to change global power dynamics—especially vis-à-vis the United States.

The domestic and global implications of China's economic success will be influenced by how policymakers—in China, the United States, and elsewhere—respond to the challenges in all three areas. And the effectiveness of the policies will, in turn, partly be shaped by policymakers' understanding of the intrinsic interrelations among the internal and external challenges.

The first section of the book addresses the domestic sustainability of China's development. Energy and water needs combined with extensive environmental damage has raised some doubts about China's ability to continue growing at the speed that it has since reforms began in the late 1970s. Even if the growth rate slows, China's leaders are under tremendous pressure to find ways for development to continue in more efficient and less toxic ways. At the same time, the institutional arrangements that have evolved between the central and local governments are insufficient in terms of finances and incentives to implement and enforce policy directives from the top. This leaves the Chinese political elite in a position of having to redesign debate within the Communist Party leadership and find ways to respond to the demands of the general population. Whereas rapid growth was enough for political legitimacy to date, people now expect redistribution to those left out of the spoils of growth, as well as adequate provision of social goods and services.

These daunting challenges could divert China's attention away from global participation for a period of time. Or they could push China to seek cooperation with other powers in order to solve some of these problems. In any case, China's resource needs, especially with respect to energy, have increased global demand significantly. They have informed China's foreign policy and foreign investment strategy, especially in developing countries, and they are bringing the country in direct competition with other powers over access to scarce natural resources.

Huge inflows of foreign direct investment and strategic development policies have made China the manufacturing powerhouse of the world, producing both cheap, labor-intensive products such as toys and clothing, and more technologically sophisticated products such as computers and cars. China's export profile is completely atypical for a country at that level of per capita income. Due to the size of its economy and labor force, China's entry into the international market has accelerated considerably the process of globalized production that started in the early 1970s, and China's competitiveness across a broad spectrum of skill-intensive production is leading to a profound change in the global geography of production and trade.

The second section of the book focuses on how the rest of the developing world must now compete with China, both in terms of China's demands for resources and its competition in domestic and third markets. China's size, low costs, and range of production capabilities increases the urgency for other countries to carve out niches further up the value chain that can serve as a basis for sustained growth and development. At the same time, China's development strategy holds out valuable lessons for other developing countries on how to achieve such a goal. Since the 1980s, most developing country governments in Africa and Latin America have adopted free market policies, the so-called Washington Consensus, with dismal results in terms of sustained growth and development. China, in contrast, has pursued a strategy where the government played a critical role—in conjunction with the emerging private sector—in advancing national industry and technological capabilities. Developing countries would be well advised to learn from this strategy to address the challenges posed by China's economic rise. If China's growth slows, for whichever reason, the degree of urgency for policy action in developing countries declines. But the need for such policies does not fundamentally change.

Along with engendering intense economic competition, China's entrance onto the global scene has created a potential for political competition. The major players, and in particular the United States, will have to adjust to new geostrategic roles that China may play. China's rise has played well domestically, creating renewed patriotism that supports the leadership's legitimacy. However, national self-confidence also means that China cannot be seen as being weak in the eyes of its people. Historical humiliation by foreigners has now been overcome, and there is no going back. Hence, there is a delicate interaction between China's foreign relations and its domestic political situation.

To place the rise of China into perspective, then, it is crucial to understand the political and economic dimensions, and their interconnectedness. The cross-disciplinary approach that emerges from the contributions in this volume is a first step beyond seeing each of these three spheres separately. While the results of China's success and challenges as they relate to other developing countries and the current power brokers may have been unintentional, they are real nonetheless, and the rest of the world is now in the process of figuring out their respective adjustments.

China's Domestic Challenges

China's Economic Reforms and Opening

China's transition from a planned to a market-oriented economy has been successful by many measures. Economic growth rates have averaged around 9 percent for many years. Gross domestic product per person was US$525 in 1980; by 2007 it had increased almost tenfold, to US$5046 (see figure 1.1). Looking at total Gross Domestic Product (GDP) measured in purchasing power parity, in 2006 China was the second largest economy in the world at US$10 trillion, behind the United States with US$13 trillion. The third largest economy was India at US$4 trillion. Serious challenges lie ahead, to be sure, but impressive growth and increases in household income have changed people's lives in dramatic ways. China's economic success has placed it on the world stage in a way that was not possible, or desired, under the leadership of Mao Zedong.

In 1978 China was a poor, developing country. Its inefficient and closed economic system resulted in low growth, minimal consumption, and backward science and technology, placing China in the bottom ranks of development in the region as well as globally. This had not been Mao's dream. The Chinese socialist system was supposed to have surpassed both the Western capitalist countries and its socialist rival, the Soviet Union (Riskin 1987). The Mao-led experiments to skip stages of production by pushing the agrarian countryside into industry and by creating a new society and a "new man" were to propel China to the forefront of the world in a short time.

A central element of Mao's approach to development was national and regional self-sufficiency. Mao's view of political economy and development emphasized self-sufficiency while critiquing the notion of comparative advantage both in capitalist economies and the Soviet Union. The goal was to build a "comprehensive and independent industrial system," which led to policies such as "grow grain everywhere" whether or not the climate and geography were appropriate (Eckstein 1977). This approach was implemented on multiple levels and across sectors, resulting in losses in

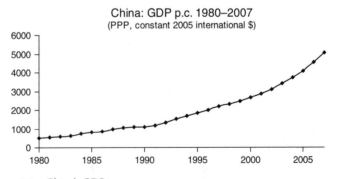

China: GDP p.c. 1980–2007
(PPP, constant 2005 international $)

Figure 1.1 China's GDP p.c.

Source: World Bank. World Development Indicators online. Accessed October 1, 2008.

output due to poor efficiency. Supporting this approach was an imposed immobility of labor and capital across geographic areas via the household registration and central planning systems. Each province, county, and city was to develop with the resources they had, and in a comprehensive way. Some of the leaders who had worked with Mao through the revolution and the construction of socialism over decades came to believe that a new path was needed.

When Mao died in 1976, an opportunity for change opened (Shirk 1993). As under the planned system, however, politics has defined the limits of economic change. Each stage of reform has seen system and policy changes combined with expanding ideological boundaries. Today China is officially a "socialist market economy," which is also sometimes described as having Chinese characteristics. This terminology supports the legitimacy and leadership of the Chinese Communist Party (CCP). Former President Jiang Zeming's theory of the "Three Represents," for example, led the ideological way to recognition of the right to private property (Prime 2004). The three factors referred to are the "advanced production forces," "advanced culture," and the "overwhelming majority of the people" (*China Daily* 2004). This theory in essence acknowledged that there are many groups in society, such as entrepreneurs, that contribute to China's socialist progress, rather than just Mao's original "progressive" groups of workers, peasants, and soldiers.

The process of reform that evolved over the next 30 years was one of political compromise and experimentation due to a combination of bottom-up pressure and top-down policy initiatives (Naughton 1996). The areas that needed change were initially identified as the "Four Modernizations," covering agriculture, industry, technology, and defense. Early on the collectivized agricultural system was decentralized to the household level, where families could contract to farm small plots of land in return for selling a portion of the output to the state at fixed prices (Zweig 1997). Any surplus could be used by the family or sold on the market. This seemingly simple change caused agricultural output to jump, and helped relieve some of the worst poverty and hunger resulting from the stagnating economy in the 1970s. It also gave political support to the reforms and leaders in charge.

Self-reliance was replaced by the now famous "opening policy" (Lardy 1992). Under Mao the goal of self-sufficiency combined with suspicion of the international, capitalist economy meant that Chinese enterprises did not participate in international trade or investment. Allowing foreign investment into China was controversial, to say the least. To get around this ideological constraint, the initial opening reforms created four Special Economic Zones (SEZs) in southern China near the border with Hong

Kong and Macao that built infrastructure and offered tax and other incentives for foreign firms to invest and export. These zones had their own borders, however, with special permission needed to enter and exit, and so were controlled to help mollify those who were against them. The zones also required most or all of the output to be exported, thus protecting domestic industry.

Hong Kong firms flocked to these zones to manufacture with vastly cheaper labor. Companies from other parts of the world soon followed suit. This region of China became the core of the global supply chain taking advantage of lower costs for manufacturing, benefiting multinationals from developed economies as well as some developing countries whose exports to China increased (Yusuf, this volume). Success in the zones led to a furthering of the opening policies in the mid-1980s when foreign investment was allowed in 14 cities along the coast. This expanded opening increased the investment options for multinationals, and also opened the China market for small and medium-sized foreign companies as well.

An important piece of China's opening was joining global institutions. Although China had been under the United Nations' umbrella for quite some time, it was only in 1980 that it became a member of the World Bank and the International Monetary Fund (IMF). To join the IMF and World Bank, the Chinese leadership had to agree to work with these institutions in terms of providing information, allowing research and project missions to visit on a regular basis, and to provide the required capital contribution. In return, China could take advantage of low cost loans, technical expertise, and perhaps most importantly, be a normal participating member of these global institutions.

In the mid-1980s some leaders in China decided to also consider joining the General Agreement on Trade and Tariffs (GATT), which later became the World Trade Organization (WTO) (Prime 2002). The idea of joining an international trade organization was controversial within China, and especially within the Chinese Communist Party and bureaucracy. In order to join, China needed to create or alter many domestic regulations, laws, and institutions to match international standards, and to open to international competition sectors that never had to compete before (Lardy 2002). In essence, China needed to establish the foundations of a market economy as defined by outsiders.

The existing members of GATT were also wary. For small, developing countries to join the process is fairly straightforward. For a country as large and complex as China, despite the obvious poverty of many of its people, joining meant negotiating its status since it neither fit the "developing" or the "developed" country category. Over time China's economic system changed in significant ways toward a market-oriented economy, and its leaders also worked diligently to meet the legal and regulatory requirements. Both within and outside of China, arguments underscoring the benefits of having China inside the global trading system also gained ground. After a decade and a half, China finally became a member of WTO in late 2001.

China's Challenges in the Next Phase of Development

As China enters its fourth decade of growth and reform, the country faces many serious challenges. Three of these are addressed in this volume: first, growing energy needs in the face of a deteriorating environment; second, growing inequalities; and third, finding new ways for the leadership to rule. How all three of these challenges are dealt with will shape China's future development path, as well as influence how China functions in the global arena.

China's economy has grown rapidly. Partly because of its large population and expanse of geography, this growth appears even more impressive than it would otherwise. But the size factor also makes sustainable growth much more difficult. The energy and environmental consequences of China's growth are enormous, for both China and the rest of the world. Kelly Gallagher's chapter in this book analyzes these connections and trade-offs.

China's growth path to date has been highly energy intensive. In recent years China's energy use has increased over 70 percent every five years (Gallagher, this volume). As China is far from self-sufficient in energy, China's addition to global demand has increased commodity prices (Klare, this volume), which is problematic for all countries, but especially for those that are less developed and also resource dependent. Energy, of course, is essential to growth, but China's energy use, especially coal, has added to environmental pressures. Various estimates of environmental damage take away anywhere from 2 to 10 percent off the growth rates recorded (Pomfret 2008). Looked at this way, China's economic growth does not look so glorious.

Environment problems are not restricted to either the cities or the countryside, but are widespread. However, rural households and those in small towns may be especially vulnerable. Often the problems are not fully recognized until many local people become ill. Closing the factories or other facilities that are causing the pollution leads to loss of jobs, again hurting the very same households that are suffering from the effects of the pollution. Solving these dilemmas is the task of local government officials, who have impossible choices to make (Wong, this volume). Of course, they are also in charge of enforcing environmental policies decided at the national level, but if these get in the way of other goals, such as employment, they may not be heeded. At the level of laws and regulations, China has made progress in environmental protection, but enforcement is systemically very weak (Gallagher, this volume).

Along with the environment-energy trade-off, a second salient challenge facing China today is the distribution of the benefits of reforms, which has become increasingly unequal. The average Gini coefficient for Asia is 38.6, while it is 46.9 in China (UNDP 2007).[1] China's inequality is now even greater than that of the United States, whose Gini coefficient is 40.8. These inequalities stand in stark contrast to the much more equal distribution of income and wealth in the former, Mao-led socialist system, and they have ideological and political ramifications for China's leaders.

Hu Jintao's current national strategy of balanced development and a harmonious society is designed to address these inequalities and political backlash (Wong, this volume). Fundamentally, the strategy means leaving the blind pursuit of growth in favor of investing resources into long-term payoffs such as a cleaner environment, and to reverse the severe urban bias that has dominated economic change since the initial agricultural reforms ran their course by the mid-1980s.

Can China reverse the trends in inequality? Wong's answer is "perhaps"—if local governments are given the ability to finance, and therefore, deliver needed services. But, for the most part, they do not have this ability now. Passing well thought out regulations, laws, and policies at the national level is one thing; creating the incentives and providing the resources to implement and enforce these decisions at the local level is quite another. Fiscal reforms in China have worked out in a way that local governments are charged with creating jobs and providing services to degrees that far exceed their ability to raise tax revenue. The transfers that the central government has provided to help fill the revenue gaps have been far too small. Hence, by many accounts, education and social services at local levels have all but collapsed, as has the center's ability to entice local governments to enforce the policies they wish to see implemented.

These issues are interrelated with a third challenge for China's sustainable growth—how to modernize the political system to maintain power while also achieving national goals. Unrest in China is widespread. Inequalities and environmental worries are two key factors behind the unrest; they both fuel a street-level sense that there is a lack of fairness. The provision of local services and the ability of government officials to respond humanely and effectively to challenges that arise within communities will be essential for the long-run cohesiveness of Chinese society. Change has occurred very quickly, leaving many without a decent livelihood or a sense of where they or the country is heading. China's next stage of development would benefit from a shift from a government whose legitimacy is based on rapid growth to one that responds to citizens' needs.

There is no consensus on how to view these challenges. Institution building has come late in the reform process for China. A relative optimistic view sees these institutions as preserving economic development for society as a whole by building internal incentives to prevent corruption from taking the spoils (Yang 2006). Rather than focus on what the next stage of reform in China should look like, some analysts are concerned about stagnation instead, or as Pei (2006) calls it, a "trapped transition." Others see virtual collapse before needed changes will be made, since those changes would undermine the current CCP power base and coveted privileges (Chang 2001). At a very minimum, China will need to learn how to deal with market downturns, as uninterrupted growth is highly unlikely now that the economy is fundamentally a market system.

Policy Choices

To solve these looming problems the relationship between the government and its citizens must change. Since a Western-style democracy does not exist and may not be a solution for China, the CCP is searching for its own way to reach the people in a decentralized and marketized context. China's leaders are counting on reforming the political process within the party, and focusing on rebalancing resources and priorities via the harmonious society agenda in order to maintain future growth and power (Li, this volume). A simple but insufficient step is to develop pride for China as a culture and a nation. More meaningful, Li argues, is the progression of debate within the CCP that reveals the development of a type of inner-party democracy. The party will build a system of much needed checks and balances, which will both be more stable and serve a wider set of needs.

China has figured out how to grow by mobilizing savings and investment, and has unleashed the private sector to help the process by creating competition where improved efficiency will be generated automatically. The next stage of progress, however, requires dealing with challenges of externalities and inequalities of the market system, such as environmental protection, provision of healthcare and education across society, and the well-being of the growing proportion of the elderly. Some analysts believe that these problems are serious enough that they could restrict China's role in the international arena, since they will require much attention and resources (Pomfret 2008). Shirk (this volume) argues that these domestic challenges in the face of a fragile political system could lead to serious international confrontation because the leadership will do whatever it takes to maintain power at home. The central leadership needs to appear willing and capable of standing up to the United States, for example. Otherwise a nationalistic populace, fueled by many grievances of its own, could rise up and challenge the status quo.

At least the Chinese government has access to resources. With its foreign exchange holdings alone, it could finance many aspects of social development (Feldstein 2008). The central government has also successfully captured a rising share of the tax revenue collected, which could be given back to localities or spent to solve these challenges (Wong, this volume). Savings is also very high in China. However, as a result, overall consumption as a share of GDP is unusually low, and has even fallen. Reversing this trend would be a helpful step in redressing some of the inequalities as well as refocusing policy attention on consumption rather than production.

The core of the current leadership's Harmonious Society and Balanced Development platform is to refocus China's resources toward those who are relatively poor and to improve the social welfare net generally. The strategy also targets improving energy efficiency, investing in the environment, and developing domestic innovation capabilities. There is no question that China's leadership faces immense domestic challenges, but to its credit, it is well aware of China's needs and is willing to shift resources to achieve sustainable development.

The Implications of the Rise of China for Developing Countries

The growth of China's economy and the globalization of the world economy have been closely interrelated, reinforcing and changing each other in profound ways. The concurrence of the dramatic decline in shipping costs with the development of containerization more than 30 years ago, the continuous fall of tariff levels in successive GATT negotiation rounds, and the liberalization of foreign trade and investment regimes in many developing countries was the genesis of a new international division of labor. Transnational corporations (TNCs) increasingly produced different parts of the value chain in different countries around the globe, wherever local production conditions best matched TNCs' global profit strategy. With globalized production expanding, it was little wonder that TNCs flocked to China, when economic reforms got under way in the 1980s, to take advantage of very low labor costs and produce an array of manufactured goods—mainly assembled from imported inputs—and then export them, mostly to developed countries.

The rapid growth of foreign direct investment (FDI) inflows and the inextricably linked rise in exports and imports have contributed significantly to China's impressive growth. At the same time, China's economic growth has been having a profound impact on the global economy. The sheer size of China's labor market and the speed of its growing participation in international markets have far-reaching consequences for the global geography of production, trade, and economic well-being in the twenty-first century. Between 2000 and 2006, China's share in world FDI inflows increased from 2.9 percent to 9.6 percent, in world merchandise imports from 3.3 percent to 5.9 percent, and in world merchandise exports from 6.0 percent to 9.8 percent (UNCTAD 2007, IMF 2007). The data in table 1.1 show the remarkable increase in China's trade with major areas of the world.

China's entry into the international economy has led to a rapid expansion of the global labor force. The global impact of this "great doubling"—in the words of Richard Freeman (2007)—is particularly far-reaching. China, along with the other emerging economies—most notably India and Eastern Europe—all have highly skilled/educated workers. Some argue that we are at the beginning of another "great transformation," with the expansion of global capitalism breaking down the current social order, a process akin to the rise of market economies and nation states destroying the preexisting

Table 1.1 China's importance in world trade

	Exports to China as Share of Area's Total Exports		Imports from China as Share of Area's Total Imports	
	2000	2006	2000	2006
Industrialized Countries	1.9	3.8	5.4	9.5
European Union	1	1.8	2.6	5.1
United States	2.1	5.3	8.6	15.9
Canada	0.9	1.7	3.3	8.7
Japan	6.3	14.3	14.5	20.5
Developing Countries	5.7	8.6	7.2	10.3
Africa	2.8	7.9	3.3	9.2
Asia	8.7	4.1	11.2	12.9
Europe	2.3	2.6	2.2	6.0
Middle East	3.5	6.0	3.4	8.1
Western Hemisphere	1.0	3.7	2.0	8.0

Source: Author's calculations based on IMF (2007).

social system in the nineteenth and early twentieth century (Standing 2007). But where Polanyi's *Great Transformation* (1944) was about the development of a national capitalist labor market, the current transformation is about the development of an international capitalist labor market. Workers across the world compete with each other much more directly and intensely, except for those working in nontraded goods and services. Mobile capital in search of regions and countries with the best production costs— wherever they may be—is undermining the ability of governments in developed countries to maintain the social contract that emerged after World War II.

China is a driving force in this globalization process, because of the size of its labor force and, equally importantly, because of the range of products in which it is competitive. Traditionally, developing countries with an abundance of unskilled labor tend to have a comparative advantage in low tech products, while developed countries with an abundance of skilled labor and innovation potential tend to have a comparative advantage in high tech products. Indeed, in a sense, the very process of economic development is about moving up the value chain—developing comparative advantages in medium-tech and eventually high tech products.

China defies the traditional expectations. Predictably, since the opening of its economy in the 1980s China has had a comparative advantage in low tech goods as demonstrated by the composition of its exports. But between 2000 and 2006, it also developed a comparative advantage in high tech goods, especially electronics, an unparalleled achievement for a country of China's income level. When the first Chinese astronaut stepped into space in September 2008, it was a glowing success for China's ambitious space program, following in the footsteps of the United States and Russia.

For developed and developing countries alike, the key question is what China's high economic growth and broad competitiveness mean for the well-being of the majority of their people. In the literature the question is often framed differently for the two sets of countries. In developed countries, the main question is whether and how the globalization of the labor market in general and China's production and export prowess in particular is undermining the viability of the welfare state of the post–World War II era. Analysts discuss whether strategic efforts to move production and employment up the value chain—combined with expanded transitional income support for displaced workers—will be able to ensure social peace and economic well-being for most workers in developed countries.[2]

For developing countries, on the other hand, the main question is how China's rise in the international economy affects their ability to industrialize and find a basis for sustained economic growth. The academic literature is only starting to address this question, though the answer affects the well-being of a much larger number of people than in developed countries. In this volume, three authors investigate the impact of China on the development prospects of developing countries. They each focus on a different developing area: Raphael Kaplinsky on Africa, Barbara Hogenboom on Latin America, and Shahid Yusuf on Asia, particularly Thailand and Malaysia. The countries in each region are, of course, not a homogeneous group. Nonetheless, countries within each region tend to be integrated into the global economy in similar ways. Many countries in South America and Sub-Saharan Africa are rich in natural resources, which dominate their exports. Asian countries, on the other hand, are generally natural resource poor and tend to be more integrated into global or regional production chains of transnational corporations. Differences in the nature of global integration are an important factor in how China impacts the economic prospects of developing countries.

Generally speaking, China's economic rise affects developing countries in three main ways: first, through economic channels, primarily trade and FDI; second, through the demonstration effect of its development model that is rather different from the free market policies pursued by many developing countries since the 1980s; and third, through the political counterweight it might offer to developing countries in their bilateral relations with developed countries, especially the United States, or in multilateral institutions.

China's Trade and Developing Countries: Commodity Price Boom and Competitive Pressures in Domestic and Third Markets

To sustain its high economic growth, China has imported large quantities of natural resources, from oil to copper to aluminum to soy beans. China's growing demand has been a driving force behind the rise in natural resource prices in recent years, in absolute terms, and relative to manufactured products. Natural resource rich countries in Latin America and Africa have benefited greatly as their foreign exchange earnings have skyrocketed. In Latin America, the primary beneficiaries are Argentina, Brazil, Chile, Peru, Uruguay (e.g., Hogenboom, this volume; Paus 2009. In Sub-Saharan Africa the benefits of rising commodity prices are concentrated in only a few countries: five countries are responsible for 90 percent of fuel exports and 12 countries for 90 percent of metals and minerals exports (Kaplinsky, this volume).

China's quest for natural resources has also been a key factor in the country's foreign direct investment projects in South America and

Sub-Saharan Africa and in its foreign policy toward developing countries (e.g., Lunding 2006). With the goal of securing access to energy supplies and other critical raw materials, Chinese companies have announced and made huge investments in resource rich developing countries in recent years, irrespective of human rights abuses by the host country government (e.g., Sudan), political turmoil in the host country (e.g., the Republic of Congo), or the host country's antagonistic relations with the United States (e.g., Venezuela).

Another group of countries that has benefited from increased exports to China are Asian countries like Thailand and Malaysia. Their production is integrated into TNCs' regional production chains, and as these TNCs have expanded assembly production in China, they have increased the production of parts in Thailand and Malaysia and subsequent parts exports to China, especially in electronics (Yusuf, this volume).

Not all developing countries have benefited from increased exports to China. But they have all been affected by the increased competitive pressures from Chinese exports, in their domestic markets and, for some countries, in third markets as well. China's ability to compete in products across the spectrum of technology intensity is reflected in the analysis of the three regions. Kaplinsky underscores China's ability to out-compete Sub-Saharan African countries in clothing exports to third markets.[3] Hogenboom highlights how Mexico has been particularly hard hit by China's exports in its own market as well as to the United States, Mexico's principal export market.[4] And Yusuf, looking ahead, argues that Malaysia and Thailand will cease to be competitive in the production of standardized electronic parts, as China is moving aggressively toward becoming competitive in the production of inputs for the electronics industry.

China's Economic Development Strategy: An Alternative to the Washington Consensus

Since the seminal works by Prebish (1950) and Singer (1950), development economists have argued that industrialization holds the key to development, as the prices of natural resources tend to fall relative to those of manufactured goods, and manufacturing generates greater productivity growth.[5] Kaplinsky provides a succinct summary of the theoretical arguments for the secular decline in the relative prices, the terms of trade (TOT), of natural resources.

There is widespread agreement now that the commodity price boom will continue into the medium term future, at least for another 10 years (e.g., Yusuf, this volume). Yet nobody is advocating, in this book or elsewhere, that industrialization—broadly defined—is no longer necessary for development. The potential knowledge and productivity spillovers from industrialization are simply too high.

Rather, the breadth of China's competitiveness and the growing competitive pressures of Chinese exports in developing countries' home markets and in third markets increase the urgency for these countries to carve out niches of competitiveness up the value chain. China's remarkable success in acquiring competitiveness across a broad range of products offers valuable lessons to developing countries. Controlled opening of China's economy to the rest of the world has been a key factor behind the country's economic miracle. Another, equally important factor has been the proactive role of the Chinese government in promoting strategic sectors, building national champions, and advancing domestic innovation capabilities. Kaplinsky, Hogenboom, and Yusuf all stress that over the past 25 years the role of the state in the promotion of development, and particularly in the movement up the value chain, has been very different in China compared to most countries in Sub-Saharan Africa and Latin America. In the latter regions, governments retreated from their active role in promoting development and embraced free market policies. In China, in contrast, the state played a strategic role in advancing key sectors and promoting R&D and productivity growth (see also, for example, Zhao et al. 2007, Rodrik 2007, Amsden 2004).

In many ways, the Chinese government has pursued the development model that had brought success to the first Asian Tigers, but with the added component of greater emphasis on innovation earlier in the development process. The success of the Chinese economic strategy stands in stark contrast to the failure of Washington Consensus policies to generate a sustained movement in production up the value chain. There is now a vast literature on the failure of the Washington Consensus to engender development (e.g., Gallagher 2005, Paus 2004, Rodrik 2001). But the very success of China's strategy provides the strongest critique yet of the Washington Consensus and a powerful example of a successful alternative development strategy.

The economic success of China's strategy has relegitimized the state as a critical actor and private sector partner in a development strategy focused on the advancement of knowledge-based assets. The need to pursue such a strategy is equally urgent for all developing countries. The particulars of any such strategy need to be defined in a country-specific context, of course. The countries that benefit from the commodity price boom and greater foreign direct investment have extra help (additional foreign exchange and possibly technology spillovers from FDI) in pursuing such a strategy. But whether governments in developing countries will have the political will and wherewithal to rebalance the market-state equation in pursuit of an aggressive move up the value chain is a different story. Hogenboom, Kaplinsky, and Yusuf all point to difficulties along the way in their respective geographic areas of analysis.

Hogenboom argues that an alternative strategy in Latin America will only be successful if it unfolds in the context of regional integration. She identifies three hurdles on the way to regional integration: first, countries need to recognize that regional cooperation is indispensable; second, they need to move beyond infrastructural integration to political, social, and institutional integration; and third, they need to agree on what the new development model will look like. A formidable set of challenges, indeed.

Kaplinsky distinguishes between countries with diffuse commodities (that can be produced in different locations) and countries with point commodities (resources in the ground). He argues that countries with point commodities tend to have "malign patterns of political coalitions" in Sub-Saharan Africa, as extraction of point commodities lends itself more readily to rent-seeking and corruption. Kaplinsky concludes that "Sub-Saharan African political economies may be in for a rocky ride."

Yusuf sketches out two possible scenarios for Thailand and Malaysia: one of no or slow government action where "industrial development could stagnate and atrophy and growth come to a crawl" and another where they "invest heavily in R&D and develop niches based on the strengths they have already." He provides no reasons for optimism that the second scenario is the more likely one to unfold.

China as Political Counterweight: Opening Policy Space?

Whether developing country governments will pursue the policies needed to address China's competitive pressures is not only an issue of internal political economics. It is also a question of available external policy space. The World Trade Organization and bilateral trade and investment agreements have dramatically restricted the policy space for many developing countries (e.g., Abugattas and Paus 2008). For example, the space for industrial policies is severely restricted by the Agreement on Subsidies and Countervailing Measures, the Agreement on Agriculture, TRIMs (Trade-Related Investment Measures), TRIPs (Trade-Related Intellectual Property), and the GATs (General Agreement on Trade in Services). The question is whether China's rise will offer developing countries possibilities to broaden this external policy space, either because they can use bilateral relations with China as a counterweight to external demands or because China is changing the dynamics of negotiations in international organizations.

China's partnering with Brazil and other advanced developing countries in the Doha negotiation round is one indication of China's potential impact on international fora (Hogenboom, this volume). China's support of repressive regimes in SSA, for example, Sudan, because of its interest in their natural resources, has allowed these governments to defy Western demands for human rights' observance. This is indeed an example of developing countries using China as a counterweight against Western industrialized countries, though not for the purpose of pursuing a more promising development agenda.

In sum, China's economic rise has increased the urgency for developing countries to adopt a development strategy that moves production up the value chain. China's own strategy contains valuable lessons for other governments. Its demand for natural resources provides extra help in this endeavor to countries exporting such commodities. And its willingness to assert itself in international fora, most importantly the WTO, might open policy space for developing countries to pursue the policies needed for a prodevelopment strategy.

How Chinese authorities respond to their internal challenges discussed before will affect developing countries primarily through the impact of these policies on China's economic growth. Greater attention to environmental sustainability or internal political unrest may well slow down China's economic growth. Slower growth reduces the degree of urgency for policy action in developing countries to address the challenge of China's competitiveness across a broad range of technological capabilities. But a slowdown in growth does not fundamentally alter the need for such policies.

The Geostrategic Implications of the Rise of China

How well China responds to its internal challenges and its relationship with the developing world also has significant implications more broadly for great power politics in the twenty-first century. In the past two decades, three events have led to a fundamental transformation of the global geostrategic landscape: (1) the collapse of the Soviet empire; (2) China's dramatic economic development; and (3) the onset of unprecedented economic globalization. The increasing importance of international economic activity and China's economic performance suggest that great power relations of the twenty-first century likely will be motivated more by economic interactions than by the Cold War style ideological cleavages, proxy wars, and nuclear standoffs.

What is unclear is whether or not China's economic interactions with the world ultimately will be marked by increased great power competition or cooperation. With its extensive set of internal challenges, China is being pulled in contradictory directions. On the one hand, some of China's internal needs and national interests, such as its demand for increasingly scarce imported raw materials and energy sources, suggest potential for competition or even conflict with other great powers. Conversely, to sustain its economic growth and development China has a vested interest in a stable and balanced international economy. To this end, China has increased its participation in several regional and international economic institutions and generally has acted as a responsible stakeholder in these institutions. The central challenge for the United States and others in the coming years will be to manage their relationship with a China that has multiple and varied interests and needs.

Potential Sources of Competition and Conflict

Traditionally, the most likely source of international conflict involving China has focused on particular East Asian flashpoints, most notably Taiwan and Japan. The future status of Taiwan remains unclear. Since 1971 when the United Nations transferred the China seat on the United Nations Security Council from the Republic of China (Taiwan) to the People's Republic of China (mainland China), Taiwan's international political status has been in limbo—neither recognized as an independent state nor considered under the jurisdiction of the PRC (People's Republic of China). The PRC maintains that Taiwan is a part of China and will eventually be unified with China under Beijing's leadership and has expressly warned Taiwan against any move toward independence. Meanwhile, the legacy of Japan's wartime occupation of China from 1932 to 1945 continues to be a source of raw national anger. Nationalist flareups are common even with relatively minor provocations. Both Taiwan and Japan remain potentially volatile issues. As Susan Shirk notes in her chapter, Chinese nationalism remains a very potent force and Taiwan and Japan are particularly "hot-button" issues. Most analysts consider that any effort to change the current status quo with Taiwan could prompt open hostilities (Harries 2003). Furthermore, China's relations with Japan are particularly sensitive and susceptible to the oscillations and whims of increasingly nationalist elites in both countries.

Today, however, debates on the geostrategic implications of China's rise transcend regional East Asian security issues. Many scholars now view China as likely to rival the United States in this century. Some warn that as China begins to rival American political and economic dominance, the world will see a difficult and potentially threatening episode of hegemonic transition (Mearsheimer 2001). Lipman in his historical overview suggests that China is reemerging as a global power—that it has a long history of involvement in the international economy. But, China's reentry in the global markets and its pursuit of raw material and energy resources in the twenty-first century may have a much more assertive political and strategic component than in the past (Menon and Wimbush 2003). China's demands for energy and raw materials will bring China in direct competition with the United States and others for the same resources. Michael Klare in this volume presents extensive data on China's current and projected energy demands to fuel its economy. Today, China is consuming almost 15 percent of the world energy use. In the next 20 years, that percentage is projected to increase to almost one-quarter of the world's energy demand. This demand has led China to look far beyond its borders in search of resources. It is now actively engaged in resource acquisition on every continent. Klare sees this competition as the central geostrategic challenge of the twenty-first century.

Furthermore, as Klare and Gallagher note in their respective chapters, China's projected future reliance on high sulfur coal will produce greater sulfur dioxide pollutants (acid rain) and greenhouse gas emissions. China already surpassed the United States as the largest polluter of greenhouse gases in 2008. Likewise, water scarcity in China has led to enormous water diversion projects that disrupt downstream water flows. The combined environmental degradation effects of these trends pose serious regional and global challenges. China increasingly will become a focal point for concern and condemnation as the threats from global warming and other environmental stresses intensify.

More broadly, questions remain as to what China's future role in the international system will be. Kishore Mahbubani, a leading East Asian intellectual, concludes that the rise of China is leading an "irresistible shift" of global power to Asia (Mahbubani 2008a). He argues that Western economic and development models, as well as the broader system of global governing structures such as the United Nations, have failed to protect or benefit vast portions of the world's population. The global financial crisis in the fall of 2008 revealed the vulnerability of the existing Western-dominated economic systems. These weaknesses and failures may open the political space for alternatives to emerge (ibid.). For example, China and other emerging markets are dramatically increasing the number and size of sovereign wealth funds. These funds give the Chinese government far greater economic and political leverage over markets and geostratically important industries (Kimmitt 2008). Whether by intent or not, China's experience and its new foreign policy may lead to a shift of global power and governance.

Conflict and Competition Are Not Inevitable

Despite these new concerns, however, not all trends and analyses are so foreboding. Many scholars have noted that China's very success has been rooted in its participation in the existing international order and that its rise will not inevitably lead to a contested hegemonic transition (Ikenberry 2008). The international system today is remarkably different from the international systems of the past. It is open and highly institutionalized with preset rules that integrate, not contest, new rising powers. For example, China is a member of the United Nations Security Council, the World Trade Organization, and dozens of other international structures. Some institutions, like the IMF and World Bank, are specifically designed to allow for greater institutional influence as a state's economy grows. Many scholars conclude that China's leaders have long recognized the benefit of these institutions and the country has joined dozens of additional international institutions over the past decade (Goldstein 2005). China increasingly has become a stakeholder in their preservation. Rather than rival American hegemony, China may well join it (Ikenberry 2008).

A second argument questions more fundamentally whether or not China's rise will continue to the point of reaching parity with the United States. Zhang notes in this volume that not all trends point toward China emerging as a peer rival. Indeed, Zhang remains skeptical that China will be able to overcome the numerous internal obstacles it faces such as high poverty, social cleavages, rural versus urban disparities, and the perverse effects of the extensive levels of environmental degradation. Despite its impressive growth rates, he concludes, China ultimately started from an extraordinarily low baseline and its internal challenges will simply overwhelm the existing political and economic trends. He concludes that China is unlikely to emerge as a superpower and it is unlikely to pose a significant threat to the United States. Indeed, even some of the pessimists acknowledge that China's low levels of per capita wealth will limit the degree to which China would be able to divert much of its new wealth into military spending (Christensen and Betts 2003:75).

Chestnut and Johnston do not necessarily share Zhang's skepticism on China's rise, but they unpack the existing trend data and argue that China's rise, while dramatic, remains a relatively long-term and incomplete process. It will take another 25–35 years for China to rival American economic and military power and much can happen in the interim to alter that trajectory. In addition, the chapters by Zhang and by Chestnut and Johnston also stress the importance of soft power to influence events and movements in today's global order. While it has impressive economic growth, China lacks a viable ideological alternative to the existing set of international rules nor does it have any significant soft power capacity to influence international behavior. Given this, China's ability to threaten the existing global order will remain limited.

What Is to Be Done?

With the sheer size of China's population and its dramatic economic performance making sense of China's rise is a difficult analytical undertaking. The authors here disagree on the degree and pace of China's rise. Klare and Shirk are somewhat more pessimistic than Zhang and Chestnut and Johnston. Yet, they are all in agreement that conflict and competition are not inevitable. Klare, perhaps the most pessimistic of the authors here, concludes that while many trend lines are not particularly hopeful, there are possible technological solutions through extensive investment in alternative energy sources. He encourages the United States and the international community to aid China in making a shift toward alternative energy sources.

All of the authors here share the concern over the security dilemma—that undertaking actions to make oneself more secure often exacerbates a stronger reaction from one's opponent (Jervis 1976). This triggers a spiral of action and reaction that leaves both states less secure over time. The authors concur that if the United States and the West assume China's rise to be both inevitable and dangerous, and if the United States takes action to challenge China's development in an attempt to offset those perceived dangers, it risks triggering a hostile reaction from Beijing. Chestnut and Johnson argue that the prevailing alarmist discourse on China's rise could well trigger the security dilemma. Exaggerated and inflated threat discourse may well signal that the United States and others hold hostile intentions toward China. This could make the emergence of hostility self-fulfilling. Shirk and Zhang both conclude that China's leaders likely will accept an accommodation stance from the West—that it does not seek conflict. But if the United States, Japan, or Taiwan were to assume seemingly aggressive postures, Chinese leaders—with full support of a nationalist Chinese population—are likely to respond equally aggressively.

In contrast to the growing number of books that analyze the Rise of China from a particular disciplinary and thematic angle, this volume highlights the interconnectivity between China's internal challenges and their impact on the global economic and political order. We firmly believe that students, scholars, and practitioners will need a greater understanding and awareness of the multiple disciplinary dimensions of China's rise than we have seen to date. This book begins this task.

Notes

1. The Gini coefficient measures perfect income equality as a zero and perfect income inequality as a 1.
2. See, for example, Burke and Epstein (2007) and Martin (2007).
3. Kaplinsky, McCormick, and Morris (2007) point to China's increasing competition for Kenyan flower exports in third markets.
4. For a more detailed discussion of the Mexican case see also Gallagher, Moreno-Brid, and Porzekanski (2008) and Dussel Peters (2007a, 2007b).
5. Ocampo and Parra (2003) show that the significant decline in the TOT during the twentieth century was not continuous, but occurred principally at two main points in time: around 1920 and around 1980.

References

Abugattas, Luis and Eva Paus. 2008. Policy Space for a Capability-Centered Development Strategy for Latin America. In *The Political Economy of Hemispheric Integration. Responding to Globalization in the Americas,* ed. Diego Sanchez-Ancochea and Kenneth C. Shadlen. New York and London: Palgrave Macmillan, 113–143.

Amsden, Alice. 2004. Import Substitution in High-Tech Industries: Prebish Lives in Asia! *CEPAL Review* 82: 75–89.

Burke, James and Gerald Epstein. 2007. Bargaining Power, Distributional Equity and the Challenges of Offshoring. In *Global Capitalism Unbound. Winners and Losers from Offshore Outsourcing,* ed. Eva Paus. New York and London: Palgrave Macmillan, 95–111.

Chang. Gordon G. 2001. *The Coming Collapse of China.* New York: Random House.

China Daily. 2004. Amendments to the Constitution. March 15. http://www.chinadaily.com.cn/english/dic/2004-03/15/content_314731.htm (accessed July 6, 2004).

Christensen, Thomas J. and Richard K. Betts. 2003. China: Getting the Questions Right. In *China in the National Interest,* ed. Owen Harries. Piscataway, NJ: Transaction.

Dussel Peters, Enrique. 2007a. La relación económica y comercial entre China y México: Propuestas para su profundización en el corto, mediano, y largo plazo.

En *Oportunidades en la relación económica y social entre China y Mexico.* Compilador. Enrique Dussel Peters. Mexico City: CEPAL, 165–228.

———. 2007b. *Oportunidades en la relación económica y social entre China y México.* Mexico City: CEPAL.

Eckstein, Alexander. 1977. *China's Economic Revolution.* Cambridge and New York: Cambridge University Press.

Feldstein, Martin. 2008. Resolving the Global Imbalance: The Dollar and the U.S. Saving Rate. *Journal of Economic Perspectives* 22(3): 113–125.

Freeman, Richard. 2007. The Challenge of the Growing Globalization of Labor Markets to Economic and Social Policy. In *Global Capitalism Unbound. Winners and Losers from Offshore Outsourcing,* ed. Eva Paus. New York and London: Palgrave Macmillan, 23–39.

Gallagher, Kevin, ed. 2005. *Putting Development First. The Importance of Policy Space in the WTO and International Financial Institutions.* London and New York: Zed Books.

Gallagher, Kevin, Juan Carlos Moreno-Brid, and Roberto Porzecanski. 2008. The Dynamism of Mexican Exports: Lost in (Chinese) Translation? *World Development* 36(8): 1365–1380.

Goldstein, Avery. 2005. *Rising to the Challenge: China's Grand Strategy and International Security.* Palo Alto, CA: Stanford University Press.

Harries, Owen, ed. 2003. *China in the National Interest.* Piscataway, NJ: Transaction.

Ikenberry, G. John. 2008. The Rise of China and the Future of the West. Can the Liberal System Survive? *Foreign Affairs* 87(1): 23–27.

IMF (International Monetary Fund). 2007. *Direction of Trade Statistics Yearbook 2007.*

Jervis, Robert. 1976. *Perception and Misperception in International Politics.* Princeton, NJ: Princeton University Press.

Kaplinsky, Raphael, Dorothy McCormick, and Mike Morris. 2007. The Impact of China on Sub-Saharan Africa. Working Paper 291. University of Sussex: IDS (Institute for Development Studies).

Kimmitt, Robert. 2008. Public Footprints in Private Markets. Sovereign Wealth Funds and the World Economy. *Foreign Affairs* 87(1): 119–130.

Lardy, Nicholas R. 1992. *Foreign Trade and Economic Reform in China, 1978–1990.* Cambridge and New York: Cambridge University Press.

———. 2002. *Integrating China into the Global Economy.* Washington, DC: Brookings Institution Press.

Lunding, Andreas. 2006. "Global Champions in Waiting. Perspectives on China's Overseas Direct Investment." *Deutsche Bank Research.* August 4.

Mahbubani, Kishore. 2008a. *The New Asian Hemisphere: The Irrisistible Shift of Global Power to the East.* New York: Public Affairs (Perseus Books Group).

———. 2008b. The Case against the West. *Foreign Affairs* 87(3): 111–124.

Martin, Hans-Peter. 2007. The European Trap: Jobs on the Run, Democracy at Stake. In *Global Capitalism Unbound. Winners and Losers from Offshore Outsourcing,* ed. Eva Paus. New York and London: Palgrave Macmillan, 131–144.

Mearsheimer, John. 2001. *The Tragedy of Great Power Politics*. New York: W.W. Norton.

Menon, Rajan and S. Enders Wimbush. 2003. Asia in the 21st Century: Power Politics Alive and Well. In *China in the National Interest*, ed. Owen Harries. Piscataway, NJ: Transaction.

Naughton, Barry. 1996. *Growing out of the Plan: Chinese Economic Reform, 1978–1993*. Cambridge and New York: Cambridge University Press.

Ocampo, Jose Antonio and Maria Angela Parra. 2003. The Terms of Trade for Commodities in the Twentieth Century. *CEPAL Review* 79: 7–36.

Paus, Eva. 2004. Productivity Growth in Latin America. The Limits of Neoliberal Reforms. *World Development* 32(3): 427–445.

———. 2009. The Rise of China: Implications for Latin American Development. *Development Policy Review*. Forthcoming.

Pei, Minxin. 2006. *China's Trapped Transition: The Limits of Developmental Autocracy*. Cambridge, MA: Harvard University Press.

Pomfret, John. 2008. A Long Wait at the Gate to Greatness. *Washington Post* July 27. http://www.washingtonpost.com/wp-dyn/content/article/2008/07/25/AR2008072502255.html (accessed July 30, 2008).

Prebish, Raúl. 1950. Growth, Disequilibrium and Disparities: Interpretation of the Process of Economic Development. *Economic Survey of Latin America 1949*. E/CN.12/164/Rev.1.

Prime, Penelope B. 2002. China Joins the WTO: How, Why, and What Now? *Business Economics* April: 26–32.

———. 2004. Funding Economic Transition in China: The Privatization Option. *Eurasian Geography and Economics* 45(5): 382–394.

Riskin, Carl. 1987. *China's Political Economy: The Quest for Development since 1949*. New York and Oxford: Oxford University Press.

Rodrik, Dani. 2001. *The Global Governance of Trade As If Development Really Mattered*. New York and Geneva: United Nations Development Programme.

———. 2007. *One Economics. Many Recipes. Globalization, Institutions and Economic Growth*. Princeton, NJ: Princeton University Press.

Shirk, Susan L. 1993. *The Political Logic of Economic Reform in China*. Berkeley: University of California Press.

Singer, Hans Werner. 1950. U.S. Foreign Investment in Underdeveloped Areas, the Distribution of Gains between Investing and Borrowing Countries. *American Economic Review, Papers and Proceedings. No. 40*.

Standing, Guy. 2007. Offshoring and Labor Recommodification in the Global Transformation. In *Global Capitalism Unbound. Winners and Losers from Offshore Outsourcing*, ed. Eva Paus. New York and London: Palgrave Macmillan, 41–60.

UNCTAD (United Nations Conference on Trade and Development). 2007. *World Investment Report 2007*. New York and Geneva: United Nations.

UNDP (United Nations Development Programme). 2007. *Human Development Report 2007/2008: Fighting Climate Change: Human Solidarity in a Divided World*. New York and Geneva: United Nations.

Yang, Dali. 2006. *Remaking the Chinese Leviathan: Market Transition and the Politics of Governance in China*. Palo Alto, CA: Stanford University Press.

Zhao, Zhonxiu, Xialing Huang, Dongya Ye, and Paul Gentle. 2007. China's Industrial Policy in Relation to Electronics Manufacturing. *China & World Economy* 15(3): 33–51.

Zweig, David. 1997. *Freeing China's Farmers: Rural Restructuring in the Reform Era*. Armonk, NY: M.E. Sharpe.

Chapter 2

The "Rise" of China:
Continuity and Change

Jonathan Lipman

Watching the awe-inspiring opening ceremony of the Beijing Olympics, most foreign commentators spoke of the "coming-out party" of China, as if that nation had been insignificant, adolescent, or somehow absent from the world until the summer of 2008. This chapter will show that impression to be profoundly false. China has been a crucial part of the world economy for over a millennium—long before Europe was—a source of everyday and luxury products, a major player in international politics, and a vital wellspring of invention and human creativity. A historian cannot *answer* this volume's central question—what does the rise of China mean in our contemporary world? But without some understanding of China's history, we might be tempted to regard that vast and complex country as a newcomer, which it is not, or as a simple, homogeneous, unitary actor on the world stage, which it has *never* been.

Instead, this historical introduction constructs a picture of China that includes continuities with its past as well as modern changes, diversity as well as national unity or consistency, similarities with ourselves as well as differences. To make China more of a living place, it addresses some well-known stereotypes about Chinese people and their identities—intelligence, work ethic, social networks, patriarchy, and women's roles. With these stories in hand, readers can approach the rest of this volume with greater awareness of China's multiplicity rather than assuming its unity or uniformity.

For most Chinese, the most important parts of the past lie in 150 years of foreign domination, weakness, and chaos, beginning the mid-nineteenth century. For them, today's China must be strong, united, and prosperous to play its proper role in the world, one stolen from it by imperialism and domestic weakness.[1] For others who think in longer terms, China should treasure its premodern culture; Chinese people should know their literature, poetry, arts, and traditions. Still others emphasize the *values* that have been extracted from China's heritage, ranging from familial solidarity to local cohesion to loyalty to the central state and its leaders. Still, as always, embodied in texts (Confucian classics, Buddhist sutras, Mao Zedong's writings), these values emphasize the discipline of the self to fulfill social roles, whether for self, family, society, or state.

But what does this have to do with China's extraordinary *economic* success, or with life in today's ultramodern Shanghai or Guangzhou? I argue that many characteristics of contemporary Chinese society have been inherited—never entirely and never without change—from the past. The dominance of the coastal cities, for example, dates from their establishment as trading centers many centuries ago as well as their more recent functions as treaty ports and entryways for European and American goods and ideas. Regions farther from maritime or riverine trading routes have not developed as quickly. The rural-urban divide, one of the most crucial in today's China, has ancient roots, as city folk often expressed humorous contempt for country bumpkins.[2] Certainly patriarchy, ethnic and linguistic diversity, a long tradition of commerce and private enterprise, and a nationalism derived from more than a century of foreign domination have all left their marks on today's China.

But so many things *are* new. Just as the nineteenth century's spread of Chinese people all over the world had never happened before, nothing in China's past can compare with the *speed* of economic growth of the past 30 years, the incorporation of hundreds of millions of rural people into urban work (especially factory labor and construction), the explosion of cities accompanied by the rise of an urban middle class of tens of millions,[3] or the intense engagement of China's economy and society with the world outside. Many less obvious phenomena, such as the speedy rise of domestic tourism and the incorporation of frontier regions through railroad and air links, have only very distant precedent in China's past. Outsiders looking at China through news and other media must be very cautious in making judgments, very careful to sort through the evidence either of connection to the past or of thoroughgoing innovation. Like all societies, China's is changing very quickly in the twenty-first century. Its economic productivity, enormous population, centrality in regional politics, and huge holdings of foreign capital and debt demand that foreigners pay close attention to and not accept either superficial resemblances or facile judgments in considering how this ancient and successful country has "suddenly risen."

The remaining sections of this chapter discuss some ways in which China has not changed too much—human and ethnic diversity, commercial success and power, some qualities of its people and the networks that bind them together, the roles and limitations of women, the extraordinary forces of nationalism and desire for social order—in order to see how history can inform our understanding of today's "rising giant." Many of the chapters in this book describe China only as an "it," a singular, unitary international actor represented by its government or a national economy characterized by Gross Domestic Product or foreign exchange holdings. Though that way of seeing China has usefulness and validity, as it does with all countries, we can only understand the "How?" of China's rise by seeing that huge nation in all its complexity and diversity, without stereotypes or essentialized descriptions. History can help us with that task by demonstrating China's internal intricacy, its human variety, so that we can imagine diverse "them" rather than justify "it."

China's Diversity

China has never been a homogeneous place inhabited only by one sort of people. Stretching from the tundra to the tropics, its many ecologies support many types of agriculture, some pastoralism, and local cultures limited by mountains, rivers, and the relative immobility of a vast farming population. Foodways, religion, language (often called "dialect"), domestic architecture, and many other aspects of life differ widely among the people we call "Chinese" in English (nowadays they usually call themselves *Han*). Localism and regionalism thrive in China, where Shanghainese, Cantonese, Beijingers, and Sichuanese have developed lively stereotypes of one another. The hot-tempered Hunan rebel, the predatory Henan bandit, the phlegmatic Shandong farmer, the feuding Fujian clans—these and many more images divide China domestically. So, too, has China been divided by the same social distinctions as other complex societies—gender, class, access to resources, education, and more.

This huge and diverse culture area has nonetheless been unified to some extent by its literate classes, all of whom read the same written characters while pronouncing them very differently, and by the vast legacy of texts produced over 3,000 years of cultural history. Since the eighth or ninth century, the most prestigious road to success for a young Chinese man lay in the imperial civil service examinations, which led to a career as a government official.[4] The "literati" (*shenshi*) who competed in those exams memorized and expanded the largest printed literature on the planet,[5] and their unifying influence penetrated to every part of the empire where ambitious families trained their sons and daughters to read. This "unity in diversity," a highly variegated agricultural and urban population unified to some extent by a homogeneously educated ruling class, has long characterized China and remains a useful description of the modern country. In recent years, the spread of print and electronic media has enabled a nationwide effort for unity (see Nationalism and National Pride, below), its effectiveness varying with time and place—in time of war or international conflict, people tend to pull together; in less troubled times or more isolated places, national identity can be weaker.

We can conceive of China more accurately by considering the problem of ethnicity—not everyone in China is simply "Chinese." The Qing empire (1636–1912), whose ruling elite were culturally Manchu rather than Chinese, conquered the Chinese Ming state (1368–1644) and then continued to expand their empire to include the territory of the Mongols, of the eastern Turks, and some of Tibet. By 1760, the Qing empire ruled a territory shaped very much like today's China (though somewhat larger), and its continuity has meant that the citizens of the People's Republic include over 100,000,000 people who are citizens of the People's Republic of China but not culturally Chinese. The Tibetans, Turks (among whom the Uygurs are the most numerous), Mongols, Thais, Manchus, Koreans, Russians, and other ethnic groups (the government counts and supports 55 of them) form a sometimes conflicted but unavoidable continuity in China's history as well as evidence of domestic diversity.

Commerce and Power

China's current rise to international economic prominence has happened before and should probably be called a "reemergence" rather than something entirely new. Indeed, of the major Eurasian economies (including Europe, the Middle East, and India), China's generated the largest share of products and wealth for eight of the past 10 centuries.[6] Historians have calculated that as much as half of the silver taken out of Latin America by the Spanish and Portuguese, precious metal usually seen as evidence of European dominance, found its way to China. The Chinese, after all, produced and exported the goods that other people desired—silk, tea, porcelain, medicine, foodstuffs, and artisanal products of all kinds, the famed "riches of the East"—and both the Ming and the Qing had established silver as one of two metals for monetary circulation (the other was copper). Lacking sufficient domestic supplies, China needed silver, and the

Europeans, who had vast quantities of silver, wanted to spend it on Chinese goods, so wealth flowed into China from the east (across the Pacific, via the Philippines) and from the west (via India and southeast Asia). The "rise of China" since the 1980s has replicated this pattern, with currency and instruments of credit replacing silver. China now holds a staggering quantity of dollars, euros, yen, and other international currencies, imported in exchange for consumer goods, a pattern easily recognizable from the eighteenth century.

The enormous Eurasian trading system of the past worked, in part, because China had a well-developed and efficient commercial economy, with water transport and plentiful food supplies to serve its burgeoning cities. Many authors have cited the orthodox Confucian bias against merchants, ranked as the lowest of China's four classes (below scholar-officials, farmers, and artisans), but this elite prejudice did not preclude a thriving market and accumulation of wealth. Despite commerce's degraded formal status, many official families eagerly participated in business to perpetuate and increase their family fortunes, publicly disdaining commerce while privately enriching themselves. At the lower end of the social scale, China's rural population has been the largest in the world for over 1,000 years, and the careful, highly adaptive labor of millions of farmers has enabled the economy to flourish.

As early as the thirteenth–fourteenth centuries, foreign travelers (the Venetian Marco Polo and Moroccan Ibn Battuta among them) gasped in amazement at the size and complexity of the urban markets they encountered in China:

> This city is greater than any in the world, and is quite 100 miles around; nor is there any span of ground that is not well inhabited...This city has also great suburbs containing more people than the city itself contains. It has twelve principal gates; and at each of these gates at about eight miles are cities larger than Venice or Padua might be, so that one will go about one of those suburbs for six or eight days...[7]

The tonnage and diversity of food brought into the cities daily, the effectiveness of financial arrangements (including long-distance credit), the honesty and reliability of the merchants, the expanse of the public markets, the wealth of the elites and the sheer numbers and diligence of the common folk—nothing in the world could compare to China.

Some of its merchants spread to neighboring kingdoms, especially to Southeast Asia, and their skill in business enabled them to control economic sectors as diverse as tin mining, plantation farming, and the transcultural trade in *materia medica*. The Ming court dispatched the great fifteenth-century fleets commanded by Admiral Zheng He, the largest carrying almost 30,000 men as far as East Africa, to do business at all the important ports of maritime Asia and expand Chinese trading networks to include Bengal, the coasts of Southern India, and the Persian Gulf.[8] From the fifteenth century until the nineteenth century, Beijing was almost certainly the largest city in the world (Edo, now Tokyo, was its closest competitor), as Hangzhou had been in the thirteenth and Chang'an (now Xi'an) long before that. Merchants and their commercial skills clearly played a large part in such widespread, long-term urbanization, supplying many cities with the goods and services they demanded.[9]

The coming of European imperialism, often described as fatal to local or regional trade networks, actually strengthened some parts of the Chinese commercial world. The British in Malaya, the Dutch in Java, and the Spanish in Manila all found Chinese merchants and laborers necessary to productivity in their colonial empires. Despite tension and some violence, Chinese traders expanded the reach of their business enterprises (including joint stock companies with sophisticated ownership and management arrangements) in the eighteenth and nineteenth centuries, reaching Hawai'i and other Pacific islands, Australia, North and South America, and the Caribbean. They imported southern Chinese workers to all of those destinations, where they formed tightly knit communities, some endogamous but others intermarrying with local people. Though the economy of China as a whole did decline rapidly in the nineteenth century—the importation of vast quantities of opium from British India had reversed the flow of silver by the 1820s—China's commercial culture flourished worldwide by the time the Qing dynasty fell in 1912. Despite the political weakness of the Republic of China, which nominally ruled the mainland from 1912 to 1949, capitalism and trade brought new opportunities to some urban Chinese, and the 1910s and 1920s have been called the "golden age of China's bourgeoisie" (Bergere 1989). So today's Chinese capitalism has deep roots as well as ultramodern causes.

History and Social Order

Beginning in 1949, the Chinese Communist Party has taken advantage of the common desire for peace and stability to reinforce its own power, claiming a large measure of legitimacy through its ability to keep China strong, independent, and relatively orderly in contrast to the century that preceded its rule. The modern world dominated by Europe and the

United States, arriving in East Asia in the early nineteenth century, had a devastating and profound impact on Chinese society. Beginning with the first Opium War in 1839, the Qing empire suffered a series of defeats at the hands of foreign powers, consequent losses of sovereignty through unequal treaties, losses of territory (such as British occupation of Hong Kong and Japanese colonization of Taiwan), and numerous indignities perpetrated by foreigners. The instability created, in part, by the foreign trade in opium and the Qing court's demonstrated weakness led to domestic rebellions on a vast scale. Thirty million people are said to have lost their lives during the mid-nineteenth century upheavals, which also devastated the economies of whole regions. Foreign designs on Korea stimulated two major wars—between the Qing and Japan in 1894 and Russia and Japan 10 years later (fought mostly in Qing territory). A foreign invasion of northern China followed the "scramble for concessions" in the late 1890s and the Boxer uprising of 1899–1900. The American "Open Door" policy, designed to prevent any one foreign power from dominating the China trade, also left little room for the Qing, or its successor governments, to protect themselves economically, militarily, or diplomatically.

When the Qing fell in 1912, no unified government arose to replace it until the late 1920s; instead, chaotic warfare between factions of former Qing officials and generals—the infamous "warlords"—laid waste the already insecure economic lives of many Chinese. Millions of men lost their liberty, and many their lives, as conscripts into the armies that marched and countermarched everywhere in the country, in many cases pillaging the townsmen and farmers' meager supplies in order to feed themselves. During this period, one foreign scholar wrote, the Chinese rural population resembled "a man up to his neck in water so that even a ripple is sufficient to drown him" (Tawney 1932:77).

When the Nationalist Party (*Guomindang*) led by General Jiang Jieshi[10] emerged victorious as a government of national unification in 1927, many Chinese hoped for some peace to rebuild their shattered farms and businesses. But both domestic conflict with the Communist Party (*Gongchandang*) and continuing confrontation with Japan impoverished and weakened the nascent central government. The industrial northeast, Manchuria, became a Japanese puppet state in 1931, and full-scale Japanese invasion of eastern China followed in 1937, including lethal bombardment of densely populated Shanghai and the horrific massacre of civilians in the Nationalist capital of Nanjing. Both Nationalist and Communist Parties conducted bloody anti-Japanese resistance for the next eight years, then—despite American attempts at mediation—deployed their huge armies against one another in a three-year civil war from 1946 to 1949.

The establishment of the People's Republic of China by the Communist Party in 1949 seemed to herald a new age of unity and national strength—as Party Chairman Mao Zedong announced, "The Chinese people have stood up!" But a year later, China was embroiled in war against the United States in Korea, and the continued existence of the Nationalist Party government on Taiwan meant seemingly permanent military preparations. The 1950s, often seen nowadays as a moment of calm, contained not only three years of war in Korea but also the social upheaval of land redistribution, rapid Soviet-style industrialization, hasty collectivization of agricultural land, and the trauma of the Sino-Soviet split. Using "mass campaigns" as a crucial technique, the new government attempted to mobilize the passions and energy of all citizens in the interest of rapid economic development, running roughshod over individual or local interests and rationality in order to "overtake England in 15 years!" One of history's most devastating famines resulted in the late 1950s, killing tens of millions.

After a brief hiatus in the early 1960s, Mao Zedong and his faction in the Communist Party again mobilized all Chinese for the ill-fated "Great Proletarian Cultural Revolution" (1966–1976). Pitting his own vision of "permanent revolution" against his colleagues' and rivals' plans for slow, steady economic development, Mao inspired hundreds of millions of Chinese to tear their own society apart in the name of ideological purity. Political and social institutions, cities, villages, families, and individuals collapsed under the strain of constant, unrelenting pressure for "revolutionary struggle."[11] After Mao's death in 1976 and a brief inner-party scuffle, Deng Xiaoping and his faction took control of the party and the government and began the reforms that resulted in the "rise of China," which is the subject of this book.

Even this drastically abbreviated history of modern China can remind an outsider that every one of the multitudes of Chinese in each era suffered *individually*, humiliated, starved, shot, diseased, tortured, or worse. Being one of a million casualties does not make the process any less awful. A member of a society that had undergone that much chaos, who had heard endless stories of imperial invasions, warfare, revolution, and suffering from history teachers and elders, might very well desire nothing more than social order and calm. After all these historical tribulations, many Chinese folks want a stable, predictable government that protects them from foreigners (especially the Japanese and the Americans) and keeps the economy growing.[12] Even if it is corrupt and repressive, as long as it allows ordinary people to earn money, take care of their families, and rebuild their social worlds, most will not resist. If that means, "go along to get along," so be it. Chinese politics have never encouraged competing political parties—Emperors used to write polemical essays against factionalism—nor an independent judiciary nor a widespread culture of voluntary association. So opposition to the party and the state, and there is plenty of it in China, remains fragmented and focused on single issues: labor rights, birth control policy, land disputes, religious freedom, ethnic autonomy, and many more.[13] No unified opposition movement has been possible beyond the local level.[14]

With over 70,000,000 members (over 5 percent of the population), the Chinese Communist Party justifies its rule by maintaining social order through both politics and violence, with its own officials and committees at the top of every level of society. Now open to capitalists as well as Marxists and revolutionaries, the party retains its historical reputation and legitimacy as China's unifier and only hope for constancy and strength, not to mention continuing economic expansion. No other regime in modern Chinese history, except the Nationalist government on Taiwan, has been able to make good on that claim. Surely that legitimacy is a crucial legacy of China's history over the past two centuries.

Intelligence, Hard Work, and Education

Racial and ethnic stereotypes change with the times. When Europeans and Americans visited China in the nineteenth century, they often commented on the laziness, sloth, indolence, and fecklessness of the heathen Chinese. Such people, they opined, were fit only to be coolies, opium-sodden servants to more motivated, assiduous nations. Even clear evidence of extraordinary artisanship and diligent work habits did not persuade the arrogant outsiders that the Chinese were capable of becoming modern, as the Japanese had done. American philosopher Ralph Waldo Emerson (who never went to China) generalized and racialized this erroneous impression—"The closer contemplation we condescend to bestow, the more disgustful is that booby nation...China, reverend dullness! hoary ideot!, all she can say at the convocation of nations must be—'I made the tea.'"[15]

Now, of course, we see only *stereotypes* of the intensely active, hard working, intelligent Chinese, busily taking over market after market, earning international prizes and securing myriad patents, earning the best grades and outsmarting the competition. Could this be the same country and people? Have the Chinese really changed so much and so recently? A careful look at China's past reveals that there have always been brilliant, innovative Chinese people. Joseph Needham's (1954) monumental study, *Science and Civilization in China*, includes many fields of scientific endeavor, from mathematics to siege artillery, from civil engineering to forestry, in all of which Chinese scientists made important discoveries.[16]

We can read the biographies of exceptional Chinese—ancient philosophers and historians, imperial officials and women poets, contemporary businessmen and novelists.[17] One of the ambitions of Chinese at many levels of society lay in "making a great name" (*chu da ming*), creating a lasting reputation.

Education constituted the main route to fame and success in premodern China, and that education focused on texts written in Chinese characters, one of the most important and problematic legacies of China's past. Among all the literate, urban civilizations, only China's still uses ideographs exclusively rather than a phonetic system for writing.[18] This has tremendous advantages in a diverse culture area where people pronounce words in very different ways—if two literate Chinese cannot understand one another's speech, they can *write* their conversation. But it also means that the Chinese ideographs, usually called "characters" in English, have little obvious relationship to sound and must be memorized in large numbers. Basic literacy requires a few thousand of them, and serious academic work many thousands more. The act of learning to read and write Chinese, therefore, takes a great deal more time than it would with a phonetic alphabet and demands a terrific memory (like English spelling).

But this certainly does not mean that *all* Chinese have always been (or are now) gifted and accomplished. In every generation, Chinese scholars have worried about the illiterate (always the majority), the foolish, the gullible, and the wicked among whom they lived. Whether as representatives of the state or as leaders in their own hometowns, the elite advocated education and self-cultivation as the keys to improving society.[19] Every human being, they argued, should nurture the innate virtues with which all are born. Indeed, a good society can only be created when every individual *disciplines the self* to perform all the social roles correctly—being a good father or son, husband or wife, king or minister, manager or employee.

That notion of self-discipline constitutes a profound historical legacy for many Chinese people today. Whether preparing for the Olympic Games or a local martial arts tournament, memorizing a difficult text for an exam or learning to identify medicinal herbs, practicing acupuncture or struggling to learn English, Chinese folks live within a powerful ideology of self-improvement. Not everyone succeeds, of course, and both ancient and contemporary literatures are filled with stories of failure, self-indulgence, and irresponsibility.[20] But the ideal of self-cultivation remains, and many Chinese respond to it. That is, contemporary China has inherited a long cultural tradition stressing individual responsibilities rather than individual rights. The European notion of "rights" has taken hold in the past century and more, but the notion of inherent human rights remains—ideologically, at least—secondary to social duties, producing serious trouble for individuals who violate established norms. We must conclude that stereotyping "the Chinese" as uniformly degenerate (as some nineteenth century Europeans did) or upwardly mobile and extraordinarily able (as many contemporary Americans do) cannot describe the vast range of abilities and potentials of a huge population.

Social Networks and Relationships (*guanxi*)

Both Chinese and foreign observers characterize contemporary China as a political culture mired in corruption and crisscrossed with webs of personal influence. Given the power of social roles and conventions, human relationships in China take on a special and urgent quality, far more important than any impersonal laws created by the government. Anyone who has traveled or lived in China knows the word *guanxi*, meaning "connections," and its importance for getting things done. From the earliest historical texts, Chinese people have portrayed themselves as imbedded in networks of *guanxi*, which extend from the youngest children to long-deceased ancestors. From child-rearing practices to funeral rituals, *guanxi* dictates hierarchies of power and how people ought to behave toward one another. When foreigners note, usually with distaste, the obsequiousness of Chinese toward superiors in rank, they unwittingly describe one way in which *guanxi* works. By giving due respect to elders and bosses, people present themselves as appropriate subordinates, willing to obey and sacrifice in exchange for favors and protection.

Ancient Chinese texts enumerate Five Relationships necessary for an orderly society—father/son, king/minister, husband/wife, elder brother/ younger brother, and friend/friend. Of these, four are explicitly hierarchical (or *vertical*), with one member clearly superior in power and privilege. Even friends, Chinese people say, organize themselves hierarchically by age and/or ability. Not only family relationships but also hometown, schoolmate, teacher/student, and patron/client ties characterize the *guanxi* networks of both modern and premodern China.

Of course, all societies have authority structures, and none of the features of Chinese *guanxi* is unique. People in most societies know-how to give appropriate gifts, make or return phone calls and dinner invitations from significant people, and do favors for friends of friends. But in a society so large, so complex, and so old as China's, such behaviors take on the power of law, and violation of *guanxi* conventions can be as severely punished as criminal acts, sometimes even more so when powerful individuals feel slighted. What is often called "corruption," in fact, seems more like "relationship building" in many Chinese contexts. That is, a substantial gift to someone who has decision-making power might be a prudent choice rather than evidence of criminal intent. In Ming and Qing times, local magistrates' salaries were set quite low, for their superiors in the bureaucratic hierarchy knew that they would be able to earn substantially more from gifts presented by litigants. These "customary fees," known and acknowledged by all, constituted an important part of the *guanxi* network among elites. When a powerful faction dominated the court, its leaders accumulated fantastic wealth through gifts passed up from each lower level of the state bureaucracy.[21]

Nowadays, Chinese people claim that all government and Communist Party officials take money and favors in exchange for their decisions, but that does not distinguish the contemporary state from its predecessors. In the old days, rural folks had to tip the tax collector or the constables in order to avoid trouble; now, aspiring business people give presents to licensing authorities in the city government in order to set up a business. The reach of the state may be longer and deeper than it was, but *guanxi* remains, and the "back door" opens for people with properly maintained relationships. Though many Chinese resent and revile this system, others see it as evidence not of a disintegrating, dishonest social order but rather of one where the *guanxi* rules ensure stability and predictability.

Patriarchy and Women's Power

Gender ideologies establish "natural" characteristics and roles that determine limits of possibility for men and women in society. To this day, China maintains a powerful, pervasive sense of gender hierarchy inherited from a long history of separation and role definition based on sex. Some of the most ancient Chinese texts—3,500 years old ideographs scratched on bones and shells used as oracles—call the birth of a royal daughter "really not good" and clearly include male superiority, *patriarchy*, as defining a virtuous society. One fundamental Chinese analysis of reality postulates the dynamic interaction of *yin* and *yang* as giving movement and change to all things, with *yin* identified as the female principle and *yang* as the male. For the cosmos to be in harmony, *yang* must properly dominate *yin*.

Conventional marriage in China meant the transfer of a young female from her natal family to her husband's family (*patrilocality* or *virilocality*); one common name for marriage was "finding a mother-in-law." Males remained in their natal families for life; females were transferred, some say "torn," from the familiarity and comfort of their natal families into another family, in which they often met with distrust as outsiders. According to the classical texts, men and women should live and work in entirely different spaces, appropriately acting out the social hierarchies of husband/wife, mother-in-law/daughter-in-law, and so on. Having a son constituted a central act of familial devotion, for descent could only be ensured through the male line (*patriliny*), and women played only minor roles (if any) in a family's genealogy.

Women's domesticity was encouraged, beginning about 1,000 years ago, by the practice of footbinding, wrapping young girls' feet tightly in cloths to prevent them from growing. With feet shortened and bowed by the binding cloths, women could not run at all and preferred sedentary, less painful activities. Very common but never universal, footbinding came to signify civilized family life, one of the ways in which "we" civilized Chinese differed from "them," the uncivilized (and unfootbound) cultural outsiders. Sitting in the family compound, making cloth or embroidering tiny shoes for themselves and female relatives, footbound women acted out some of the proverbs that defined their roles—"Men plough, women weave"; "In women, lack of talent is virtue"; "Men and women must be separated."

Though this patriarchal culture seems entirely constraining, historians and anthropologists have found that Chinese women did find ways to control their own lives, to express their emotions, to be more than household servants or sex objects. Elite women might learn to read and write, some exceeding their brothers and husbands in calligraphy or composing poetry (Mann 2007). Women in all classes of society made use of conventional social hierarchies to garner respect from younger members of their families, especially their sons, who were enjoined to include their mothers in the practice of *filial piety*, personal and ritual respect for parents. Age, and the death of husbands, gave many women the opportunity to head their households—though rarely could they be officially recognized—and to control the family businesses and finances. Many women made notable contributions to the family and local economies by producing or managing production. All of the most interesting characters in *The Story of the Stone*,[22] one of China's most famous novels, were female, and the elite household at its center was dominated by the oldest woman, Grandmother Jia, who easily controlled her sons and grandsons, despite their masculinity and official titles.[23]

In the late nineteenth century, footbinding came under attack as a "shame to the nation" and a weakening of China's human resources in the face of imperialist aggression. Modernizers wanted to enlist women's energy, both as "wise mothers" to train the sons of New China and as activists in their own right. In their view China, endangered by division at home and aggressors from abroad, needed everyone's contribution. Footbinding disappeared, but patriarchal ideas and institutions die slowly, and today's China still maintains many remnants of patrilocality and patriliny. During the 1960s, political radicals attempted to eliminate all vestiges of "feudal patriarchy," but they failed, and the conflicted legacy of premodern gender ideology and modern equality continues to be part of China's contemporary society. Chinese women have risen to equality with men in some areas—academics, business, and the professions—but biology remains destiny for hundreds of millions of Chinese women today.

Nationalism and National Pride

The contemporary world has seen Chinese people react to international crises with widespread bursts of nationalism—the American bombing of the Chinese embassy in Belgrade perceived Japanese designs on some of "our" islands, the race for Olympic medals. This has not always been the case. An ancient Chinese proverb, commenting on the relationship between ordinary people and the government, said, "The sky is high, and the Emperor is far away." That distance prevented most people from feeling the intimacy and engagement with "our country" that we call nationalism. Modern nationalism requires participation, a sense that we (Chinese, Americans, Italians, Nigerians, etc.) are in it together, that our community belongs to us all.

Certainly some Chinese felt that way, even in the distant past, when they contrasted their own (civilized) culture with other (barbaric) peoples. But the elites who envisioned "Chineseness" in this way also contrasted themselves sharply with the common Chinese folk, the "black-haired masses," upon whom they called only to pay their taxes, do their civilian labor service, and stay out of trouble. The cultured elite saw the common people as uncivilized, ignorant, and thus very different from themselves, and people from one part of the emperor's realm perceived themselves as very different from folks from other parts. Only in modern times did "we Chinese" become a national collective, an "us" in contrast to the aggressive foreigners ("them") who threatened to dismember China in the nineteenth and twentieth centuries. Beginning in the first decade of the twentieth century, "Save the nation!" became a rallying cry, first for students and elites, then for politically aware business people and ordinary urbanites, and finally for the vast population of China's rural areas.

Since then every Chinese government—warlord, Nationalist, or Communist—has used the language and the passion of nationalism to mobilize people and resources, sometimes sincerely, sometimes cynically. When Beijing students protested against Japanese imperialism in 1919, or against Communist Party corruption and nepotism in 1989, they did so in the name of "the Chinese people," our nation. When the Nationalist Party called for resistance to Communism or resistance to Japan, they did so in the name of the nation. When Chinese worldwide rejoiced at the People's Republic's first space voyagers or the awarding of the 2008 Olympics to Beijing, they explicitly identified themselves as members of the Chinese nation.

That identification does not only derive from government and media manipulation. Rather, it includes a powerful sense of history, of the antiquity and greatness of China and Chinese culture, of pride in China's long classical tradition and achievements—the invention of paper and the compass, the construction of the Great Wall and the Grand Canal, the creation and preservation of Confucian family values, and much more. Whether fulfilled by China's productivity or its art, its elegant poetry or its famous warriors, the narrative of China's past has become a crucial part of the Chinese nationalist project. Chinese children learn in school that *their* country produced a great culture and that *their* country was oppressed by imperialist foreigners. The martyrdom of resistance heroes and the Communist Party's final victory entirely legitimize the rule of the current government as the embodiment of the nation. Certainly the Communist Party and government benefit from people thinking that way, but so do ordinary folks, who can identify with something larger and more powerful than their village, family, county, or province, especially when China opposes foreign rivals (especially Japan and the United States) and acts successfully in the world.

So when Tibetan militants protested violently against the Chinese state in 2008 and sympathizers worldwide rallied in their favor, millions of Chinese reacted with deeply felt nationalist sentiment. Chinese students from Tokyo to New York to Paris marched in support of their government, though many of them recognize it as corrupt and repressive, because they felt personally were attacked by what they saw as foreign desire to weaken or even dissect their homeland. "These are internal affairs!" they cried, echoing the Communist Party, and anyone who meddles will feel the wrath of over one billion loyal Chinese. In other words, whether studying physics in Berkeley or hauling bricks in Sichuan, vast numbers of people have come to identify themselves as *Chinese*, belonging to the nation (as well as to families, towns, regions, professions, etc.), and this constitutes an extremely powerful continuity of modern China's history.

An End to Essences

Finally, foreign observers must never allow themselves to be seduced by stereotypes, whether of the Chinese as homogeneous or of the Chinese as upside down, completely different from everyone else. Some Chinese do well in math and go to Qinghua University or Harvard, while others build substandard school buildings or work in dingy factories for very low wages. Some Chinese stay home and care for their families, while others run off to distant islands. Some Chinese women become corporate executives, while others marry young and live as rural housewives. Which is the "typical Chinese?" And how different are those choices from those made by non-Chinese? Like "the lessons of history," Chinese people vary widely, and outsiders must respect their diversity, study their culture, and understand them as human beings.

Notes

1. This simple narrative of China's past—exploitation and oppression by imperialist foreigners followed by national revival under the Communist Party's reform agenda—does have *some* truth value, but as we will see, it only tells part of the story.
2. Zhang Yimou's 1993 film, "The Story of Qiu Ju" (*Qiu Ju da guansi*), deals in part with this theme.
3. Over half of the world's cities with populations of 1,000,000+ are in China.
4. By the eighteenth century, the enormous number of candidates in the examinations had reduced an individual's chance of success to about seven thousand to one. See Miyazaki and Schirokauer (1981).
5. Scholars estimate that in 1750, half of the printed books in the world were in Chinese.
6. For the best summary of this argument, see Marks (2002).
7. From the account of Odoric de Pordenone, cited in Gernet (1970).
8. These fleets dwarfed the tiny ships and crews of Columbus's expeditions across the Atlantic half a century later. The *Nina*, *Pinta*, or *Santa Maria* could have been carried on the main deck of any one of Zheng He's dozens of large ships. Zheng He did not, however, circumnavigate the globe or discover the Americas.
9. For a sampling of the goods available in Chinese cities in various eras, see Schafer (1985) for the Tang; Gernet (1970) for the Song; and Brook (1998) for the Ming.
10. General Jiang is usually called Chiang Kai-shek in English.
11. Readers unfamiliar with this history can consult a textbook, such as Spence (1999). On the especially traumatic Cultural Revolution period, see MacFarquhar

and Schoenhals (2006). Contemporary Chinese filmmakers have made many movies that deal effectively and poignantly with elements of this history: Zhang Yimou, *To Live* (1994), based on Yu Hua's wonderful novel of the same name (Anchor Books, 2003); Tian Zhuangzhuang, *The Blue Kite* (1994); and Wang Xiaoyan, *The Monkey Kid* (1995), to name a few. After 1978, Chinese writers produced an enormous, heart wrenching "scar literature" trying to deal with the suffering and loss of moral compass of those years, including novels (Zhang Xianliang, *Half of Man Is Woman*, for example) and memoirs—Liang Heng, *Son of the Revolution*; Yue Daiyun and Carolyn Wakeman, *To the Storm*; and Gao Yuan, *Born Red* are three among many available in English.

12. Gallagher (2005); Lardy (2000); Whyte (2000); Zhao (2004).

13. For essays on these and other resistance to the state in China, see Perry and Selden (2003).

14. Some local communities did band together to resist, but the state responded with overwhelming violence. For example, the Muslim town of Shadian, in Yunnan province, organized in the early 1970s to oppose some of the antireligious excesses of the Cultural Revolution and was flattened by the army's artillery, suffering over 1,000 casualties.

15. Cited in Cohen (1984:59).

16. The late Prof. Needham's students continue his extraordinary work, currently in two dozen volumes and still growing. For a general overview of Needham's work, and his personal relationship to Chinese people and culture, see Winchester (2008).

17. A tiny sampling of important biographies might include Watson (1958); Rowe (2001); Mann (2007); and a wonderful collection, Wills (1994).

18. Japanese people still use thousands of Chinese characters in their writing system, and Koreans use a few, but both have phonetic representations of their languages as well. Chinese people do not, except for the *pinyin* romanization commonly used along with ideographs on street signs and in textbooks.

19. To this day, Chinese elites research, think, and write endlessly about the problem of "raising the quality" of the Chinese people through education, genetic engineering, population control, and other techniques.

20. We see the less savory, less "self-cultivated" aspects of China in the production of lead-tainted toys, chemically adulterated foods, and substandard products. This impression must be balanced by the successful adaptation of Chinese companies to international standards and quality control evident in China's vast outpouring of consumer goods.

21. The most notorious, and wealthiest, such factional leader was the late eighteenth century Manchu minister Hesen, whose personal fortune exceeded that of the Imperial treasury. See Nivison (1959:209–243).

22. *Shitou Ji*, also translated as "The Dream of the Red Chamber" (*Hong lou meng*).

23. At the other end of the social scale, Ning Lao-t'ai-t'ai, narrator of *A Daughter of Han: Autobiography of a Chinese Working Woman*, demonstrates that even a poor, illiterate woman could create meaning and agency in life as a domestic servant.

References

Bergere, Marie-Claire. 1989. *The Golden Age of the Chinese Bourgeoisie, 1911–1937.* Trans. Janet Lloyd. New York: Cambridge University Press.

Brook, Timothy. 1998. *The Confusions of Pleasure: Commerce and Culture in Ming China.* Berkeley, CA: University of California Press.

Cohen, Paul. 1984. *Discovering History in China: American Historical Writing on the Recent Chinese Past.* New York: Columbia University Press.

Gallagher, Mary. 2005. China in 2004: Stability above All. *Asian Survey* 45(1): 21–32.

Gernet, Jacques. 1970. *Daily Life in China on the Eve of the Mongol Invasion, 1250–1276.* Palo Alto, CA: Stanford University Press.

Lardy, Nicholas. 2000. The Challenge of Economic Reform and Social Stability. In *China under Jiang Zemin,* ed. Hung-mao Tien and Yun-Han Chu. Boulder, CO: Lynne Rienner.

MacFarquhar, Roderick and Michael Schoenhals. 2006. *Mao's Last Revolution.* Cambridge, MA: Belknap Press of Harvard University Press.

Mann, Susan. 2007. *The Talented Women of the Zhang Family.* Berkeley: University of California Press.

Marks, Robert. 2002. *The Origins of the Modern World: A Global and Ecological Narrative.* Lanham, MD: Rowman & Littlefield.

Miyazaki, Ichisada and Conrad Schirokauer. 1981. *China's Examination Hell: The Civil Service Examinations of Imperial China.* New Haven, CT: Yale University Press.

Needham, Joseph. 1954. *Science and Civilization in China.* New York: Cambridge University Press.

Ning L. T'ai-t'ai, Lao T'Ai-T'ai Ning, and Ida Pruitt. 1945. *Daughter of Han: Autobiography of a Chinese Working Woman.* Palo Alto, CA: Stanford University Press.

Nivison, David S. 1959. Ho-Shen and His Accusers: Ideology and Political Behavior in the Eighteenth Century. In *Confucianism in Action,* ed. David S. Nivison, Arthur F. Wright, William, and Theodore De Bary. Palo Alto, CA: Stanford University Press.

Perry, Elizabeth and Mark Selden, eds. 2003. *Chinese Society: Change, Conflict and Resistance.* 2nd edition. London and New York: Routledge.

Rowe, William. 2001. *Saving the World: Chen Hongmou and Elite Consciousness in Eighteenth Century China.* Palo Alto, CA: Stanford University Press.

Schafer, Edward. 1985. *The Golden Peaches of Samarkand: A Study of T'ang Exotics.* Berkeley, CA: University of California Press.

Spence, Jonathan. 1999. *The Search for Modern China,* 2nd edition. New York: W.W. Norton.

Tawney, R.H. 1932. *Land and Labor in China.* New York: Harcourt.

Watson, Burton. 1958. *Ssu-ma Ch'ien, Grand Historian of China.* New York: Columbia University Press.

Whyte, Martin King. 2000. Chinese Social Trends: Stability or Chaos? In *Is China Unstable? Assessing the Factors,* ed. David L. Shambaugh and Thomas P. Bernstein. Armonk, NY: ME Sharpe.

Wills, John E. 1994. *Mountain of Fame: Portraits in Chinese History.* Princeton, NJ: Princeton University Press.

Winchester, Simon. 2008. *The Man Who Loved China: The Fantastic Story of the Eccentric Scientist Who Unlocked the Mysteries of the Middle Kingdom.* New York: HarperCollins.

Zhao, Suisheng. 2004. China's Perception of External Threats to Its Security and Stability. In *Searching for Peace in Asia Pacific: An Overview of Conflict Prevention and Peacebuilding Activities,* ed. Annelies Heijmans, Nicola Simmonds, and Hans Van De Veen. Boulder, CO: Lynne Rienner.

Part 2

The Chinese Dragon: Domestic Challenges

Chapter 3

China's Political Trajectory: Internal Contradictions and Inner-Party Democracy

Cheng Li

Introduction

The year 2000 marks the thirtieth anniversary of China's policy of "reform and opening," which was initiated by Deng Xiaoping in 1978. Over the course of the past three decades, China's meteoric economic growth, profound societal transformations, and multifaceted integration with the outside world have been widely recognized by both policymakers and the general public in the United States. Yet, the American China studies community seems to have been struck by a prolonged and peculiar sort of political blindness. The early signs of Chinese political experiments, such as genuine local elections and regional representation at the national leadership, have largely been overlooked.[1] Some important socio-political forces unleashed by the country's transition toward a market economy, including the emergence of an entrepreneurial class and a middle class, are commonly perceived as factors that are more likely to consolidate the existing authoritarian political system than to challenge it (Dickson 2003). The prevailing view in the United States is that, despite the economic dynamism exhibited by present-day China, the governing regime is still Communist in nature and is, thus, resistant to significant political change (Mann 2007, Pei 2006, Nathan 2003, 2006).

This chapter focuses on two interrelated and potentially far-reaching political trends in present-day China that reveal significant changes in the nature of the political system: the growing internal contradictions in Chinese society and the experiments of inner-party democracy within the leadership. Three decades of market reforms have not only brought forth a wealthy entrepreneurial elite group and an ever-growing Chinese middle class, but have also created many less fortunate and increasingly marginalized socioeconomic groups. At the same time, China confronts many daunting challenges including economic disparity, employment pressure, environmental degradation, and the lack of a social safety net. As a result, Chinese leaders have come to realize that the country's political system is inadequate in dealing with the complicated, sometimes contradictory, needs of the Chinese economy and society and therefore are moving toward change.

By both design and necessity, the Chinese leaders have recently developed the notion of "inner-party democracy," embracing the idea that the Chinese Communist Party (CCP) should institutionalize checks and balances within its leadership. To a certain extent, a Chinese style bipartisanship, characterized by two informal and almost equally powerful coalitions within the CCP leadership, has already emerged. Competition between these two coalitions over power, influence, and policy initiatives reflects the growth of conflicting interests in this rapidly changing country. The socioeconomic classes (both old and new) have also become more consciously sought after for their support of representatives in the leadership. These new dynamics in state-society relations will either lead to political deadlock or contribute to a more responsible and representative political system that will enable the leadership to deal with the various challenges that the country faces. Such new political trends are profoundly important for our assessment of China's political trajectory. Ultimately, China's rise to prominence in the twenty-first century in the international arena will depend on its strength in various domains, including political resilience and openness. Military and economic might are undoubtedly important, but a country that is not viewed by its own citizens to be politically legitimate cannot claim to be a rising world power.

Economic Development and Socio-Political Change

Of course, China's political development in the reform era, though intriguing and potentially consequential, has been far less fundamental or systemic than changes in the economic realm. Yet, it is too simplistic to think that the earthshaking socioeconomic changes that have transformed China over the past three decades have taken place within a political vacuum, with no corresponding changes in the Chinese political system. Those who adhere to the view of concurrent Chinese economic development and political stagnation must ask themselves: How is it possible that the supposedly inert ruling party was able to accomplish China's first peaceful political succession in 2002–2003? How has the widely perceived monolithic ruling elite been able to drastically and successfully alter the course of the country's socioeconomic development from a single-minded emphasis on GDP growth to an approach that places greater emphasis on social cohesion and the fair distribution of wealth? Are the recent and frequent speeches by top Chinese leaders and their advisors about political democracy and inner-party elections purely political rhetoric?[2]

Critics of the Chinese regime are right to condemn China's widespread human rights violations, strict media censorship, and one-party rule. These problems are real, and they not only reveal serious deficiencies in the present Chinese political system but also explain why China's international reputation remains poor. Yet, even in these frequently cited problem areas, there have recently been some remarkable, and potentially far-reaching, positive changes. For example, over the past decade, the Chinese term for "human rights" (*renquan*) has shed its negative connotation, transitioning from implying Western anti-China hypocrisy to gaining such a positive luster that the Chinese government has expressed a willingness to engage in a dialogue on this issue with the outside world.

Perhaps more importantly, a clause asserting that it is the government's responsibility to ensure the protection of citizens' human rights was added to China's constitution in 2003. The issue of human rights, especially the rights of those vulnerable social groups such as migrant workers, has increasingly become a central concern in the public discourse within the People's Republic of China (PRC). Meanwhile, despite tremendous efforts by the Chinese authorities to control the media and the Internet, the commercialization of the media and the unprecedented telecommunications revolution are making the flow of information easier and faster, bringing new perspectives to the Chinese public, and offering new voices for the country's increasingly pluralistic interest groups.[3]

With respect to political competition, the CCP seems neither willing to give up its monopoly on political power, nor interested in moving toward a Western-style system based on a tripartite division between the executive, legislative, and judicial functions of government. But this does not mean that the Chinese leadership is a monolithic elite group whose members all share the same values, outlooks, political backgrounds, and policy preferences. The political factions currently competing for power seem to represent the interests of different socioeconomic classes and different geographical regions, thus creating something approximating a mechanism of checks and balances in the government decision-making process. To a certain extent, this development reflects an important transition away from the previous political system, one that relied on arbitrary decision-making power held by one individual leader, such as Mao or Deng. Today, Chinese politics are much different—characterized by a system of collective leadership that functions according to commonly accepted binding rules. With a few noticeable exceptions, these subtle but important political changes have not received as much attention in the Western academic discourse as they deserve.

Chinese Society: Contending Forces and Conflicting Interests

A recent report on the PRC by the Council on Foreign Relations' Task Force observed that China is a paradox of numerous contrasts: "modern and ancient, Communist and capitalist, rich and poor, reforming and resisting change, homogenous and diverse, repressive and freewheeling, conservative and revisionist, passive and aggressive, strong and weak" (Hills and Blair 2007). Many factors, such as China's sheer size, large population, and lasting historical legacies, have contributed to these dichotomies. The rapid economic transformation, especially the emergence of new socioeconomic forces, has also added to the complexity and growing pluralistic nature of Chinese society.

Beneficiaries of the Reform

One of the most fascinating developments in China during the reform era has been the swift rise of three related but not identical new socioeconomic forces, namely, entrepreneurs, the middle class, and state corporate interest groups. These three classes are the main beneficiaries of economic reform.

By definition, entrepreneurs are engaged in risk-taking businesses in a market economy. In the Chinese context, entrepreneurs mainly refer to business owners and/or managers of private firms; but if one employs a broader definition of the term, it may encompass the managers of collective, public, or joint venture enterprises.[4] The upward social mobility of China's contemporary entrepreneurs represents a historical change in

Chinese society (Nee 1996). Traditional Chinese society, which was dominated by the scholar-gentry class, tended to devalue merchants (now called entrepreneurs). The antimerchant discrimination reached its climax during the first few decades of the PRC. Throughout the Mao era, the role of entrepreneurs was strictly restrained. The 4 million private firms and stores that had existed in China prior to the 1949 Communist Revolution had all disappeared by the mid-1950s.[5] Since 1978, however, private enterprises have played an increasingly important role in the PRC, radically transforming the social standing of business owners. Factors that have contributed to the rise of entrepreneurs in the post-Mao era include the rapid development of rural industries, rural-urban migration, urban private enterprises and joint ventures, the adoption of a stock market and land lease practices, foreign trade and investment, and technological revolution, especially the birth of the Internet.

The composition of the Chinese entrepreneurial class has been diverse and dynamic ever since its emergence in the 1980s. Yet, three distinct groups, largely based on the different means through which they have become rich, are particularly noticeable. Each of these groups has a distinctive occupational background and reflects the particular socioeconomic environment from which it ascended. The first consists largely of people who became rich as the result of the rapid growth of the township and village enterprises (TVEs) in rural China or who opened private restaurants and shops in urban areas in the 1980s. The second is comprised mainly of corrupt officials and their children. They emerged after the late 1980s, especially after Deng Xiaoping's famous southern journey in 1992, and took advantage of the two-track pricing system, making huge fortunes by issuing certificates, business permits, tax breaks, land leases, and quotas. The third group of entrepreneurs emerged during the late 1990s, largely as a result of the Internet and the rapid development of the computer industry. A new Chinese term, *zhibenjia* (knowledge capitalist), has been created to refer to this third class of entrepreneurs. In contrast to the term *zibenjia* (capitalist), it suggests that at a time when information technology transforms economies, the primary capital is knowledge. Knowledge elites, especially those who work in the IT sector, are often seen as the leading force in the so-called information age. The three major subgroups of entrepreneurs are all very active in today's China. They will likely coexist and share the country's wealth for many years to come.

According to a Chinese official source, in 2006, China had about 5 million private enterprises, accounting for 57 percent of the total business firms in the country and contributing one-third of tax revenue.[6] In addition, about 45 million other people ran their own small businesses. Many owners of private enterprises are members of the Chinese Communist

Party; and their percentage in the total private entrepreneurs increased significantly during the past 15 years—from 13 percent in 1993 to 34 percent in 2004.[7] A recent study by *Forbes* magazine revealed that 35 percent of the 500 richest people in China in 2006—all of them multimillionaires or even billionaires—are CCP members.[8]

While some entrepreneurs may also be considered members of China's middle class, urban professionals—including government employees, office workers in foreign firms, college professors, journalists, and lawyers—constitute the main body of China's fastest growing socioeconomic bracket. Ironically, China analysts generally did not recognize the existence of the Chinese middle class until the late 1990s. At the close of the twentieth century, however, with a large and growing number of urban Chinese who owned their private homes and cars, analysts in both China and abroad suddenly began to take note of the existence of a middle class in China.[9] In 2002, the Chinese Academy of Social Sciences (CASS) reported that the country had a middle class of 80 million people.[10] What makes someone a member of the Chinese middle class is the combination of income, consumption, and lifestyle.[11] A recent report by McKinsey & Co. estimates that by 2025 China's middle class will consist of about 520 million people.[12]

China's entrepreneurs are disproportionately distributed along the southeast coastal area. In the city of Shenzhen, for example, about 2 million people belong to the middle class. They are usually young, well-educated, and there is some evidence that they are increasingly interested in opportunities for political participation.[13] Emerging young professionals contribute to the rapid growth of China's middle class. During the past decade, the number of registered lawyers and law school students, for example, has increased significantly.[14] In the early 1980s, there were only three thousand lawyers in a country of over one billion people. In 2004, China had a total of 114,000 lawyers in 11,691 registered law firms, and this number will probably double in the next few years.[15] China today has 620 law schools and departments that produce roughly 100,000 law graduates a year (Cohen 2004). The number of enrolled students at the Law School of Beijing University in 2004, including those studying part time, equaled the total number of law students trained at the institution over the course of the past 50 years.[16] Despite the rapid growth of the Chinese legal profession, however, it is still too early to say if an increase in lawyers will lead to the expansion of the rule of law in China. An encouraging phenomenon is, however, that some lawyers have actively engaged in human rights issues and many now work in nongovernment organizations (NGOs).[17]

While the emergence of entrepreneurs and the middle class is often considered to be a positive development, the corporate and industrial interest groups have created much public resentment. The Chinese business interest groups consist mainly of two clusters. The first refers to those economic elites who work in the state monopolized industries such as oil, electricity, coal, telecommunications, aviation, and shipping; and the second refers to the lobby groups who work for foreign or private firms in sectors such as real estate. These lobbying groups often have strong ties with local governments. In general, local governments also have vested interests in these business deals, which may result in increased tax revenues for their municipalities.

It has been widely reported in the Chinese media that business interest groups have routinely bribed local officials and formed a "wicked coalition" with local governments.[18] Some Chinese observers believe that the various players associated with property development have emerged as one of the most powerful special interest groups in the present-day PRC.[19] According to Sun Liping, a sociology professor at Qinghua University, the real estate interest group has accumulated tremendous economic and social capital during the past decade.[20] Ever since the early 1990s real estate bubble in Hainan, this interest group has consistently attempted to influence government policy and public opinion. The group includes not only property developers, real estate agents, bankers, and housing market speculators, but also some local officials and public intellectuals (economists and journalists) who promote the interests of that group.[21]

This could explain in part why the central government's macroeconomic control policy (*hongguan tiaokong*) has failed to achieve its intended objectives, as analyzed in detail in this volume by Christine Wong. A survey of 200 Chinese officials and scholars conducted in 2005 showed that 50 percent believed that China's socioeconomic reforms, especially the central government's macroeconomic control policies, have been constrained by "some elite groups with vested economic interests" (*jide liyi jituan*).[22] In 2005, for example, the real estate sector remained overheated with a 20 percent increase in the rate of investment despite the central government's repeated call for the cooling of investment in this area.[23] In the same year, the State Council sent four inspection teams to eight provinces and cities to evaluate the implementation of the central government's macroeconomic control policy in the real estate sector. According to the Chinese media, most of these provincial and municipal governments did nothing but organize study groups that discussed the State Council's policy initiatives.[24]

Not surprisingly, a large number of corruption cases are related to land leases and real estate development. For example, among the 13 total number of provincial and ministerial level leaders who were arrested in 2003, 11 were primarily accused of illegal pursuits in land-related decisions.[25]

Meanwhile, a large portion of mass protests directly resulted from inappropriate compensation for land confiscations and other disputes associated with commercial and industrial land use. According to a recent study by the Institute of Rural Development of the CASS, two-thirds of protests by peasants since 2004 were caused by local officials' misdeeds in the handling of land leases.[26] The annual number of mass incidents in the country, including protests, riots, and group petitioning, rose from 58,000 in 2003, to 74,000 in 2004, and to 87,000 in 2005—almost 240 incidents per day! These public resentments associated with land leases reveal the growing tensions and conflicts between "winners" and "losers," between haves and have-nots, and between wealthy beneficiaries and vulnerable social groups in China's economic reforms.

Economic Disparity and Vulnerable Social Groups

Despite rapid economic growth, China has been beset by the growing economic gap between urban and rural areas, coastal and inland regions, and new economies and traditional economic sectors. Within a generation, China has transformed itself from one of the most equitable countries in the world in terms of income distribution to one of the least equitable. Jiang Zemin's theory of "three represents," which broadens the CCP's power base by recruiting entrepreneurs, or capitalists, into the party, is often regarded by the public as a ploy by the ruling party that represents only the rich and powerful.

Regional economic disparity has increased significantly in the past decade. Among China's 100 wealthiest counties in 2004, 92, including all of the top ten, were located in the coastal region. In 2003, the average revenue of 8,477 towns in the east coast region was 28.3 million yuan, in contrast to only 4.8 million yuan on average for 5,748 towns in China's western region (Ru, Lu, and Li 2005:7). The ratio of the GDP per capita between the coast and inland regions increased from 1.86 in 1991 to 2.33 in 2000 to 2.52 in 2003 to 3.2 to 1 in 2005 (National Bureau of Statistics of China 2006). The ratio of GDP per capita between Zhejiang Province and Guizhou Province increased from 2.7 in 1991 to 5.6 in 2003.[27] The difference in GDP per capita between Shanghai and Guizhou increased from 7.3 times in 1990 to 13 times in 2003.[28] In contrast, the ratio of the GDP per capita between the richest and poorest of the European Union's (EU) 24 regions in 2002 was 2.4, which in fact was an incentive for the EU to reduce this gap.[29]

Arguably the most important sources for social disturbance in China today are the growing number of landless migrants. During the past decade, China has been engaged in probably the largest "enclosure" movement (*quandi yundong*) that the world has ever seen. A vast area of agricultural land has been "enclosed" for commercial and industrial uses. Land leases for foreign companies, infrastructure, and transportation projects, and real estate development have forced a large number of people, in both urban and rural areas, to relocate. The recent wave of new "university cities," where universities build new campuses together on the outskirts of urban areas, has also driven many farmers out of their homelands. According to a Chinese official source, from 1996 to 2004, China's arable land decreased by 150 million *mu*, about 5 percent of the country's total arable land.[30] Meanwhile, about 40 million people have become "landless migrants."

By 2006, the country had a total of 150 million migrant workers, and this ever-expanding group constitutes an important force for social and political change.[31] Migrant laborers are unique in the Chinese context—they are considered "workers in occupation" and "farmers in identity." Like all citizens, they want to have a decent salary, a safe work environment, basic social welfare rights, education for their children, and respect from society. But in reality, they can get hardly any of these.[32] They are second, or even third, class citizens in the PRC.[33] But as Liu Kaiming, director of the Shenzhen Social Research Institute, observed, China's migrant laborers are also experiencing a generational change. The new generation of migrant laborers is better educated and is more conscientious about protecting their interests.[34] They often use cell phones to disseminate information and are potentially more interested in political participation. They were, for example, the main participants in worker strikes in Shenzhen and other coastal cities during the past few years.

Contradictory Needs and Concerns

These dynamic new forces in Chinese society—entrepreneurs, the middle class, and corporate interest groups on the one hand, and migrant workers and other vulnerable social groups on the other hand—will remain important for China's political and socioeconomic development in the years to come. Now more than during any previous period in PRC history, the elite interest groups and the general public are aware of ways to advance and protect their economic interests. Chinese decision makers will likely be increasingly sensitive in addressing the needs and concerns of these potentially contentious groups. The most daunting challenge for the Chinese leaders is perhaps to obtain the wisdom and leadership skills needed to achieve the best possible equilibrium between contradictory needs in the country. The Chinese leaders need to be very delicate in balancing these contradictory concerns. The following list summarizes the most important concerns:

- They need to accelerate the market reforms required by international standards to assist China's growing integration in the global economy, but at the same time they must use policy decisions to assist vulnerable areas and to establish a social safety net.
- They have to deal seriously with rampant official corruption in order to avoid political backlash, while at the same time avoiding chaos.
- They must respond to the growing demands of societal forces, including emerging NGOs and migrant workers, while at the same time not undermine the governing capacity of the authoritarian regime. They need to broaden the power base of the CCP by recruiting entrepreneurs, lawyers, and other professionals, but at the same time avoid portraying the CCP as an elitist party that represents only the interests of the rich and powerful.
- They need to give more autonomy to provincial and local governments without undermining national integration and the governing capacity of the central government.
- They need to allocate more resources to the inland region and issue more state bonds for its development, but this should not be achieved at the expense of the more efficient coastal region.

Most importantly, from the perspective of China's top leaders, they need to initiate a new leadership structure or a new political system to correspond with the ever-changing socioeconomic environment, but at the same time, be careful to not undermine the system of one-party rule. The idea of inner-party democracy seems to be particularly appealing to top leaders such as Hu Jintao, Wen Jiabao, and Zeng Qinghong.

Chinese Leadership: One Party, Two Coalitions

The inner-party partisanship in the CCP, which is currently characterized by checks and balances between two factions or two informal coalitions in the CCP leadership, did not come to the fore simply as a result of the ideas of China's top leaders. As a matter of fact, dual trends have contributed to this remarkable change in Chinese elite politics. Unless China dramatically reverses its course, these trends will most likely continue, if not accelerate, in the future, and will change the political course of China.

Ending "Strong-Man" Politics

The first trend is a gradual transformation from an all-powerful, god-like, and charismatic single leader to a collective leadership. A review of the leadership politics of the PRC four generations (Mao, Deng, Jiang, and Hu) illustrates this profound transformation.

Throughout the Mao era, especially during the Cultural Revolution, the Chairman wielded enormous power. As an example, Mao treated succession as if it was his own private matter; discussion of the transition of power was taboo. The omnipresent slogan "Long Live Chairman Mao" reinforced the illusion of Mao's "immortality."

During the Deng era, political succession and the generational change in the Chinese leadership became a matter of public concern. Yet, because of his legendary political career, no leaders dared to challenge Deng's authority, even when he did not hold an important leadership position following the Tiananmen crisis. For many years during the 1990s, people in China and Sinologists abroad speculated about when the geriatric Deng would die, often causing stock markets in Hong Kong and China to fluctuate wildly.

Jiang Zemin has neither the charisma nor the revolutionary experience that Deng had. To a large extent, Jiang has remained in power since 1989 primarily through coalition building and political compromise. During the 2002 Party Congress, for example, the political spotlight focused on Jiang's scheduled retirement. The bifurcation of the military and civilian leaders also contributed to the end of both "strong-man politics" and "the soldier as a king-maker."

Hu Jintao's generation of leaders relies even more on power sharing and consensus building. Hu is known for his low profile personality and his skills in coalition building reflect a defining characteristic of the fourth generation of Chinese leaders. During the past few years some foreign observers have even wondered whether "Hu is in charge." To a certain extent, Hu is largely the "first among equals" in his generation of leaders. He could not even appoint one of his protégés to be his successor. Instead, a model of dual successors was introduced at the Seventeenth Party Congress.[35]

The shift in Chinese public sentiment from "whether Mao would ever die" to "when will Deng die" to "when will Jiang retire" to "whether Hu is in charge?" shows the consistent trend toward a more collective leadership replacing "strong-man" politics. As a result of this change, political negotiation and compromise in the leadership are taking place far more often than before.

Increasing Institutional Restraints

Nepotism in various forms (e.g., blood ties, school ties, regional identities, bureaucratic affiliations, or patron-client ties) has played a profoundly important role in the selection of leaders during the reform era. But, at the same time, institutional mechanisms such as formal regulations and informal norms have been more effectively implemented to curtail various forms of favoritism. These institutional developments include

- *Elections with more candidates than seats (cha'e xuanju).* For example, if the CCP Central Committee plans to elect 200 full members, it will offer 5 percent more candidates (210) on the ballet.
- *Term limits.* With some exceptions, a term limit of five years has been established for top posts in both the party and the government. An individual leader cannot hold the same position for more than two terms.
- *Age limits for retirement.* Based on CCP regulations or norms, leaders above a certain level cannot exceed a set age limit. For example, all the members who were born before 1940 retired from the Central Committee at the Seventeenth Party Congress.
- *Regional representation on the CCP Central Committee.* On the CCP Central Committee, each of the 31 provincial-level administrations has 2 full members.
- *"Law of avoidance" in selection of local top leaders.* For example, provincial party secretaries are often nonnative outsiders who were transferred from another province or the central government.

These institutional rules and norms generate a sense of consistency and fairness in the selection of leaders. Consequently, no individual, faction, institution, or region can dominate the power structure. These developments have reinforced the norm of checks and balances in the Chinese leadership and affected elite behaviors. New leaders are far more interested in seeking legitimacy through institutional channels than were their predecessors.

Three Features of Factional Dynamics

Institutional development in China does not reduce factional tensions; instead, it makes factional politics more dynamic. These new factional dynamics have three main features: (1) the current coalitions represent two different socio-political and geographical constituencies; (2) they have somewhat contrasting policy initiatives and priorities; and (3) they compete with each other over some issue areas but cooperate on others.

The Elitist Coalition versus the Populist Coalition: Social and Geographical Contrasts

These two coalitions cannot be simplistically divided into ideological predispositions such as liberals and conservatives, or reformers and hardliners. More appropriate labels would call the coalition led by former party chief Jiang and his protégé, Vice President Zeng Qinghong, the "elitist coalition" and the other coalition, led by current party chief Hu and Premier Wen Jiabao, the "populist coalition."[36] The elitist coalition and the populist coalition represent two starkly different socio-political and geographical constituencies. These differences are largely reflected in their leaders' distinct personal careers and political associations.

The core faction of the elitist coalition consists of *princelings*, children of former high ranking officials. Many have advanced their careers in the areas of finance, trade, foreign affairs, IT industries, and education. Some are returnees from studies abroad, (*haiguipai*). The leaders in the elitist coalition often represent the interests of economic and cultural power players as well as the most economically advanced coastal regions. Jiang, Zeng, and Xi Jinping (one of the dual possible successors to Hu) all come from the privileged families of high ranking officials and advanced their political careers in Shanghai. Like his mentor Zeng, Xi has also spent almost all his leadership career working in coastal regions such as Fujian, Zhejiang, and Shanghai.

In contrast, none of the top three populist leaders, Hu, Wen, and Li Keqiang (the other possible successor to Hu), has strong political family ties and all spent many years working in China's poorest areas. Hu has spent most of his adult life in some of the poorest provinces in China's inland region—14 years in Gansu, 3 years in Guizhou, and about 4 years in Tibet. Similarly, Wen spent the 15 years after college graduation working in extremely arduous conditions, also mainly in Gansu. Li Keqiang worked in Henan and Liaoning for almost 10 years before moving to Beijing in 2007. The fact that Hu, Wen, and Li come from China's poorest regions suggests that they are more sensitive to the needs and concerns of the inland provinces and weaker social groups.

The core faction of the populist coalition is the Chinese Communist Youth League (CCYL), the so-called *tuanpai* who worked in the national or provincial leadership in the League in the early 1980s when Hu Jintao was in charge of the organization. Hu's *tuanpai* officials alone occupy 86 seats in the 371-member Central Committee selected at the Seventeenth Party Congress in October 2007, accounting for 23 percent of this decision-making body. Most of the members of the populist coalition advanced their political careers through local and provincial administrations, often in poor inland provinces, and many have worked in the areas of youth affairs, rural administration, party organization, propaganda, united front work, and legal affairs. Like many members of the populist coalition, both Hu and Wen focused on party organizational work for many years.

In the newly formed Politburo and Secretariat of the Seventeenth Central Committee, there are 8 members now in their fifties. These eight leaders can be equally divided into two groups in terms of their factional affiliations. Four leaders—Li Keqiang, Li Yuanchao, Wang Yang, and Ling Jihua—are in the populist camp. All advanced their careers primarily from the CCYL and are known as long-time protégés of Hu Jintao. The other four—Xi Jinping, Wang Qishan, Bo Xilai, and Wang Huning—belong to the elitist camp. The first three are princelings, while Wang Huning is a member of the Shanghai Gang. These four leaders are all protégés of Jiang Zemin and Zeng Qinghong.

A vicious power struggle between these two camps is, of course, hardly inevitable. Political competition in China is by no means a zero sum game. Fifth Generation leaders are smart enough to understand that they are all "in the same boat." It is, therefore, in their best interest to demonstrate political solidarity publicly when facing enormous economic and sociopolitical challenges.

Having said that, the diverse demographic and political backgrounds of China's top leaders can be seen as a positive development that may contribute to political pluralism in the country. Collective leadership, one might even argue, is not only a mechanism of power sharing through checks and balances among competing political camps, but is also a more dynamic and institutionalized decision-making process through which political leaders come to represent various social and geographic constituencies and thus develop better policies to meet new and complicated socioeconomic environments.

From Jiang to Hu: A Policy Shift

The Jiang era was known for the rapid development of Shanghai. Jiang allocated a disproportionately large amount of economic resources to Shanghai and other coastal cities while allowing many inland provinces to lag behind. Since that time, China has paid the enormous cost of environmental and ecological degradation for its narrow-minded focus on economic growth.

Upon his ascension to power, Hu quickly sensed that his mandate was to fix the serious problems associated with Jiang's leadership. Over the past few years, Hu has outlined his development strategy under new catch phrases such as "scientific development," and the "harmonious society." Christine Wong (this volume) describes these policies in detail. With this strategy Hu has already changed China's course of development in three important ways: (1) from obsession with GDP growth to greater concern about social justice; (2) from the single-minded emphasis on coastal development to a more balanced regional development strategy; and (3) from a policy in favor of entrepreneurs and other elites to a populist approach that focuses on the interests of farmers, migrant workers, the urban unemployed, and other vulnerable social groups. The emphasis on more balanced regional development has already placed some inland cities such as Chongqing and Xi'an on the fast track to economic growth. For example, a new industrial renovation project in Chongqing has a fixed asset investment of 350 billion *yuan* (US$43.5 billion) over the next five years.[37]

In their first term, Hu and Wen took many popular actions: reducing the tax burden on farmers, abolishing discriminatory regulations against migrants, ordering business firms and local governments to pay their debts to migrant workers, visiting AIDS patients and the families of coalmine explosion victims, and launching a nation-wide donation campaign to help those in need. These policy changes and public gestures by Hu and Wen suggest that current top Chinese leaders are not only aware of the tensions and problems confronting the country, but also are willing to respond to them in a timely and often proactive fashion.

Competition, Cooperation, and Complicated Interdependence

While these two coalitions represent different regional and socioeconomic interests as well as divergent policy priorities, both have valid socio-political concerns. Neither the elitist coalition nor the populist coalition is willing to, or capable of, defeating the other in terms of monopoly of power and policy agenda. These two coalitions compete against each other in some areas, and cooperate in others. This dynamic is creating a complicated factional interdependence.

Each coalition has its own strengths that the other does not possess. *Tuanpai* officials are well-endowed in terms of organizational and propaganda skills and often possess experience in rural administration, especially in poor inland regions, although they are usually less qualified to handle the international economy. *Tuanpai* officials' credentials may not have been valuable in a Jiang era that stressed foreign investment and economic globalization, but are essential at a time when the Hu administration emphasizes the need to focus on social problems and political tensions among various interest groups. My recent study of 22 prominent *tuanpai* leaders found that none of them has had work experience in foreign trade, foreign investment, finance, or banking (Cheng 2005).

The divergent work experiences and administrative skills of these two coalitions suggest that the *tuanpai* and the princelings need each other. *Tuanpai* officials' lack of credentials in economics, especially in foreign trade and finance, is an inherent disadvantage for this powerful elite group. Consequently, Hu's *tuanpai* officials must cooperate—and share power— with other elite groups. This highlights the fact that, although Hu is in charge, other political forces may be able to restrain his power. Such tension creates a healthy political dynamic that may help prevent Hu and his protégés from wielding excessive power or achieving social fairness at the expense of economic development. To a great extent, both coalitions share a common purpose: to ensure the survival of the CCP rule at home and retain China's status as a major international player abroad. This makes Chinese bipartisanship sustainable. In my judgment, this "one Party, two factions" formula will likely remain a dominant feature of Chinese elite politics for the next 10–15 years.

Concluding Thoughts

Inner-party democracy is not true democracy, but it may pave the way for a more fundamental change in the Chinese political system. The democratic transition of the world's most populous nation, if it occurs, will certainly be no easy task. At present, political power in China is monopolized by the CCP, which prohibits the formation of competing political parties or an independent judiciary. In the absence of a broad-based and well-organized political opposition in the PRC, it is unlikely that the country will develop a multiparty political system in the near future. This fact actually makes the ongoing experiments with inner-party bipartisanship even more important, as the Chinese leaders often assert that China's democracy should take a path based on the country's cultural and historical circumstances.

Despite its dynamics, the Chinese inner-party bipartisanship has some serious limitations. Factional politics and political coalitions within the party, although not completely opaque to the public, lack transparency. Unlike factional politics in democracies such as the LDP-hegemony period in Japan, factional politics within the CCP are not yet legitimated by the party constitution. Chinese bipartisanship may provide checks and balances in the Chinese political system and thereby revitalize the CCP leadership. But the CCP as currently constituted cannot survive indefinitely, partly because societal forces will become increasingly active in the Chinese political process, and partly because inner-party bipartisanship itself will lead to further political changes. The inner-party elite groups are increasingly seeking support from certain socioeconomic classes through new policy initiatives. These initiatives largely represent the interests of one or another populace group. Jiang Zemin's theory of "the three represents" aimed to advance the economic interests and political power of entrepreneurs while Hu Jintao's call for building a harmonious society pays more attention to vulnerable social groups such as farmers and migrant workers. These major policy changes are real, not just political rhetoric.

This evolving arrangement is not just a top-down process. China's new socioeconomic groups have a strong effect on the formation and the policy orientation of the new leadership. It is important to point out, however, that due to the incremental nature of this institutional development, the competition—or even the possible split—within the CCP in the future can potentially be achieved in a nonviolent way. The leadership's shared concern for avoiding chaos and the fact that two major political coalitions are almost equally powerful makes China's inner-party bipartisanship sustainable for years to come. Elections and competition within the CCP might one day even be extended to general elections in the country as some top Chinese leaders and their advisors recently stated.[38] Ultimately, China's rise to prominence in the twenty-first century will depend on its ability to adapt to global governance norms, including political pluralism, openness, transparency, and the rule of law.

China's emerging bipartisanship within the ruling party has profound implications for the outside world, especially the United States. It will be a mistake if China watchers continue to consider the Chinese leadership a monolithic group or perceive Chinese factional politics in ideological terms such as hardliners versus liberals, communists versus reformers. China analysts and policymakers should pay greater attention to the dynamics and constraints in Chinese elite politics, as more comprehensively articulated in this volume by Susan Shirk. U.S. policy toward China will be far more effective if it is formulated and delivered in a way that is more sensitive to the tensions in the social forces within Chinese society and the competition of elite groups in the leadership.

On the other hand, the next 10–15 years will test the political instincts, strategic vision, wisdom, humility, and capabilities of the Chinese leadership. These two coalitions in the upcoming Fifth Generation have been allotted an equal number of the seats in China's most important decision-making organs, indicating the intensity of factional competition, especially for the upcoming political succession. In a far more important sense, this period will also test whether China can make a major step toward a more institutionalized transition to power sharing. One must hope that the next generation of Chinese leaders is up to this task. If it fails, this most populous country—and the entire world—will be profoundly affected.

Notes

The author also thanks Christina Culver, Scott W. Harold, Robert O'Brien, and Penelope Prime for suggesting improvements in the chapter.

1. For example, since the Fifteenth National Party Congress held in 1997, each and every one of the provincial-level Party Committees has two representatives serving as full members on the Central Committee of the Chinese Communist Party formed at the Congress.
2. Buckley, Chris. 2008. "Elite China Think-Tank Issues Political Reform Blueprint." Reuters. February 18. http://www.reuters.com/article/worldNews/idUSPEK20590720080219 (accessed February 18, 2008).
3. John L. Thornton recently observed that, as independent Chinese publications seek readers and advertisers, they report stories that are of interest to the public, and, like their counterparts in the West, they have discovered that investigative journalism sells (Thornton 2008).
4. Chinese scholars define an entrepreneur as "a manager and/or owner of private property—a person who has managed to possess property either through capitalization of personal income, or through the private operation of a collective, public or joint venture enterprise" (Houyi 1995).
5. *China News Analysis*, No. 1501, January 1, 1994, p. 2.
6. http://news.xinhuanet.com/politics/2007-10/12/content_6870696.htm (accessed March 5, 2008).
7. *Xingdao ribao*, December 13, 2004, 1.
8. See "Hu Run's List of the 500 Richest People in China in 2006." http://news.xinhuanet.com (accessed October 11, 2006). Also, see Dickson (2008).
9. According to the Chinese official media, China will "have 140 million automobiles plying its roads by 2020, seven times more than the number in 2004." See http://www.chinadaily.com.cn/english/doc/2004-09/04/content_371641.htm (accessed March 5, 2008).
10. Lu Xueyi, "Dandai zhongguo shehuijieceng yanjiu baogao" (Research Report on Social Strata in Contemporary China) (Beijing: Shehui kexuewenxian chubanshe, 2002), 254–256.

11. For a detailed discussion of the definition of the Chinese middle class, see Zhou Xiaohong and others. *Zhongguo zhongchan jieji diaocha* (A survey of the Chinese Middle Class). Beijing: Shehui wenxian chubanshe, 2005.

12. Quoted from *Zhongguo jingying bao* (China Business Daily), July 9, 2006, p. 1. According to this McKinsey report, in 2006, the percentage of the Chinese urban families that have an annual income below 25,000 yuan will drop from 77 percent in 2006 to 10 percent in 2025. For a comprehensive discussion of the definition of the middle class in China, see Zhou Xiaohong and others. *Zhongguo zhongchan jieji diaocha.*

13. *Yangcheng wanbao* (Guangzhou Evening News), February 19, 2007.

14. Ji Shuoming and Wang Jianming, *Zhongguo weiquan lushi fazhixianfeng* (China's Lawyers for Human Rights Protection: Vanguards of the Rule of Law). *Yazhou zhoukan* (Asia Week), December 19, 2005.

15. Jean-Pierre Cabestan, "Zhongguo de sifa gaige" (China's Judicial Reform). news.bbc.co.uk/hi/chinese/china_news/newsid_2149000/21492061.stm (accessed July 27, 2002).

16. *Renmin ribao* (People's Daily), May 19, 2004, p. 15.

17. Ji and Wang, *Zhongguo weiquan lushi fazhixianfeng.*

18. *Zhongguo xinwen zhoukan* (China Newsweek), January 13, 2006, *Liaowang* (Outlook), December 5, 2005, and also see http://www.chinesenewsnet.com, December 12, 2005.

19. The other powerful interest groups include the monopoly industries such as telecommunications, oil, electricity, and automotive. They have a huge stake in government policies. See Sun Liping, "Zhongguo jinru liyi boyi de shidai" (China Is Entering the Era of the Conflict of Interests)," http://chinesenewsnet.com, February 6, 2006.

20. Sun, "Zhongguo jinru liyi boyi de shidai."

21. Jin Sanyong, "Zhongyang difang cunzai mingxian boyi" (The Open Game that the Central and Local Governments Play). See http://www.zisi.net, February 10, 2006.

22. China's Reform Institute (Hainan) conducted this survey. See http://chinanews.com, January 19, 2006.

23. See http://www.news.soufun.com, February 10, 2006.

24. Ibid.

25. Ibid.

26. Qianshao (Frontier), No. 10 (2005), p. 83.

27. Ru, Lu, and Li, *2005 Zhongguo shehui xingshi fenxi yu yuce*, p. 86.

28. Ibid., p. 180.

29. Ibid.

30. *Liaowang dongfang zhoukan*, December 30, 2004, p. 35.

31. This is based on data from China's Ministry of Agriculture, see (cnc.nfcmag.com/ReadNews-12400.html. [July 15, 2007]).

32. *Zhongguo xinwen zhoukan* (China News Weekly), December 28, 2004, p. 1.

33. www.chinesenewsnet.com (accessed December 28, 2004).

34. *Zhongguo xinwen zhoukan* (China News Weekly), December 28, 2004, p. 1. Also see Harney (2008).

35. Cheng Li. 2007. "China: Riding Two Horses at Once." *Foreign Policy Online*, October. http://www.foreignpolicy.com/story/cms.php?story_id=4033.
36. A part of this discussion is based on my article on intraparty partisanship in the CCP. For a full discussion of the concept of intraparty partisanship, see Cheng (2005a).
37. *Diyi Caijing ribao* (The First Economics and Finance Daily), February 6, 2006. And also see http://finance.sina.com.cn/g/20060206/01222317519.shtml (accessed March 5, 2008).
38. For more discussion of China's political roadmap, see Yu (2008).

References

Cheng Li. 2005a. Hu's Policy Shift and the Tuanpai's Coming-of-Age. *China Leadership Monitor* No. 15.
————. 2005b. The New Bipartisanship within the Chinese Communist Party. *Orbis* 49(3): 387–400.
Cohen, Jerome. 2004. Can, and Should, the Rule of Law Be Transplanted Outside the West? Paper presented at the Annual Meeting of the Association of American Law Schools, Washington, DC, January 4.
Dickson, Bruce J. 2003. *Red Capitalists in China: The Party, Private Entrepreneurs, and Prospects for Political Change.* New York: Cambridge University Press.
————. 2008. *Wealth into Power: The Communist Party's Embrace of China's Private Sector.* New York: Cambridge University Press.
Harney, Alexandra. 2008. *The China Price: The True Cost of Chinese Competitive Advantage.* New York: Penguin Group.
Hills, Carla A. and Dennis C. Blair. 2007. U.S.-China Relations: An Affirmative Agenda, a Responsible Course. Independent Task Force Report, Council on Foreign Relations, No. 59. New York.
Houyi, Zhang. 1995. The Position of the Private Entrepreneur Stratum in China's Social Structure. *Social Sciences in China* 16(4): 33.
Mann, James. 2007. *The China Fantasy: How Our Leaders Explain Away Chinese Repression.* New York: Penguin Group.
Nathan, Andrew J. 2003. China's Changing of the Guard: Authoritarian Resilience. *Journal of Democracy* 14(1): 6–17.
————. 2006. Present at the Stagnation: Is China's Development Stalled? *Foreign Affairs* 85(4): 177–182.
National Bureau of Statistics of China. 2006. *China Statistical Yearbook 2006.* Beijing: China Statistical Press.
Nee, Victor. 1996. The Emergence of a Market Society: Changing Mechanisms of Stratification in China. *American Journal of Sociology* 101(4): 910.
Pei, Minxin. 2006. *China's Trapped Transition: The Limits of Developmental Autocracy.* Cambridge, MA: Harvard University Press.

Ru Xin, Lu Xueyi, and Li Peilin, eds. 2005. *Zhongguo shehui xingshi fenxi yu yuce* (Analysis and Forecast on China's Social Development, 2005). Beijing: Social Sciences Academic Press.

Thornton, John L. 2008. Long Time Coming: The Prospects for Democracy in China. *Foreign Affairs* 87(1): 2–22.

Yu, Keping. 2008. *Democracy Is a Good Thing: Essays on Politics, Society and Culture in Contemporary China*. Washington, DC: Brookings Institution Press.

Chapter 4

The New Social and Economic Order in Twenty-First Century China: Can the Government Bring a Kinder, Gentler Mode of Development?

Christine Wong

Introduction

Entering the twenty-first century, the Chinese government has called for building a "Harmonious Society," under a new "scientific" development paradigm that emphasizes more balanced, sustainable growth, with development that will "put people first." Starting with the communiqué of the Sixteenth Party Congress in September 2002, when the new administration of Hu Jintao and Wen Jiabao commenced, the call was sounded for emphasizing the *quality* of growth and downplaying the traditional stress on quantitative growth targets. This change was spelled out in more specific terms in Premier Wen Jiabao's Report to the National People's Congress on March 5, 2004, when he called for[1]

- Reorienting China's development strategy to one that emphasizes balanced, sustainable, and "people-centered" growth;
- Strengthening social protection;

- Solving fiscal problems of the rural sector;
- Curbing corruption and government abuse; and
- Putting China on a timetable to achieve "*xiaokang* society" (well-off society).

Since that time, the change in discourse has been striking. From government ministries to think tanks in Beijing, the talk is of a "scientific concept of development" that will be "people-centered," that rejects a narrow focus on Gross Domestic Product (GDP) growth to emphasize social development, as well as a balanced, more inclusive growth. Premier Wen Jiabao, in particular, has repeatedly called for redressing the current inequalities by "tilting" toward the rural sector through promulgating policies that offer more favorable treatment of the "three agricultures"—agricultural production, rural villages, and farmers. In support of these policies, he instructed the Ministry of Finance to come up with a plan to "extend public finance to the rural villages," to improve the delivery of public services to the rural sector. These preferences were built into the Eleventh Five-Year Plan (2006–2010), which formally adopted the "strategic concepts of Scientific Approach to Development" and "Constructing a Harmonious Socialist Society."

This is a timely, long overdue adjustment of the development path China has taken since beginning its remarkable transition to a market economy some 25 years ago, whose stunning achievements have been marred by an increasingly obvious divide between the country's "haves" and "have-nots."[2] This chapter addresses the new turn in China's paradigm and assesses its prospects, focusing especially on whether the government will be able to reverse the trend of growing inequality and improving rural public services. These prospects are not at all straightforward, since the massive reallocation of resources that will be required will undoubtedly meet bureaucratic and political opposition (Wong 2007). Moreover, the central government's capacity to implement policies at the grassroots levels has been severely eroded through the transition (World Bank 2002, 2008). This chapter will focus on fiscal policies, which are not only the primary instrument for implementing the new paradigm, but, as I will argue below, were a principal driving force of the growth of inequalities in China over the past 25 years.

The "Old" Paradigm and the Impetus
for Change

It would be unfair to characterize the "old" paradigm (ca. 1978–2000)—the one intended to be replaced, as the "blind pursuit of GDP growth" decried by the People's Daily headline of March 2004, "China Says Goodbye to Blind Pursuit of GDP Growth."[3] However, it is undeniable that achieving economic growth was assigned top priority through the past two decades. The most concrete manifestation of this was the enshrinement of GDP growth at the top of performance indicators used in the cadre evaluation system at all levels of the administrative hierarchy (Whiting 2001). The old paradigm also tolerated a higher degree of inequality under the call of Deng Xiaoping, its chief architect, at the outset of reform to "let some people get rich first." The logic behind the call appeared to be that, if market reform brought with it rising inequality, it was the price to pay for faster growth, to lift the country out of the abject poverty that Maoist policies had brought.

Achievements of China's liberalization and market transition are spectacular and well-known.[4] Since 1978, China has experienced a prolonged growth spurt that saw an eightfold increase in per capita GDP—a record unparalleled in world economic history.[5] What has been even more remarkable was the extraordinary rate at which China has joined the global economy. Starting out as an autarkic economy largely insulated from world trade, Chinese exports doubled every three years. By 2002 China had become the fifth largest trading nation in the world; in 2004 it was the third largest. In this process, China achieved impressive rates of productivity growth and improvement in global competitiveness; today it dominates world trade in a number of light manufactures including consumer electronics. In the twenty-first century, China's economic ascendancy has made it an "engine of growth" increasingly courted by world leaders. By International Monetary Funds (IMF) estimates, China accounted for nearly one-quarter of world economic growth in 2004, a remarkable feat given that the Chinese economy remains small compared to the major countries—it is just one-eight the size of the U.S. economy and less than 5 percent of the world GNP (World Bank 2004).

Fueling this performance was the rapid structural transformation of the economy—some 25 percent of China's labor force moved from low productivity agricultural sector jobs to higher productivity jobs in the industrial and service sectors. As productivity rose across the board, as many as 400 million people were lifted above the official poverty line, making this the most successful poverty alleviation program in world history (World Bank 2001).

Time for a Course Correction

Given these spectacular successes, it might have seemed surprising for the new, at that time untested, administration of Hu Jintao and

Wen Jiabao to call for a significant change in development strategy. The reasons are several-fold. First, while achieving this economic miracle, China also acquired a reputation as a country that has abandoned its socialist past and embraced a particularly virulent form of capitalism. The evidence includes a rapid rise in interpersonal income inequalities as measured by Gini coefficients, which rose from an estimated 0.28 in 1978 to 0.45 at the end of the twentieth century—a level that puts China in the same league as Latin American economies, and far worse than its East Asian neighbors.[6] A major cause is an urban-rural income gap that is among the biggest in the world. Having grown secularly since the mid-1980s, the ratio of average urban to rural income is now estimated to be more than three. The ever-growing divide between coastal and inland provinces also contributes to making China among the most unequal countries in the world. These large disparities are reinforced by the *hukou* system, a system of residency controls retained from the Maoist era, which imposes a caste-like divide between urban and rural populations. While rural-urban migration, prohibited for two decades during the 1960s and 1970s, has resumed and accelerated, rural migrants are still denied access to social services such as schooling, health care, and welfare provisions in the urban centers, hindering their permanent settlement and integration.

Since the 1990s, there have been increasing signs of social tension, fanned by the emergence of a muckraking press. Demonstrations and protests have become commonplace throughout the country: According to Public Security Minister Zhou Yongkang, in 2004 there were more than 74,000 "mass incidents" involving some 3.76 million people (Cody 2005). Protestors range from pensioners, laid-off workers, and teachers marching on city hall to complain about defaults on payment of salaries and benefits, to farmers protesting against rising fees and levies, to citizens protesting against unlawful/unreasonable evictions in the name of urban development, to violence that just explodes on perceived injustices, and so on. Social surveys conducted in recent years consistently find increasing concerns about income inequalities, official corruption, and economic security. The environmental degradation in many parts of the country—chemical run-offs ruining rivers and contaminating ground water supplies, large cities choking from polluted air, and so on, have also brought increasing calls to reexamine the strategy of pursuing growth at all costs. Finally, leadership successions are opportunities for the introduction of bold policy initiatives, as the new leaders try to prove their worthiness and put their marks on the country's direction, undoubtedly this is partly the motivation of Hu Jintao and Wen Jiabao as well.

Fiscal Policies: China's Decentralized System and the Growth of Inequalities in the 1980s and 1990s

Fiscal policies—how government raises revenue and allocates spending and transfers directly and indirectly affect the distribution of income across sectors, regions, and individuals. In China, how revenues and spending are divided between the central and subnational governments are equally important in shaping distributional outcomes (Wong and Bird 2008).

To understand the central role played by the intergovernment fiscal system in China, we start with some stylized facts. First, China is the most decentralized country in the world by expenditure shares: the central government accounts for only 30 percent of total budgetary expenditures. The rest are distributed across four levels of local government.

The reason the central government share is so small is because in China, many costly public services are financed by local governments.[7] Among the most notable are that cities and counties have sole responsibility for pension pooling, unemployment insurance, and social welfare programs such as the minimal living stipends scheme. Counties, districts, and townships together account for 61 percent of public expenditures on education, including all basic education in the rural sector. They also account for 44 percent of public subsidies to the health sector and 64 percent of national outlays for social welfare and relief.[8]

China is virtually unique in assigning pension pooling, social welfare, and unemployment insurance to local governments. In other countries, because of their ballooning costs and potentially large requirements for fiscal subsidies, social security is almost always provided by the central (or federal) government, except in a few former Soviet republics.[9] Safety net mechanisms are almost always jointly financed by the national government because these large, cyclical expenditures are difficult for local budgets to accommodate especially as they run counter to economic cycles (i.e., with expenditures rising during economic downturns, when tax receipts are falling). Responsibilities for basic education and public health are similarly often shared with the provincial and central governments because of their costliness, important spillover effects, and concerns for maintaining minimum standards of provision.

These unusual expenditure assignments in China are the unreformed legacies from the planned economy. During the 1950s–1970s, in China the central government was responsible for national defense, economic development (capital spending, R&D, industrial policy, universities and research institutes), and administration of national institutions such as the judicial system. Local governments had responsibilities for delivering day-to-day public administration and social services such as education (except universities), public safety, health care, housing, and other local/urban services. Social security (pensions) was mostly the responsibility of state-owned enterprises.[10] These assignments were unproblematic because they were financed by the central budget through revenue sharing arrangements.

Decentralization by Default Rather Than Design

Through the 25 years of transition to a market economy, the expenditure assignment rules have remained largely intact, while expenditure shares have shifted significantly to local governments. The rules remain that local governments are mainly responsible for public administration and "local social needs," while the central government focuses on issues of national scope. However, several changes occurred to raise the local share of expenditures:[11]

1. Under the planned economy, a large portion of central spending went to capital investments and providing financing for state-owned enterprises. By the mid-1980s, the financing for state-owned enterprises had been transferred from the budget to the banking system, as were the bulk of capital investments. These reduced central spending relatively.
2. Responsibilities for capital investments in support of local economic development were decentralized to local governments.
3. Social expenditures that had been borne by state-owned enterprises—including housing, pensions, education, and health care—were gradually transferred to local governments.
4. Retrenchment in the state-owned enterprise sector led safety net expenditures to rise rapidly—unemployment stipends, early retirements, and increased pension payouts.
5. Rapid wage increases during the transition have raised the cost of labor-intensive services such as public administration, education, health, and other social services, affecting disproportionately local expenditures.
6. Local government expenditures also rose with the rising standards of provision for education, health care, and so on, due to national policy as well as popular demand.

7. Urbanization, increased mobility of population, and the growing diversity of economic entities brought increased costs of infrastructural and other urban services including public safety, judicial, and procuratorial services, most of which are local responsibilities.

Even without a revision of functional assignments, these changes combined to raise the local share of total budgetary expenditures from 45 percent in 1980 to 70 percent by the 1990s. In the meantime, though, revenue sharing rules were being changed repeatedly by the central government in response to macroeconomic pressures and attempts to stimulate revenue mobilization, and the link between local revenues and expenditure needs was weakened and then severed.[12]

Changes in Revenue Sharing Rules

Under the planned economy, all revenues belonged to the central government, but were collected by local governments and remitted upward. Revenue sharing with local governments was ex post facto, negotiated annually, and adjusted to finance local government functions. Market reforms brought a rapid and dramatic erosion in the traditional tax base of the planned economy—state-owned enterprise profits, and revenue collection declined steeply. Central revenues were especially hard hit as local governments in rich regions often shielded local enterprises from taxation to avoid sharing revenues with central government.[13] The results can be seen in figure 4.1, where budget revenues fell from more than 30 percent

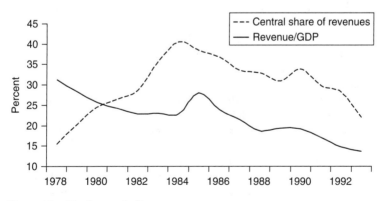

Figure 4.1 The "two ratios"

Source: NBS. Various years.

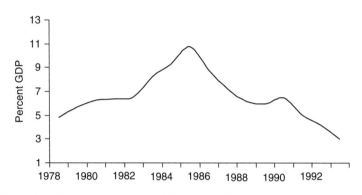

Figure 4.2 Resources under central budgetary allocation

Source: NBS. Various years.

of GDP to less than 15 percent during 1978–1993. At the same time, the central government's share of revenues was also declining as revenue assignments adjusted to the rising expenditure needs at the local levels.

The resultant squeeze on central resources is shown in figure 4.2, where the net result of the trends in overall revenues and the central share meant that resources under central government allocation fell from the mid-1980s, to only 3 percent of GDP at the nadir.

The Tax Sharing System Reform (1994) and Recentralization of Revenues

Fiscal contracts were not enough to solve the central government's financial problems, as revenues continued to decline due to continuing problems of state-owned enterprises (SOEs) profitability and persistent credibility of the central government. Moreover, as the generous terms of the contracts gave local governments a disproportionate share of new revenues, the central share of revenues continued to fall, to just over 20 percent in 1993.[14] By then, the central government managed only 3 percent of GDP through its budget.

This desperate situation spurred a drastic reform: introduction of the Tax Sharing System (TSS) in 1994. The TSS fundamentally overhauled the revenue sharing system by shifting to tax assignments, under which taxes were assigned to central government, local government, or shared. By assigning the biggest tax, the value added tax (VAT), as a shared tax and claiming 75 percent of its receipts, the central government reclaimed a majority portion of total revenues.[15]

The Broken Intergovernmental System and the Growth of Inequalities

The Tax Sharing System made the system much more favorable to rich localities. First, by sharing VAT revenue with local governments at a uniform rate by origin, the TSS is inherently disequalizing. This was exacerbated by the new system of transfers, which was dominated by tax rebates that also favor the rich (figure 4.3).[16]

Through the 1980s and 1990s, the coherence of the intergovernmental fiscal system was steadily chipped away by the piecemeal, incremental changes that occurred. By changing only one component of the intergovernmental system—revenue assignments, and delinking them from expenditure needs, the reforms have left local governments saddled with unusually heavy and unsustainable expenditure assignments, especially at low levels of government. As the fiscal decline had weakened the central government's capacity to aid poor regions, intergovernmental transfers also withered, to only 1 percent of GDP or less during 1993–1996 (Wong 2008).

During this period, then, local governments were largely self-financed, with no supporting system of transfers to ensure minimum standards of service provision across regions. As economic growth also became increasingly concentrated in coastal regions during the 1990s, income disparities accelerated, and the fiscal system provided no palliative. The outcomes show a significant worsening of the distribution in both economic and fiscal resources across provinces through the 1990s, and the trend has continued (see table 4.1).

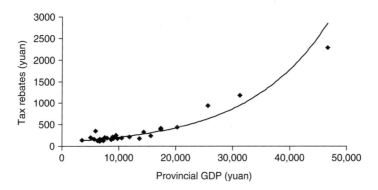

Figure 4.3 The distribution of tax rebates by province (2003)
Source: MOF. 2004a.

Table 4.1   Fiscal and economic concentration in rich and poor provinces

	1990 (%)	1998 (%)	2006 (%)
Five richest provinces[a]			
Share of GDP	20.8	22.8	28.4
Share of population	12.5	12.3	12.9
Share of revenue collections	18.0	12.2	15.6
Share of government expenditures	11.8	14.8	17.6
Five poorest provinces[b]			
Share of GDP	11.0	9.7	9.3
Share of population	16.8	17.0	16.5
Share of revenue collections	8.4	5.7	3.9
Share of government expenditures	9.8	9.5	9.2

a Shanghai, Beijing, Tianjin, Zhejiang, and Jiangsu.
b Guizhou, Gansu, Yunnan, Anhui, and Guangxi.

Source: Calculated from data assembled from CSY, various years.

Given that the TSS had recentralized revenues but left expenditure assignments unchanged, many local governments were left with inadequate resources for financing their expenditure responsibilities, and had little help from central transfers. As a result, many defaulted on their responsibilities and were unable to provide services mandated by law/regulation. Although the Education Law called for nine years of compulsory education for all children, for example, in 2004 some 17 percent of rural counties could not provide it, all of them in remote rural areas.[17] One scholar has estimated that during 1985–2000, as many as 150 million rural youths did not receive 9 years of schooling, due to the combination of undersupply and the high fees that were often charged by schools (Zhang 2003).

Likewise, the urban-rural gap in public services is large. For example, in 2003 the per capita recurrent expenditure on education is three times higher in city districts than in the rural communities, and health expenditures were almost three times as high in urban areas compared to those in rural (UNDP 2005). Figures for 2002 show the number of doctors per 1000 persons was 5.2 in urban areas, but only 2.7 in rural (MOF 2004). Similar urban-rural differences exist with respect to infrastructural services such as water, sanitation, roads, and information and communication technology. These urban-rural differences produced stark consequences for the rural population. For 2003, China's human development index was estimated to be 0.81 for urban and only 0.67 for rural areas (UNDP 2005). Aside from the differences in income, this reflects the lower life expectancy in rural areas, which, at 69.6, was 5.6 years less than in urban areas. It also reflects the differences in levels of education: the share of population between 15 and 64 years of age without any formal education was 8.7 percent in rural areas—more than three times the urban rate.[18]

In an important sense, then, the intergovernmental fiscal system was broken: implementation of decisions made at the top could not be assured at the lower levels given the existing financial arrangements (Wong 1997, 2007, World Bank 2002, 2008). Noncompliance by local governments has become a bottleneck to national policy implementation (World Bank 2002).

The Challenge of Reversing the Inequalities

Attempts to improve equalization had in fact begun under the Zhu Rongji administration. Since around 1998, a number of new programs have been introduced that had the effect of "tilting" toward the poorer regions. This effort received a big boost from the fiscal stimulus program introduced in 1998 to counter the effects of the Asian Financial Crisis with deficit spending. The program injected 100 billion yuan into capital spending, mostly on infrastructural investments, and the decision was taken to "tilt" them toward promoting economic growth in inland provinces.

In aggregate terms, central transfers to local governments more than tripled, from 328.5 billion yuan in 1998 to more than 1 trillion yuan in 2004, during a period of virtually 0 inflation. As shown in table 4.2 this was achieved by the central government devoting three-quarters of its budgetary revenues growth during the period to transfers. In the process, it raised the share of its revenues devoted to transfers from two-thirds to nearly three-quarters. Moreover, nearly three-quarters of this growth in transfers was outside of tax rebates—that is, devoted to equalization purposes. At present local governments depend on transfers to fund fully one-half of their expenditures (figure 4.4). Reversing the inequalities would

Table 4.2   Increased central transfers (1998–2004)

(Billions Y)	Central revenues	Transfers	Transfers as share of central revenues	Transfers net of tax rebates
1998	496.67	328.5	66.1%	120.3
2004	1450.31	1037.88	71.6%	632.8
change	953.64	709.35		512.52
of which		74%		72%

Source: China Fiscal Yearbook 2005.

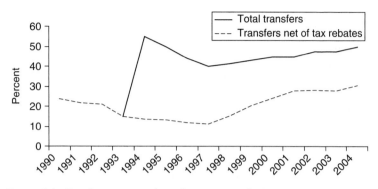

Figure 4.4 Local government dependency on transfers*

*Defined as transfers divided by local expenditures.

Source: Calculated from Budget speeches to the NPC, Lou (2000), Wong (1997), and Li and Xu (2006).

Table 4.3 Growing disparities in per capita budgetary expenditures by province*

	1990	1994	1998	2002	2004
Highest (1) Shanghai	609	1207	3337	5516	7875
Lowest (2)—Henan	104	130	362	680	899
Ratio of (1) to (2)	5.9	9.3	9.2	8.1	8.8
Average	254	374	861	1684	2066
Absolute gap	505	1076	2976	4835	6977
Coefficience of variation**	0.57	0.71	0.75	0.75	0.75

*Deflated to 1990 yuan, and excluding Tibet.

**The Coefficient of variation is calculated as standard deviation divided by the mean across
provinces for each of the years reported.

Source: MOF Compendium of Local Fiscal Statistics and CSY.

seem to require only increasing transfers and increasingly their equalization content.

Data presented in table 4.3 show that fiscal disparities remained very
large across provinces in 2004 despite the valiant effort of the past six
years. Per capita budgetary expenditures (own revenues + transfers) were
7875 yuan in Shanghai, the richest provincial-level unit, and just 899 yuan
in Henan, the province with the lowest fiscal capacity. The range of 8.8
to 1 from the richest to the poorest is large by international standards.
These interprovincial disparities were aggravated by the TSS reform in
1994. The disparities appear to have moderated somewhat since then, but
the coefficient of variation has remained at 0.75 since 1998, indicating
that fiscal disparities remain stubbornly large across provinces. Given that

very large differences remain, the size of the equalization effort required is huge.

If transfers were designed to produce perfect equalization, then they would vary by province to produce bars that are of equal length for each province. The reality in China was that, in 2004, transfers produced no clearly discernible pattern of equalization across provinces, in spite of the improved central effort of recent years. Studies focusing on county level data find much the same (absence of) pattern.[19]

Redoubling the Effort: The Harmonious Society Program

As noted at the outset of this chapter, the main thrust of the changes introduced under the administration of Hu Jintao and Wen Jiabao is to increase redistribution and effect a rebalancing of the economy, aimed at reversing some of the inequalities that have emerged, addressing social grievances and relieving tensions.

Many new programs have been rolled out that have a clear propoor, prorural thrust. For the sake of simplicity, in the rest of this chapter I will refer to these broadly as the "Harmonious Society Program" (HSP). Aside from the rural fee reform, they include free rural basic education, new cooperative medical insurance for farmers, building the "new Socialist Countryside," rural *dibao* (minimum living stipend), training and job placement support for rural out-migration, and social security schemes for farmers. Table 4.4 offers some details of the programs.

These programs represent major steps forward in improving public services in the rural sector, with increased commitments of central government support that is aimed at creating a "floor" for minimum standards of provision of vital services. They point clearly to a more activist role for the central government in promoting national standards.

Constraints to Implementing the Harmonious Society Program

Because of the large numbers of people served, the HSP will be expensive. Paradoxically, however, financing will not be the main problem. Since introduction of the Tax Sharing System in 1994, overall budgetary revenue collection has recovered robustly in China, and now reaches 20 percent of GDP—a level comparable to the prereform period given that capital

Table 4.4   Key new programs for rural education and health

Program	Launch Date	Policy Objective	Policy Content
"Two-exemptions and one subsidy"	2003	To reduce financial costs of schooling to families for nine years of compulsory education in order to expand access.	Government provides funding to replace revenues from the textbook and miscellaneous fees and provides a subsidy to boarding students from "poor" families.
Free Rural Compulsory Education	2006–2007	To take on nine years of compulsory education financed by public resources; to reduce financial costs to families in order to expand access.	Government provides funding to replace revenues from "miscellaneous fees" (*zafei*) at an average of RMB140 per student p.a. for all rural primary school students, and RMB180 per student p.a. for all rural junior middle school students. By 2007 this will cover 150 million students.
New Rural Cooperative Medical Scheme (NCMS)	2005	To provide risk-pooling for major illnesses, to reduce the financial risks of farmers falling into poverty due to illness.	Designed mainly for in-patient services; run at the county level, scope of coverage and reimbursement rates are stipulated; participation is voluntary and on a household level; counties are permitted to set up a NCMS when 70 percent of households agree to participate. The minimum funding was initially set at RMB 30 p.a., with cost-sharing: Center RMB10; subnational governments RMB10–20 per participant toward the annual premium; RMB10 by the participant. The central and local government contributions were doubled in 2006, raising the total premium funding to Y 50. In early 2008 the central government again doubled its own contribution, to Y 40.
Rural Dibao (minimum living stipend)	2005	To provide income support to the poor	All households with incomes below the local stipulated minimum will receive a "top-up" from the government. To be rolled out in all counties by year-end 2007. This is modelled on the successful urban "dibao" program.

Source: Adapted from World Bank (2008).

expenditures have been moved off-budget. The central government is especially flush with new revenues, and, as noted in the last section, has been generous in putting resources into improving equalization.[20] What is perhaps even more problematic is getting central resources through the several layers of administrative hierarchy to reach the grassroots levels.

Since the central government accounts for less than 10 percent of budgetary expenditures on social services such as education, health, and social relief, its control over social outcomes in the rural sector is at best attenuated. Even when the central government injects resources to support local services, these resources pass through provinces and municipalities before reaching counties. Leakages can occur at each level, and at present the central government has few levers for holding local governments accountable.

Under China's highly decentralized systems of fiscal management and administration, the central government employs extensive delegation of authorities in a nested, hierarchical setting. The central government delegates authorities to the provinces, and depends on the provinces to carry out their responsibilities. The provinces in turn delegate to the municipalities, and depend on them to "deliver" their assigned responsibilities, and so on downward through the hierarchy (figure 4.5). This decentralized administration can be an asset for cost-effective service delivery, if local governments can be held accountable for performance. At present, though, the accountability relationships are weak on multiple levels, with the result that compliance with central policies is not always assured at the local levels, and central transfers are not always used as intended.

Likewise contributing to the often low effectiveness of public expenditures is the weak accountability relationship between service providers—which are mostly public institutions—and local governments. Just as the central government has few levers to enforce compliance by local governments, local governments often lack effective levers over service providers. Finally, the downward accountability of both service providers and local governments to citizens is also weak, and most services are provided without significant participation by citizens or communities.

Central government $\longrightarrow$ Provinces
Provincial government $\longrightarrow$ Municipalities
Municipalities $\longrightarrow$ Counties
Counties $\longrightarrow$ Townships
Townships $\longrightarrow$ Villages/farmers

Figure 4.5 Hierarchical delegation in China

These are in part legacies of the long fiscal decline, during which incremental reforms had focused narrowly on reviving revenue collection, especially central revenues. In the process revenue and expenditure assignments were delinked, and the withering away of transfers led ultimately to a breakdown of the intergovernmental fiscal system. Despite significantly increased transfers and improved equalization since 1998, underfunding remains a fundamental obstacle to the central-local accountability relationship today, as the intergovernmental fiscal system still does not ensure sufficient funding to counties and townships in the western and central provinces (World Bank 2007). This is true for overall amounts as well as for specific programs, since the system still lacks mechanisms for ensuring that mandated services can be financed in poor counties. Moreover, the assignment of responsibilities across local governments is murky—with many programs requiring joint financing among the many levels but no clear divisions, and local governments do not have clearly articulated roles and functions against which they can be held accountable.

The accountability relationship with public service providers is similarly undermined by underfunding, as many of them are not adequately funded for their public service tasks. Instead, these providers are often expected to cross-subsidize their public service from money-making activities (World Bank 2005).

Weak accountability also stems from the weak information base for policy analysis in China, especially for rural public services, which undermines efforts to judge the performance of local governments and service providers. Even though a huge amount of information is routinely reported, China lacks a system for vetting and reconciling the data reported by the different ministries and agencies, and their figures can vary widely. For budgetary expenditures on rural compulsory education, for example, figures reported by the Ministry of Finance are 10 percent greater than those from the Ministry of Education. Large discrepancies also exist for data reported by different levels of the administrative hierarchy. In 2004, for example, the sum of central and provincial expenditures on education exceeded the "national consolidated" figure by 22 percent (China Fiscal Yearbook 2005). Data on social indicators and service outputs are weaker still—figures for school enrollments, hospital bed usage, and so on are widely considered unreliable.

In sum, piecemeal reforms to the system of public finance over the past 25 years have repaired the revenue mechanism, but left expenditure management in substantial disarray. As a result, the central government faces significant difficulties in implementing social policies through the present system of delegated governance.

Conclusion

In Wong (2007) I had argued that rural interests tend to be left out in the competition for central transfers, so that Wen Jiabao's prorural policies will have an uphill struggle to get sufficient funding. In this chapter I have reviewed the new Harmonious Society policies being implemented, focusing not only on funding levels, but also policy implementation mechanisms to argue that because the government has delayed institutional reform in the public sector, the central government's capacity to achieve stated social objectives is weak. Under the current intergovernmental arrangements, on average, local governments do not have the wherewithal to implement the HSP, nor do they have unambiguous incentives for doing so. Under these circumstances, even though the central government has the will and the ability to provide funds, it will find it difficult to channel them toward delivering services at the grassroots levels of Chinese society. This inability of the central government to implement policies in support of the national vision of a Harmonious Society points to a fundamental weakness in the foundation on which China is building its hopes for the twenty-first century.

More worrisome is that the gap between government promises and its capacity to deliver is very large and growing rapidly on the many components of the Harmonious Society Program—on the environment, on health care and education reforms, and on "tilting" toward the ethnic minority regions, and so on. On every front, there are daunting institutional challenges. On the environment, the government will have to undertake large realignment of relative prices and significantly raise tax rates on energy resources, as well as tackle the issues such as giant SOEs, for example, Sinopec, CNOOC, power companies capturing huge economic rents that keep resource regions impoverished and production methods backward and inefficient. To improve health care and education, provider incentives will have to be fundamentally altered.

The challenges are great. The government has shown willingness to acknowledge problems and seek solutions. The current piecemeal approaches, however, will unlikely suffice, especially since the central leadership remains stuck in the mindset that it can mandate policy changes, and spends too little effort building public support for its programs. The ratcheting up of promises by top leaders in the past two–three years carries significant political risks, since they are building expectations that the machinery of government may not have the capacity to deliver.

Notes

1. Traditionally, the Premier appears at the annual National People's Congress meetings in March to present a report on the work of the government. This report reviews the achievements of the past year and outlines the main undertakings for the coming year. This report is the occasion for presenting major new policies and changes in direction.
2. For recent accounts of the growing inequalities in China, see Shue and Wong (2007), Gustafsson, Li, and Sicular (2008), UNDP (2005), and Dwayne et al. (2008).
3. *People's Daily Online* (English), March 5, 2004.
4. For an overview of China's economic achievements through the first 20 years of transition, see World Bank (1997).
5. In recent world economic history, Japan and South Korea underwent growth spurts of similar magnitudes, but China has maintained the growth spurt for longer duration and at higher rates.
6. See, for example, Li Shi (2005) and Wang Shaoguang (2005).
7. In this chapter, unless otherwise stated (e.g., in table 4.2), "local" government is used interchangeably with "subnational" government, and refers to government at the provincial, municipal, county, and township levels.
8. Ministry of Finance (2004).
9. In the early 1990s in Brazil the states and municipalities were allowed to opt out of the national social security scheme, and many established their own schemes. The poor design and management of these local schemes have led to the creation of contingent liabilities on local governments that amount to as much as 500 percent of GDP. Yvonne Sin presentation at the World Bank, March 17, 2005.
10. Unemployment was not recognized as a problem and no provision was made for it.
11. See Wong (1991) for a discussion of these effects on increasing local government fiscal burdens, most of which had occurred during the 1980s.
12. This process is discussed in detail in World Bank (2002) and Wong (2007).
13. For example, under the planned economy Shanghai remitted more than 80 percent of its revenues to the central government. This high "tax" on Shanghai revenues created incentives for collusion between the municipal government and its subordinate enterprises and the potential for informally sharing the "saved revenues" within Shanghai. For analyses of this evolution, see Oksenberg and Tong (1991) and Wong (1991, 1992).
14. This was largely because the contracts had failed to anticipate the high inflation rates through the late 1980s and early 1990s, when revenues grew at an annual rate of 12 percent from 1987 to 1993 while remittances grew at low single digit rates.
15. The VAT accounts for nearly half of all tax revenues in China. It is also a reliable tax whose revenues go up with GDP regardless of profitability, and thus less cyclical than income or profit taxes.

16. As a concession to gain support for the TSS from the coastal provinces, the government committed to returning to provinces a portion of the "growth" in VAT and excise taxes, also by origin, in tax rebates. Tax rebates accounted for three-quarters of central transfers to the provinces in the mid-1990s, while equalization transfers were only 1–2 percent (World Bank 2002).
17. Information from Ministry of Education.
18. Data from 2000 census, National Bureau of Statistics (NBS).
19. See, for example, World Bank (forthcoming) and Shih and Zhang (2007).
20. In another paper, I proposed a "start-up Harmonious Society Program" that substantially increases central funding for the five programs underway, on rural education, rural health, rural dibao, and so on, at a cost of RMB 205 billion, an amount that was equal to 12 percent of central revenues in 2005, and less than the amount of "unbudgeted" revenue increase that year (Wong 2008).

References

Cody, Edward. 2005. China Grows More Wary Over Rash of Protests. *Washington Post* August 10.

Gustafsson, Bjorn, Li Shi, and Terry Sicular, eds. 2008. *Inequality and Public Policy in China.* Cambridge and New York: Cambridge University Press.

Li Ping and Xu Hongcai, eds. 2006. *China: Intergovernmental Fiscal Relations.* Beijing: China Public Finance Economics Press.

Li Shi. 2005. Empirical Analysis on Rising Income Inequality in China at the Beginning of the New Millennium. Paper presented at the International Symposium on Income Distribution during the Economic Transition, Shanghai Academy of Social Sciences, January.

Lou, Jiwei, ed. 2000. *Xin Zhongguo 50 Nian Caizheng Tongji* (Fifty Years Financial Statistics of New China). Beijing: Jingji Kexue Chubanshe.

MOF (Ministry of Finance). 2004. *Compendium of Local Fiscal Statistics.* Beijing.

NBS (National Bureau of Statistics of China). 2007. *China Statistical Yearbook.* Beijing: China Statistics Press.

Oksenberg, Michel and James Tong. 1991. The Evolution of Central-Provincial Fiscal Relations in China, 1971–1984: The Formal System. *China Quarterly* 125: 1–32

Shih, Victor and Zhang Qi. 2007. Who Receives Subsidies? A Look at the County Level in Two Time Periods. In *Paying for Progress in China: Public Finance, Human Welfare, and Changing Patterns of Inequality,* ed. Vivienne Shue and Christine Wong. London: Routledge.

Shue, Vivienne and Christine Wong, eds. 2007. *Paying for Progress in China: Public Finance, Human Welfare and Changing Patterns of Inequality.* London and New York: Routledge.

UNDP (United Nations Development Programme). 2005. *China Human Development Report 2005.* Beijing: United Nations Development Programme.

Wang Shaoguang. 2005. A Framework for the Study of Inequality. Background paper for the UNDP *China Human Development Report 2005*.

Whiting, Susan H. 2001. *Power and Wealth in Rural China: The Political Economy of Institutional Change*. New York: Cambridge University Press.

Wong, Christine. 1991. Central-Local Relations in an Era of Fiscal Decline: The Paradox of Fiscal Decentralization in Post-Mao China. *China Quarterly* 28: 691–715.

————. 1992. Fiscal Reform and Local Industrialization: The Problematic Sequencing of Reform in Post-Mao China. *Modern China* 18(2): 197–227.

————, ed. 1997. *Financing Local Government in the People's Republic of China*. Hong Kong: Oxford University Press.

————. 2007. Can the Retreat from Equality Be Reversed? An Assessment of Redistributive Fiscal Policies from Deng Xiaoping to Wen Jiabao. In *Paying for Progress in China: Public Finance, Human Welfare, and Changing Patterns of Inequality*, ed. Vivienne Shue and Christine Wong. London: Routledge.

————. 2008. Assessing the Fiscal Power of the Chinese State: Assessing the Central Government's Capacity to Implement National Policies. In *Power and Sustainability of the Chinese State*, ed. Keun Lee, Joon-Han Kim, and Wing T. Woo. London: Routledge.

Wong, Christine and Richard Bird. 2008. China's Fiscal System: A Work in Progress. In *China's Great Transformation: Origins, Mechanism, and Consequences of the Post-reform Economic Boom*, ed. Loren Brandt and Thomas Rawski. New York: Cambridge University Press.

World Bank. 1997. *China 2020: Development Challenges in the New Century*. Washington, DC: World Bank.

————. 2001. *The Alleviation of Poverty in China*. Washington, DC: World Bank.

————. 2002. China—National Development and Sub-national Finance: A Review of Provincial Expenditures. Washington, DC: World Bank Report 22951.

————. 2004. World Development Report 2004: Making Services Work for Poor People. Washington, DC: World Bank.

————. 2005. China—Deepening Public Service Unit Reform to Improve Service Delivery. Washington, DC: World Bank Report 32341.

————. 2007. China: Rural Public Finance for a Harmonious Society. Washington, DC: World Bank Report 41579.

————. 2008. *China: Public Services for Building the New Socialist Countryside*. Washington, DC: World Bank.

World Bank. Forthcoming. Reforming Intergovernmental Finance in China: A Study of the Northeast. Washington, DC: World Bank.

Zhang Yulin. 2003. The Urban-Rural Gap under the System of Schools Run at Separate Levels of Government...*Investigation of Chinese Villages* (1).

Chapter 5

The Voracious Dragon: Environmental Implications of China's Rising Energy Consumption

Kelly Sims Gallagher

Introduction

How China could and might balance its voracious desire for energy services with the urgent need to protect the environment and public health, both of which are fundamental to human well-being, are two of the central questions regarding the rise of China in the twentieth century. In China, as is often the case elsewhere, human well-being rests on a foundation of three pillars: (1) economic conditions and processes, such as employment, income, wealth, markets, and trade; (2) socio-political conditions and processes, such as national and personal security, rule of law, justice, education, health care, the pursuit of sciences and the arts; and (3) environmental conditions and processes, such as air, water, soils, minerals, biota, and climate (Holdren 2008). Most of China's most obvious and pressing environmental challenges—choking urban air pollution, acid rain, regional haze, and greenhouse gas emissions—come from current quantities and modes of coal consumption, which in turn are driven by China's rapid economic development.

This chapter explores the centrality of energy to economic development in China, and how energy consumption can and must be decoupled from economic growth if the burgeoning public health and environmental problems are to be resolved. The centrality of coal in China's energy system is also explored in some detail since the basic fact of China's heavy reliance on coal is a primary contributor to the environmental crisis that is unfolding in China. The environmental consequences of China's coal consumption are profound. China is home to the world's most polluted cities; China became the largest emitter of greenhouse gases in 2007, China is the largest emitter of sulfur dioxide (SO_2) emissions in the world, and acid rain affects most of China's southeastern agricultural lands. These and other environmental challenges are reviewed and analyzed here.

The political and policy response to the self-evident environmental problems in China has been inconsistent. Top leaders express great concern about environment and public health in their speeches and the central government has passed many laws and regulations. However, partly due to the incentives imbedded in central-local government relations (Wong, this volume), the provincial and local governments fail to enforce the regulations more often than not. Environmental activism is on the rise with sporadic bursts of activity that pierce the appearance of equanimity, but for the most part, environmental advocacy groups limit themselves to public education activities.

Possible strategies for a more effective response on the part of the government include slowing down population or economic growth, changing the composition of the economy to move to lighter industry, increasing energy prices, and/or imposing environmental taxes, switching to cleaner fuels, enabling more effective public participation, imposing and enforcing more stringent energy efficiency and environmental standards and regulations, and investing in innovation.

Energy, Environment, and Economic Development Connections

China's energy-related challenges are many, including the need for energy to sustain economic growth, its increasing foreign dependency for oil and gas, the need to provide modern forms of energy to China's poor, its increasingly severe urban air pollution, its already massive acid deposition, the growing concerns domestically and internationally about global climate change, and access to affordable, advanced energy technologies to address all of the above challenges. Simply put, energy is at the heart of the environmental problem, and environment is at the heart of the energy problem (Holdren 2008). Total energy consumption in China increased 70 percent between 2000 and 2005, and total coal consumption increased by 75 percent during the same time period (World Bank-SEPA 2007).

This astonishing rate of growth indicates that China's entire energy system has been doubling in size every five years so far in this century.

Economically, China's growing energy consumption presents both challenge and opportunity. Energy sustains economic growth by providing fuel for factory boilers, electricity for lighting and machinery, and provision of transportation services, such as getting goods from factory to ports. Of course, energy provides heating and cooling services as well. During periods of energy shortages in China, factories are shut down entirely, or moved into a rotation where each factory must cease production periodically—once a week, or every other night. During the summer of 2004, for example, factories on the outskirts of Shanghai were forced to close two days a week due to the high demand for electricity to power air conditioners and insufficient supply (Fallon 2004). More recently, heavy snowstorms in central China in January 2008 contributed to severe electricity shortages and brownouts in 31 provinces, caused primarily by an acute shortage of coal. This shortage was exacerbated by several factors, namely strong and persistent demand for coal, the closing down of small, unsafe coal mines, rising coal prices, and price controls on electricity. Because Beijing sets electricity prices, as coal prices rise but electricity prices stay the same, profit margins shrink until power producers are forced to shut down. As a result of the coal shortages, the Chinese government suspended coal exports for two months, causing coal prices to shoot up to all-time high in the United States, Europe, and Asia. In Asia, coal prices rose 34 percent in just a few weeks. China's largest copper producer, Jiangxi Copper Co., shut down some plants due to the high coal prices and lack of availability, as did some steel, zinc, and aluminum producers (Oster and Davis 2008).

The economic costs of China's air pollution are very high. According to a recent report from the Chinese government and World Bank, conservative estimates of morbidity and premature mortality associated with ambient air pollution in China was 157.3 billion yuan in 2003, equivalent to 1.16 percent of China's Gross Domestic Product (GDP). If premature death was valued somewhat higher than the convention at 1 million yuan per person, still arguably low, then the economic damages rise to 3.8 percent of GDP. Acid rain, caused mainly from SO_2 emissions from coal combustion, is estimated to cost US\$30 billion yuan in crop damage and US\$7 billion yuan in material damage annually. This damage, in turn, causes an estimated 1.8 percent of the value of the crop output, especially for vegetable crops. Although water pollution is less directly tied to coal consumption, it is still fundamental to human well-being, and it too has become a major drag on overall economic growth. Health damages from water pollution are estimated to account for 0.3–1.9 percent of rural

GDP, not including the morbidity associated with cancer. Adding all the calculable economic damages from air and water pollution together, the total costs of air and water pollution in China in 2003 were estimated at 362 billion yuan, or about 2.68 percent of China's GDP that year (World Bank-SEPA 2007).

Despite the perception that China has become an industrial power-house and the impressive fact that since the Cultural Revolution more than 400 million have been pulled out of absolute poverty, there are still many poor people in China. One-hundred and thirty-five million Chinese still live in absolute poverty (less than US$1 per day) and millions more remain just above that arbitrary poverty divide. Between 10 and 25 percent of rural residents are estimated to subsist at a level of around US$1 per day (World Bank 2003). With millions still in poverty, there is a tremendous political and social imperative to foster economic development and high economic growth rates in order to provide better jobs for rural inhabitants, reduce rural-urban inequality, and maintain internal stability. Providing better energy services to the poor in order to improve the quality of life for those still reliant on traditional forms of energy such as charcoal, crop wastes, and dung is thus very important, and a preoccupation of the Chinese government. Nationally, 96 percent of rural households have access to electricity, although in some provinces the figure is much lower, such as in Guizhou where 80 percent of households lack access (LBNL 2004). Because of China's gigantic population of more than 1.3 billion people, even if everyone consumed a very small amount of energy, China's total energy consumption and greenhouse gas emissions would be very large.

One rising concern is that as China imports greater amounts of energy, prices of these commodities will rise until supply catches up, and price spikes will be especially likely during supply disruption events. After China became a net oil importer in 1994, its demand for global oil supplies grew rapidly as it became the second largest consumer of oil in 2004, and it is now the third largest oil importer in the world. China's rapidly escalating demand contributed strongly to the rise in world oil prices during the first part of this century as suppliers scrambled to catch up. It appears that China is beginning to affect world coal prices as well. In the first six months of 2007, China imported more coal than it exported for the first time in history. This trend is likely to continue in part because China is not rich in coking coal and so it has been importing it from Australia, which can provide good quality coking coal at a relatively low price (Shenhua 2008). Rail capacity to transport coal is also a bottleneck. Overall, China's coal demand grew nearly 9 percent in 2007, indicating that Chinese coal demand could double by 2015.

The other big challenge is the need to supply enough energy, especially in the form of electricity, to meet the very high demand created by Chinese industry. Industry consumes the majority of electricity supplied, accounting for 74 percent of total demand (National Bureau of Statistics of China 2006). The power sector has been through several boom and bust cycles because when electricity shortages emerge, the industry responds by adding huge quantities of new capacity as fast as it can, and then there is some oversupply for a time until the economy catches up and a new shortage emerges. As already discussed, the shortages have been intermittently harmful to the Chinese economy whenever electricity is rationed and factories are forced to shut down. On the opportunity side, the Chinese energy sector is already large and growing rapidly so it represents an exciting market opportunity for Chinese and foreign energy services companies alike. As of 2000, China had an electricity capacity of approximately 320 billion Watts (GW). Between 2001 and 2005, 176 GW of new capacity was added. Then, in 2006, China installed 101 GW of new coal-fired power capacity in a single year, 90 GW of which was thermal power. By the end of 2007, China had a total installed capacity of 713 GW, of which 554 GW (78 percent) was thermal power, most of which is coal (China Electricity Council 2008). To put these astounding numbers in perspective, Germany's entire electricity system in 2005 was 124 GW (Eurostat 2007).

Since the beginning of this century, China emerged as a major consumer of oil, and there is strong potential for China to become a major natural gas consumer as well, especially if it tries to reduce its greenhouse gas emissions. About half of China's oil imports come from the Middle East, but Angola became the largest supplier in 2006, and indeed, China has invested heavily in energy resources in Africa. Although there have been several new oil discoveries in China recently, Chinese reserves are on the decline. China has relatively few natural gas reserves domestically, and therefore uses virtually no natural gas in its power sector. It is trying to increase production of coal-bed methane. If China decides to increase its reliance on natural gas, China will likely import natural gas through LNG import terminals on the coast or by pipeline over land from central Asia or Russia. If China begins to import large quantities of natural gas from either the Persian Gulf or Russia, the geopolitical implications would be serious because China would be a major source of natural gas demand, which could cause prices to rise dramatically. China's long-term energy security is not only dependent on having sufficient supplies of energy to sustain its incredible rate of economic growth, but it will be equally dependent on its ability to manage the growth in energy demand without causing intolerable environmental damage.

In China's big cities, most of the air pollution comes from motor vehicles. The car population in China has grown dramatically, going from less than 100,000 in total in 1990 to approximately 25 million in 2007. All the new cars on the road are causing oil imports to rise, and China is now the second largest consumer of oil in the world and the third largest oil importer. By 2000, total Chinese automobile oil consumption equaled total oil imports at 1.2 million barrels per day (Xu 2002). Although the growth in new cars has been astounding, the total number is still small compared with the situation in the United States, which has a car and sports utility vehicle (SUV) population of 230 million. With 20 percent of the world's population, the Chinese only own 1.5 percent of the cars in the world (ORNL 2007).

The Centrality of Coal

China's main energy resource endowment is coal. Coal accounts for 93 percent of China's remaining fossil fuel resources. In China, 74 percent of the electricity is derived from coal, at 526 GW in 2007.[1] Hydropower provides 20 percent of electricity capacity, nuclear 1 percent, and wind power half of 1 percent. Although nuclear and wind power have been growing rapidly in recent years, coal is so dominant that it is unlikely that the current mix of electricity supply can be significantly altered any time soon. Natural gas is not commonly used for power generation due to the high price and lack of availability of the fuel in China due to limited domestic resources and China's historic reluctance to import natural gas from the most obvious supplier, its neighbor Russia. China is aggressively pursuing renewable energy, and ranks number one in the world in some respects, such as in its installation of solar hot water and small hydropower. It ranks fifth in the world in terms of installed wind capacity, and fourth in terms of ethanol production (REN21 2008). Still, China's nonhydro renewable capacity is a tiny fraction of primary energy, which is completely dominated by coal.

Environmental Consequences of Coal Consumption

Environmentally, coal is at the heart of China's environmental woes. Most of China's air pollution emissions come from the industrial and electricity sectors. Particulate matter from coal is a major air pollutant. Concentrations of PM10 (particles the size of 10 microns or less that are capable of penetrating deep into the lungs) in China's cities are extremely high, ranging from the extreme of Panzhihua's average concentration of 255 to 150 in Beijing, 140 in Chongqing, and 100 in Shanghai. These numbers can be compared to 45 in Los Angeles, and 25 in New York. PM10 can increase the number and severity of asthma attacks, cause or aggravate bronchitis and other lung diseases, and reduce the body's ability to fight infections. Certain types of people are especially vulnerable to PM10's adverse health effects, including children, the elderly, exercising adults, and those suffering from asthma or bronchitis (CARB 2003).

Sulfur dioxide emissions from coal combustion, a major source of acid deposition, rose 27 percent between 2001 and 2005. Acid rain predominantly affects southeastern China, and Hebei Province is most severely affected, accounting for more than 20 percent of crop losses from acid rain. Hunan and Shangdong Provinces are also experiencing heavy losses from acid rain. Eighty percent of total losses are estimated to be from damage to vegetables (World Bank-SEPA 2007).

In terms of global climate change, coal is the most carbon-intensive of the fossil fuels. Coal accounts for approximately 80 percent of China's carbon dioxide (CO_2) emissions. As of 2000, electricity accounted for 52 percent of China's CO_2 emissions (and 75 percent of China's electricity is consumed by industry), cement accounted for 28 percent, iron and steel for 9 percent, and transportation for 8 percent. At this point, annual emissions from Chinese coal are three times U.S. emissions from transportation, which means that if all cars, trucks, ships, and airplanes came to a halt in the United States for an entire year, emissions from Chinese coal would compensate in just a few months. But, U.S. transport emissions are 17 times larger than Chinese emissions from transport (IEA 2007).

The possible impacts of climate change on China are not as well studied as they have been in the United States, but it is clear that there could be very adverse impacts with respect to water supply, agriculture, and sea level rise. Precipitation decreased 50–120 mm/year along the northern Yellow River between 1956 and 2000, an already arid region. Precipitation increased by 60–130 mm/year along the southern Yangtze river from 1956 to 2000, an area that has been plagued by heavy flooding. The mountain glaciers on the Tibetan plateau are receding rapidly, with major implications for fresh water supply in already water-stressed northern China. The glacier that is the source of the Urumchi river on the Tianshan Mountain, for example, shrank 11.3 percent between 1962 and 2001. A sea level rise of 30 cm would cause massive coastal inundation, which Chinese scientists estimated would cause 56 billion RMB in economic losses to the Pearl River Delta area, 9.6 billion RMB in losses for the Yangtze Delta area, and 52 billion RMB in losses for the Yellow River delta, including the Gulf of Bohai.

The other major environmental problem in China, scarce water resources, is less attributable to energy consumption, although energy plays an important role here too. Two-thirds of China's cities lack sufficient water resources, and 110 cities suffer severe water shortages. The inefficient agricultural sector is mainly to blame for overuse, though industries certainly add to the problem. Water pollution is pervasive. The Chinese government estimates that 30 percent of China's river water is unfit for agriculture or industry, and 75 percent of the river water that flows through urban areas is unfit for human consumption (Economy 2007). One-third of China's cities does not have waste water treatment plants (CCICED 2008). Some of the largest hydropower installations in the world are in China, most infamously the Three Gorges Dam. These hydropower stations have more localized but no less severe environmental impacts, causing loss of habitat, forcing human relocation, inundation of agricultural lands, and impacts on biodiversity. On the other hand, hydropower projects can help with flood control, irrigation, and in the provision of low-emission electric power. Coal-fired power plants are also the fourth-largest source of waste water in the country (Sinton et al. 2000).

Political and Policy Response to Challenges

China has already taken important steps to moderate future growth in greenhouse gas emissions, largely through energy efficiency and renewable energy measures. Energy intensity (amount of energy used to generate economic activity—usually expressed as total energy consumption divided by GDP) dramatically declined in China from 1980 to 2004. This means that China's overall energy efficiency improved, air pollution was less than it could have been, and significant growth in greenhouse gas emissions was avoided. In other words, energy consumption was partially decoupled from economic growth during this period because GDP grew faster than energy consumption. But, despite these improvements, China's overall energy efficiency is still considerably worse than is the case in most industrialized countries and, unfortunately, during the past few years, it appears to have reversed from a long trend of general improvement to actually become more intensive rather than less.

The central government has set forth aggressive policies and targets for energy efficiency for the next decade. Because so much of China's energy depends on coal, efficiency measures that result in reduced coal combustion will greatly help to reduce greenhouse gas emissions. The Eleventh Five-Year Plan (2006–2010) calls for a 20 percent reduction in energy intensity by 2010. This goal is already proving hard to achieve since Chinese energy intensity *increased* slightly in 2006 rather than decreasing by the planned 5 percent. The energy intensity target was also at the heart of the climate change plan that the Chinese government announced in June 2007 in advance of the G-8 summit. By improving thermal efficiency, the government estimated that it could reduce carbon dioxide emissions by 110 million tons by 2010 (NDRC 2007). Notably, the Chinese government also issued its first fuel efficiency standards for passenger cars in 2005, and these were strengthened in 2008. China also implemented vehicle excise taxes so that if a buyer purchases a car or SUV with a big engine, she will pay a much higher tax than if she purchased a car with a small, energy-efficient engine. In both cases, these policies are considerably more stringent than comparable ones in the United States. The Chinese government also adopted aggressive efficiency standards for appliances. The China Energy Group at Lawrence Berkeley National Laboratory estimates that those standards are already reducing greenhouse gas emissions in China substantially, and that even more stringent minimum appliance standards could reduce carbon emissions by 19 million metric tons per year by 2020 (Lin 2006).

The Chinese government has also aggressively promoted low carbon energy supply options especially renewable energy, hydropower, and nuclear energy. If you exclude large hydropower but include small hydropower, China has twice as much installed renewable power capacity than the United States. In fact, China leads the world in terms of total installed capacity of renewable energy at 42 GW (compared with 23 GW in the United States) as of 2005. China accounts for 63 percent of the solar hot water capacity in the world, and as of 2005, China had installed 1.3 GW of wind capacity. China passed a Renewable Energy Law in 2005 that requires grid operators to purchase electricity from renewable generators, and China set a target of having 10 percent of its electric power generation capacity come from renewable energy sources by 2010 (not including large hydro). By expanding renewable energy (including bioenergy), the Chinese government estimated it could reduce carbon dioxide emissions 90 million tons by 2010. The Chinese has exploited its large hydro resources at some social and ecological cost due to forced relocations of communities, loss of ecosystems, and decreased river flow, but it believes it has substantial scope for increasing small-scale hydropower, and in fact, it estimated that it could achieve a reduction of 500 million tons of carbon dioxide by 2010 with increased small-scale hydro. Compared with coal and hydro, however, China has scarcely begun its expansion of nuclear power. By 2020, the Chinese government plans to have built 40 GW of new nuclear power plants, but even if they succeed in expanding so rapidly, the 40 GW would only account for about 4 percent of the anticipated total capacity by then.

The Chinese government is also devoting a substantial portion of its R&D dollars to the research, development, and demonstration of advanced energy technologies. During the Eleventh Five-Year Plan, the Ministry of Science and Technology's (MOST) budget for energy research, development, and demonstration is about 3.5 billion RMB (approximately US$425 million). The budget for advanced coal technology is about 0.7 billion RMB (approximately US$85 million). This accounts for 21 percent of the total energy budget. Five coal coproduction and gasification demonstration projects are planned for the next five years, in collaboration with Chinese industry. If all are actually built, there will be more coal gasification and coproduction plants in China than there are in the United States.

In terms of so-called conventional (nongreenhouse gas) air pollution control, the record is at best mixed. The government has promulgated regulations that require that new coal-fired power units must be equipped with flue-gas desulfurization (FGD) equipment, and all old plants must install FGD equipment by 2015 in order to reduce SO_2 emissions. Sulfur desulfurization equipment has been installed on 200 GW of coal-fired power plants, which is approximately 40 percent of thermal power plant capacity in China (Zeng 2007). The government offers a preferential price for electricity from power plants utilizing FGD technology, and subsidizes some advanced coal technology demonstration projects. The Eleventh Five-Year Plan called for a 10 percent reduction in SO_2 emissions by 2010, but China is not on track to meet the goal. As mentioned earlier, there has actually been an increase in total SO_2 emissions even though there are standards for emissions concentrations for both SO_2 and NO_x and emissions fees for noncompliance. One reason for this poor record is that even though FGD equipment is required to be installed in power plants today, the equipment is not always operated (Zhao and Gallagher 2007). The emissions fees are so low that factories would prefer to just pay the fees rather than comply, and this suits local enforcement officials because they collect the revenue from the fees. This set of problems gets to the heart of one of the central government's most daunting challenges, the enforcement of environment, energy, and public health regulations at the local level.

Environmental protection is complex politically. While no Chinese leader would publicly disparage the urgent imperative to better protect China's natural resources and the health of her people, in practice environmental protection takes a backseat to economic growth. While China has many good laws that have already been passed, it fails to strictly enforce most of them (though there are some conspicuous examples of enforcement). As of June 2005, China has promulgated 2,296 environmental regulations and standards: of these 87 pieces of laws on environmental protection and relevant laws were issued by the state; 205 pieces of administrative regulations and legislations were released by the State Council; and 330 pieces of rules and regulations were made by the environmental protection departments (CCICED 2008). The problem is compounded by the lack of wherewithal to enforce because of the paucity of the Ministry of Environmental Protection's human and financial resources. The Ministry of Environmental Protection currently has approximately 300 employees in Beijing plus 30 in regional inspection offices, compared with 17,000 in the U.S. Environmental Protection Agency (Gang 2008). Enforcement is carried out at the local level by Environmental Protection Bureaus (EPBs). EPBs receive virtually no support from the central government Ministry of Environment, and instead must rely upon their local government for all financial support, including provision of budgets, salaries, offices, employee housing, and so forth. Naturally, then, EPBs are more responsive to the concerns of the local governments (e.g., jobs and economic growth) than those of the Ministry of Environmental Protection (Economy 2005). In a few of the more developed cities in the East, the local EPBs are being encouraged by their municipal or provincial governments to be more aggressive with environmental protection as was clear during the 2008 Olympics in Beijing and as we will see as Shanghai prepares for the 2010 World Expo.

The central government has tried to remedy the problem that the local governments are not providing incentives for environmental protection by tying promotions for local officials to the environmental performance of the region. In addition, leaders of the country's large state-owned enterprises (SOE) risk losing promotion opportunities or even jobs if their companies fail to meet energy-saving and pollutant-reduction targets (Fu 2007). But still, ambiguity in laws, the unavailability of notice and comment in rule-making, the gradual implementation of laws, and the lack of liability for inflicting environmental harm all leave much room for improvement in environmental governance (Ferris and Zhang 2005).

Strategies for Reconciling Economic Growth with Environmental Sustainability

It is difficult to imagine China achieving true environmental sustainability, just as it challenges the imagination to picture the United States achieving sustainability, if one defines a truly sustainable process or condition as "one that can be maintained indefinitely without progressive diminution of valued qualities inside or outside the system where the process operates or the condition prevails" (Holdren et al. 1995). But even if one cannot fathom an environmental system that isn't being somewhat diminished in China, it is not, in fact, difficult to imagine environmental conditions being vastly improved, just as they were in the United States during the twentieth century.

To achieve dramatic environmental improvements in China a comprehensive and far-reaching incentive system would have to be created. Experience to date suggests that even though much more energy-efficient and cleaner technologies exist, and are used both within China and internationally, they are not deployed and used widely and consistently in China. The proposition that countries like China would "leapfrog" to the most environmental technologies available has not been borne out, and in fact, many limits to leapfrogging have been identified. Most importantly, it is clear that the processes of leapfrogging, technology transfer, and accelerated deployment of environmental technologies are not automatic (Ohshita and Ortolano 2002, Gallagher 2006, Lewis and Wiser 2007). In order to achieve leapfrogging in environmental technologies, the government must intervene to create an incentive system, and this will require improved governance not only at the central government level, but also at the provincial and municipal levels as well.

The Chinese government is actively tackling most of these environmental challenges and is making some progress. They have issued strong targets for energy efficiency and renewable energy, though the progress toward meeting these goals has been uneven. China has issued six main environmental laws and nine natural resources laws, though again, enforcement of these laws is inconsistent. So, what are the key elements of improved governance that will enable China to reconcile China's voracious demand for energy with environmental sustainability? The following are seven possible strategies, none of which are mutually exclusive, but some will clearly be more desirable than others from the Chinese government's perspective.

Slow Down Population Growth or Economic Activity

The first option many think of for reducing energy consumption is to reduce population growth. China's large population of 1.3 billion people presents a constant challenge because even if each person is extremely energy efficient, the multiplier effect is so strong that total energy consumption is large. As is widely known, the Chinese government long ago implemented a population control policy, and this has undoubtedly helped to reduce total energy consumption below what it otherwise would have been. The other option is to try reining in the economy in order to prevent faster growth in energy consumption since energy consumption and the resulting pollution are strongly correlated with economic growth. Industry accounts for approximately three-quarters of China's energy consumption, so if industrial demand can be moderated or reduced, then energy consumption will be reduced. Economic growth could be reduced through measures such as restricting access to capital, imposing higher corporate taxes, and slowing down government-funded projects, among many other strategies. Two other ways to reduce industrial demand are to introduce more efficient energy technologies and to change the composition of Chinese industry, as discussed next.

Structural Economic Changes—Shifting into Lighter, Less Energy-Intensive Industry

Fundamentally, there are three ways to reduce the pollution intensity of an economy: reduce the scale of economic activity overall (as discussed above), change the composition of the economy, and introduce cleaner or more efficient technologies, known as the "technique" effect (Grossman and Kruger 1991). The Chinese government has already recognized the multiple advantages of shifting into lighter industry, not only because China can reduce its demand for natural resources, but because there is typically more value added in service industries as opposed to heavy industry. In its Tenth Five-Year Plan, the Chinese government wrote that a primary goal with respect to energy consumption was to "Rationally read just the industrial structure and the product mix, vigorously develop the tertiary industry and high and new technology industries with low consumption of energy, transform traditional industries with high and new technologies, and increase the added value of products" (SETC 2003). For its current Eleventh Five-Year Plan, the emphasis on shifting the economy toward tertiary service industries became even more prominent. In a 2006 speech about the Eleventh Five-Year Plan, the Chairman of the National Development and Reform Commission, Ma Kai, commented that "The service industry lags behind, with its ratio dipping from 41.7% in 2002 to current 40.3%. Such an economic mix has not only increased the pressure on resources and environment, but has also affected the improvement of total economic quality and benefits" (Kai 2006). Thus, the second major goal identified in the plan is to transform economic growth to being driven by a more "balanced" development of the primary, secondary, and tertiary industries. Cement, iron and steel, and pulp and paper industries account for approximately 40 percent of China's greenhouse gas emissions alone, so if those three industries could be partially replaced with cleaner and more efficient ones, then major progress would have been made.

Fuel Switching

From an environmental point of view, coal is the most challenging fuel. Although different types of coal have varying characteristics, when combusted it typically releases sulfur dioxide, particulates, nitrogen oxides, mercury, and, of course, the greenhouse gas carbon dioxide. Of all the fossil fuels, coal is by far the most greenhouse gas intensive. Since China relies so completely on coal, switching to cleaner fuels can go a long way to reducing the environmental harm associated with energy consumption. In the electricity sector, this could mean using more natural gas, nuclear, or renewable energy sources such as wind and solar. In the industrial sector, this could mean using more natural gas or electricity in factories. It is not a simple matter to simply switch fuels because of the large existing infrastructure that has been built to accommodate coal. Most of China's power plants are coal-fired power plants, and most of the industrial boilers are coal-burning boilers. But, new power plants and factories could be built to use these fuels, and eventually older coal-burning factories and plants can be replaced with cleaner ones. This option is not particularly attractive to the Chinese government since coal is China's most abundant fossil fuel resource. China has very little domestic natural gas, and imports are expensive. Nuclear power is likewise expensive, plus it has all of the liabilities and risks associated with proliferation, reactor accidents, and waste disposal. Renewable energy options remain more expensive than coal, and have proven hard to scale up to the size of Chinese demand aside from large hydropower. These are some of the trade-offs faced by the Chinese government.

Pricing

Presently, the Chinese government subsidizes most forms of energy for the Chinese public and industry. It subsidizes the retail price of gasoline and diesel, and it manages the price of electricity. Coal prices have been somewhat liberalized as they are allowed to fluctuate within a band. It is estimated that Chinese government oil and gas subsidies for 2008 were US$40 billion dollars, up from US$22 billion in 2007 (Bradsher 2008). When energy prices are held artificially below market levels, there is little incentive on the part of consumers to be more efficient. To compound matters, oil and gas prices do not reflect all the environmental and public health costs associated with their use. If the environmental "externalities" were included in oil and gas prices, they would be even higher than current market prices. So, if the Chinese government is really serious about improving energy efficiency, it not only will have to let energy prices reflect market values, but also incorporate the environment and health costs into those prices with taxes. The Chinese government may want to consider a carbon tax so as to not only encourage more energy efficiency but also promote climate-friendly alternatives. Chinese government's fears of inflation and the potential regressive impacts of higher energy prices on the poor have been the main two reasons why the government has not freed energy prices. There are, of course, ways to compensate lower income segments of the population for higher energy prices.

Public Participation in Environmental Protection

In 2006, Minister Zhou Shengxian of China's State Environmental Protection Administration (SEPA) announced that there were 51,000 environmental protests in 2005, nearly 1,000 per week (Economy 2007). In many of these cases, dumping of hazardous wastes and toxic substances into local water supplies is a primary cause of protest. But, the sheer number of protests belies the poor environmental conditions that many must live with in China. The Chinese public could be a potent source of help for enforcement of environmental regulations and standards in China, but currently, the public is not empowered to help with environmental protection. First, data about emissions and accidents is not consistently reported, collected, or made available to the public so Chinese citizens don't have any idea what chemicals or pollutants are being released into their local environment, or whether local factories and businesses are in compliance with regulations or not. There is no Chinese equivalent to the U.S. Toxic Release Inventory, which makes such information available to everyone over the Internet. Although environmental hotlines have been established in many municipalities, there is no guaranteed response mechanism when someone reports a potential infraction. Critically, there is no legal recourse for Chinese citizens or nongovernmental environmental organizations that wish to sue companies for failure to comply with the law. Given China's vast geography and the large number of factories across its landscape, and how constrained government resources are for enforcement, it would clearly be environmentally beneficial to provide the public with the tools and resources to report noncompliance. Political sensitivities to this type of citizen involvement remain high, however.

Environmental and Energy Efficiency Standards

The Chinese government has promulgated many environmental and energy efficiency standards. China's vehicle efficiency standards were already discussed. China's coal-fired power plant efficiency has improved from 27 percent in 1974 to 33 percent in 2003 (Zhao and Gallagher 2007). Still, there are many small and inefficient plants that keep the overall efficiency much lower than is desirable given the Chinese's government's official target of improving the overall energy efficiency of the economy by 20 percent by 2010. The government intends to shut down many of the small plants and replace them with larger scale efficient plants. In addition, the State Environmental Protection Administration issued emissions standards for air pollutants from thermal power plants that took effect from January 1, 2004. These standards require reductions in NO_x and SO_2 emissions, but enforcement of these emissions standards has been weak. The government seems committed to strengthening China's various environmental regulations and standards, but unless the government finds a way to better enforce these standards, their effectiveness will be muted.

Innovation

Innovation in energy and environmental technologies can provide new solutions to environmental problems, and also bring down the cost of existing technologies to enable them to penetrate the marketplace more effectively. Through the Ministry of Science and Technology, the Chinese government has placed a high priority on research, development, and demonstration (RD&D) for clean and efficient vehicles, and advanced coal technologies. While continued and increased investments into the RD&D of these technologies are clearly needed, the government must also work to connect the research and development stages to the market. The government must create markets for cleaner technologies so that there is also an incentive for the private sector to innovation to meet market demand. The Chinese government can create these markets through energy pricing and green taxation, new regulations and standards, and better enforcement of existing environmental laws.

Conclusion

This chapter aimed to clarify the enormity of the challenge of reconciling China's rapidly rising energy consumption with environmental sustainability. Most of China's greatest threats to human well-being arise from its voracious energy use, which is mainly fueled by coal. The government's response to the environment and public health consequences of China's energy use has been strong and effective at times, but wholly inadequate to date. Improved governance and a stronger commitment on the part of the Chinese government to face the challenges are essential.

Note

1. China Electricity Council, various years.

References

Bradsher, Keith. 2008. Fuel Subsidies Overseas Take a Toll on U.S. *New York Times* July 28.
CARB (California Air Resources Board). 2003. Air Pollution—Particulate Matter. Sacramento: California Environmental Protection Agency. http://www.arb.ca.gov/html/brochure/pm10.htm.
CCICED (China Council for International Cooperation on Environment and Development). 2008. Report of Task Force on Innovation (forthcoming).
China Electricity Council. 2008. Nation-Wide Power Sector Statistics Newsletter for 2007 (in Chinese). http://www.cec.org.cn.
Economy, Elizabeth C. 2005. *The River Runs Black: The Environmental Challenge to China's Future.* New York: Cornell University Press.
———. 2007. The Great Leap Backwards? *Foreign Affairs* 86(5): 38–59.
Eurostat. 2007. Infrastructure—Electricity—Annual Data. December 6. http://epp.eurostat.ec.europa.eu.

Fallon, Bridget. 2004. Energy Shortage Hits Chinese Firms. *BBC News* September 1. http://news.bbc.co.uk/2/hi/business/3602678.stm (accessed February 8, 2008).

Ferris, Richard J. and Hongjun Zhang. 2005. Environmental Law in the People's Republic of China: An Overview Describing Challenges and Providing Insights for Good Governance. In *China's Environment and the Challenge of Sustainable Development*, ed. Kristen A. Day. Armonk, NY: ME Sharpe.

Fu, Jing. 2007. SOE Heads' Careers Linked to Green Targets. *China Daily*, August 30. http://chinadaily.com.cn/bizchina/2007-08/30/content_6067680.htm.

Gallagher, Kelly Sims. 2006. Limits to Leapfrogging? Evidence from China's Automobile Industry. *Energy Policy* 34(4): 383–394.

Gang, He, 2008. China's New Ministry of Environmental Protection Begins to Bark, but Still Lacks in Bite. *EarthTrends*. Washington, DC:World Resources Institute. July 17. http://earthtrends.wri.org/updates/node/321.

Grossman, Gene M. and Alan Kruger. 1991. Environmetnal Impacts of a North American Free Trade Agreement. National Bureau of Economic Research, NBER Working Paper W3914.

Holdren, John P. 2008. Science and Technology for Sustainable Well-Being. *Science* 319 (5862): 424–434.

Holdren, John P., Gretchen C. Daily, and Paul R. Ehrlich. 1995. The Meaning of Sustainability: Biogeophysical Aspects. In *Defining and Measuring Sustainability: The Biogeophysical Foundations*, ed. Mohan Munasinghe and Walter Shearer. Washington, DC: World Bank.

IEA (International Energy Agency). 2007. *World Energy Outlook 2007: China and India Insights*. Paris: IEA and OECD (Organisation for Economic Cooperation and Development).

LBNL (Lawrence Berkeley National Laboratory). 2004. *China Energy Data Book Version 6.0.* China Energy Group.

Lewis, Joanna I. and Ryan H. Wiser. 2007. Fostering a Renewable Energy Technology Industry: An International Comparison of Wind Industry Policy Support Mechanisms. *Energy Policy* 35(3): 1844–1857.

Lin, Jiang. 2006. *Mitigating Carbon Emissions: The Potential of Improving Energy Efficiency of Household Appliances in China*. Lawrence Berkeley National Laboratory, Report No. 60973.

Kai, Ma. 2006. *The 11th Five-Year Plan: Targets, Paths and Policy Orientation.* Briefing at the National Development and Reform Commission. March 19. http://en.ndrc.gov.cn/newsrelease/t20060323_63813.htm.

National Bureau of Statistics of China. 2006. *China Statistical Yearbook 2006.* Beijing: China Statistical Press.

NDRC (National Development and Reform Commission, People's Republic of China). 2007. China's National Cliamte Change Programme. http://www.ccchina.gov.cn/website/CCChina/UpFile/File188.pdf.

Ohshita, Stephanie B. and Leonard Ortolano. 2002. The Promise and Pitfalls of Japanese Cleaner Coal Technology Transfer to China. *International Journal of Technology Transfer and Commercialisation* 1(1/2): 56–81.

ORNL (Oak Ridge National Laboratory). 2007. *Transportation Energy Data Book, Edition 26.* Oak Ridge, TN: ORNL and U.S. Department of Energy.

Oster, Shai and Ann Davis. 2008. China Spurs Coal-Price Surge. *Wall Street Journal* February 12.

REN21. 2008. *Renewables 2007 Global Status Report.* Paris: REN21 Secretariat and Washington, DC: Worldwatch Institute.

SETC (State Economic and Trade Commission). 2003. The 10th Five-Year Plan for Energy Conservation and Resources Comprehensive Utilization.

Shenhua. 2008. Personal Communication with Official from Shenhua Group, Shanghai, March.

Sinton, Jonathan E., David G. Fridley, Jeffrey Logan, Guo Yuan, Bangcheng Wang, and Qing Xu. 2000. *Valuation of the Environmental Impacts of Energy Use in China.* Washington, DC: World Resources Institute.

World Bank. 2003. China: Promoting Growth with Equity. Washington, DC: World Bank, Country Economic Memorandum Report No. 24169-CHA.

World Bank-SEPA. 2007. Cost of Pollution in China: Economic Estimates of Physical Damages. World Bank and China State Environmental Protection Administration: Washington, DC.

Xu, B. 2002. Arrangement on Auto Fuel Economy Standards and Fuel Efficiency Promotion Policies of China. Workshop on Cleaner Vehicles in the U.S. and China. Beijing. Harvard University, China Ministry of Science and Technology and China Automotive Technology and Research Center (CATARC).

Zeng, Peiyuan. 2007. Speech delivered by Vice Premier of People's Republic of China, Beijing.

Zhao, Lifeng and Kelly S. Gallagher. 2007. Research, Development, Demonstration, and Early Deployment Policies for Advanced-Coal Technology in China. *Energy Policy* 35(12): 6467–6477.

Part 3

Under the Chinese Shadow: What Future for Developing Countries?

Chapter 6

China and the Terms of Trade: The Challenge to Development Strategy in Sub-Saharan Africa

Raphael Kaplinsky

Introduction

Beyond the minutiae of everyday, annual, and five-year cycles of policy lies the choice of development strategy. This shapes the trajectory of the economy over long periods, affecting not only the rate of economic growth but also its welfare and environmental impacts. It is customary (at least for economists) for this strategic choice to be located as a technical issue. "Which sectors should be privileged?" "what should be the balance between public and private actors in resource allocation?" and "what price signals will lead to the optimal outcome" are seen as decisions of economic rationality.

It is widely recognized that the core strategic choice in the development agenda has for some centuries been the commitment to industrialize and to reduce the relative importance of the commodity sectors of the economy. There are both powerful historical and analytical reasons rationalizing this strategic choice. But recent developments in the global economy, largely associated with the rise of China and India (the "Asian Drivers") challenge the logic of the commitment to industrialize at the expense of the commodity sectors. What implications does this hold for development strategies in general, and for the poor economies of Sub-Saharan Africa in particular?

And, in what political context and with what political configurations will these challenges to core development strategy be associated?

I argue that China-induced changes in relative prices undermine the feasibility of industrial development in an open economy. Without protection and other state measures designed to foster the industrial sector, Sub-Saharan Africa (SSA) will be driven even further backward into specialization in commodities. Furthermore, the distribution of the benefits among and within countries is likely to be limited in nature.

Industrialisation as a Core Development Strategy

After an initial focus on the agricultural sector following Independence in 1947, a severe drought and associated famine during the first half of the 1950s led India to commit its development strategy to a path of industrialization. In this choice Indian planners were not only influenced by powerful theoretical factors (see below), but also by the demonstration effect of Soviet Russia's rapid industrialization as a defense against hostile powers during the 1920s and 1930s.

Most of the developing world mirrored this strategic commitment to industrial development during the second half of the twentieth century. But it was not just the demonstration effect of India, or Soviet development (and indeed, the earlier experience of England, continental Europe, and North America) that rationalized this strategic choice. Nor was it the evident association between countries with high levels of per capita income and high shares of industrial development. There were also clear analytical reasons why industry should be favored at the expense of other sectors. Particularly important here was the trend in relative prices of manufactures and commodities, the terms of trade.

Until the 1950s it was widely believed that the terms of trade would turn against manufactures, and in favor of agricultural products. It was Hans Singer, and then Raul Prebisch, who deflated this belief in the early 1950s (Singer 1950, Prebisch 1950). They showed that in reality, the terms of trade were turning in favor of manufactures and against commodities (figure 6.1 shows the data for the second half of the twentieth century, but in fact the relationship goes back until at least the 1870s). In demolishing this orthodoxy, Singer and Prebisch explained these trends in terms of trade as resulting from a number of factors—the lower income elasticity of demand and higher price elasticity of demand of commodities;[1] the development of synthetic substitutes for primary products; and the fact that

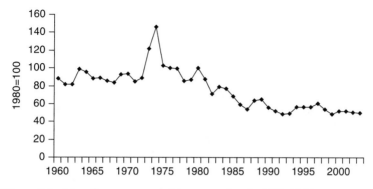

Figure 6.1 Manufactures-commodities terms of trade, 1960–2004

Source: Data provided by Mr Sami Gayi, UNCTAD, October 29, 2005.

commodities were only one of many inputs into final manufactures meant that a proportionate increase in the price of manufactures would have a lower impact on commodity-producer incomes compared to those arising in the production of commodities.

The import of this observation on the terms of trade is that long-run income growth would be fostered by moving out of price-sensitive (and, as Singer and Prebisch observed, price-volatile) primary products into income-elastic and price-inelastic manufactures, in other words by making a strategic commitment toward industrial development.

From the late 1970s, a twist was given to this widespread strategic commitment to industrialization. Based on the extraordinary growth-success of Japan and then the Asian Tigers, the strategic agenda was not just a commitment to industrialization, but to export-oriented industrialization. This increasingly became a strategic orthodoxy. For example, the World Bank's influential assessment in 2002 of the link between poverty and deepening globalization forcefully promoted the case for further globalization, notably through rapid growth in developing country exports of manufactures (World Bank 2002:xi).

Heavily influenced by this multilateral- and bilateral-agency policy agenda, and drawing on the successful growth and manufactured export experience of the first generation of Asian NICs (newly industrializing countries), SSA economies have increasingly oriented their long-term growth objectives to a graduation from the export of primary products to the export of manufactures. The demonstration effect of the astonishing recent emergence of China as a major global exporter of manufactures and its relatively successful performance in meeting the US$1/day Millennium Development Goal has provided further impetus to this policy consensus.

Are the Asian Drivers a Disruptive Force in the Global Economy?

On current trends, China will be the second biggest economy in the world by 2016, and India the third largest by 2035. A cluster of other countries in the Asian region, such as Thailand and Vietnam, are also growing rapidly. These newly dynamic Asian economies can collectively be characterized as the "Asian Drivers" of global change (hereafter the ADs). The two key AD economies are China and India. They disrupt the strategic and policy environment, and pose major and distinct challenges for the global and developing economies, for five major reasons.

The first is as a consequence of their size. As figure 6.2 shows, from the beginning of their growth spurts (1979 and 1992 respectively), neither Gross Domestic Product (GDP) nor export growth in the two largest AD economies were unique. In recent years other Asian economies (e.g., Japan and Korea) have experienced similarly rapid growth paths. However, while China accounted for 20 percent of the world's population and India for 17 percent in 2002, at no time did the combined population of Japan and Korea exceed 4 percent of the global total. So, unlike the case of Korea and Japan, who could grow without severe disruption to the global economy, we have to suspend the "small-country assumption" in the case of the ADs. The very high trade intensity of China's growth makes its big-country effect particularly prominent. Between 1985 and 2006, China's exports rose from US$50 billion to US$969 billion, transforming China into the world's third largest trading nation.

Second, the rise of the ADs has been associated with very significant, and growing, imbalances in the global economy. China's current account surplus has grown from a mere US$1.6 billion in 1996 (0.3 percent of GDP) to US$239 billion in 2006 (9.1 percent of GDP).[2] A related imbalance is in financial stocks. By mid-2007 China held foreign exchange reserves in excess of US$1.4 trillion, with India holding in excess of US$200 billion. These reserves compare with the total value of Foreign Direct Investment (FDI) stock in the United States of US$1.7 trillion. Depending on how these reserves are utilized (e.g., "sovereign wealth funds"—government-owned entities—acquiring assets of large Western firms) there is potential for substantial conflict and the possible impositions of controls over foreign ownership in the large previously dominant industrialized economies, undermining the mobility of global financial flows.

The third reason why the ADs may disrupt the global economy is that China (especially) and India embody markedly different combinations of state and capitalist development compared with the industrialized world.

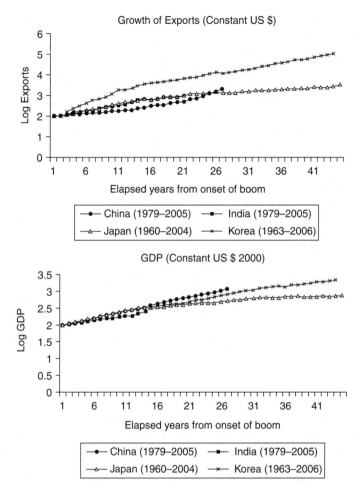

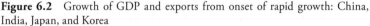

Figure 6.2 Growth of GDP and exports from onset of rapid growth: China, India, Japan, and Korea

Source: Calculated from World Bank, World Development Indicators, accessed May 9, 2008.

Chinese enterprises have their roots in state ownership, usually arising from very large and often regionally based firms (Nolan 2005, Shenkar 2005). They reflect a complex and dynamic amalgam of property rights. With access to cheap (and often subsidized) long-term capital, these firms operate with distinctive time horizons and are less risk averse than their Western counterparts (Tull 2006). Associated with these complex forms of ownership and links to regional and central state bodies, Chinese firms often operate abroad as a component of a broader strategic thrust. This is particularly prominent in China's advance in SSA in its search for the energy and commodities required to fuel its industrial advance (Kaplinsky, McCormick, and Morris 2008). This means that AD firms tend to invest with much longer time horizons, are less averse to risk than their Western counterparts, and are able to call on active state assistance when this is required. Moreover, their base in low income economies means that they are not subject to the same pressures regarding corporate and environmental social responsibility as are the previously dominant Western firms.

The fourth reason why the ADs present a new and significant challenge to the global and developing economies is that they combine low incomes and low wages with significant innovative potential. This means that they are able to compete across the range of factor prices. The oft-stated belief (and hope?) that China will run out of unskilled labor is belied by the size of its reserve army of the unemployed, estimated at around 100 million compared to the 83 million people employed in formal sector manufacturing in 2002 (Kaplinsky 2005). Moreover by 2030, India, also with a large reserve army of underemployed, is likely to have a larger—and younger—population than China. But China and India are not content to operate in this world of cheap labor and mature technologies, and are investing heavily in the building of technological capabilities. China, for example, overtook Japan to become the world's second largest investor in R&D in 2006 (Keeley and Wilsdon 2007).

A fifth disruptive consequence of the rise of the ADs is their quest for secure supplies of raw materials and energy (Klare, this volume). In the 2005–2007 period this was an agenda largely played out in SSA, and largely in relation to access to energy. China became an active investor in Sudan, Angola, and Somalia in the search for secure oil supplies, running against established policy agendas of the hitherto dominant Western powers, and displacing Western energy firms. In Sudan this led to an easing of the pressure over Darfur; in Angola it allowed the government to escape pressure exerted by the Paris Club on transparency in government, and in Somalia there is conflict within the state apparatus itself as to the legitimacy of the concession granted to Chinese companies. In Angola, China and India competed directly for access to the fuel deposits, in other cases (as in West Africa) they concentrated on different countries. But it is not just oil that the ADs have targeted in SSA. China has become a heavy investor in the Zambian copper fields, and in various mineral sectors in South and West Africa. Similarly, it is not just in SSA or in oil that their resource hunger is likely to be felt as a disruptive factor. A shortage of softwood in the global building industry in 2007 was a direct consequence of China's demand for timber, and water, too, has begun to loom on the horizon as a potential source of conflict.

As a consequence of these impacts, the ADs are beginning to disrupt the "political compact" that has underwritten the extension of globalization in post–World War II era. China and India are increasingly active in global institutions, demanding greater say in the regulation and shaping of the global economy. Their own experience belies the efficacy of the Washington Consensus policy agenda, and China and India provide a different policy role model for many developing economies, with the possible rise of a "Beijing Consensus" to rival the Washington Consensus (Ramo 2004).[3] These dynamics represent a transition from a quasi-unilateral U.S.-dominated world order to a multipolar power constellation. This is likely to lead to new turbulences and conflicts between the rising and the declining powers within the global governance system (Gu, Humphrey, and Messner 2008).

How disruptive are the ADs? Although China's growth spurt began in the late 1970s and India's in the early 1990s, their presence in global markets and their global environmental impacts only really began to be felt at the turn of the millennium. Indeed, India's impact is much more latent than real at present, although it is likely to become more significant in the future. It is perhaps too soon to conclude that they represent a historically decisive paradigm challenge to policy in SSA. However, as I will show below, their impacts are nonmarginal and the pace of change has been, and continues to be, extremely rapid. If this is the case, how are these disruptive forces transmitted to other economies, including those in SSA?

India's presence in Africa is predominantly of historical significance, although it is likely that this will change in the future as it too runs short of raw materials and increases its exports of manufactures. By contrast, China has a large and rapidly growing presence in SSA, and it is this presence that I will consider in the discussion below.

How Are These Disruptive Forces Transmitted to SSA?

The impacts of the ADs on SSA are complex. They arise from a variety of direct interactions between the ADs and Africa. But they also arise as an indirect consequence of AD interaction with the global economy. An overview of China's links with SSA distinguishes different channels of impact transmission, the distinction between complementary and competitive impacts, and between direct and indirect impacts.

Channels of Interaction

There are a variety of different channels through which individual countries interact with other economies, in their regions and elsewhere. Clearly, these channels are contingent—they change over time, and vary in importance depending on factors such as location, resource endowment, trade links, and geostrategic significance. Six key channels stand out in importance—trade links; investment flows (FDI and portfolio investments); aid; institutions of global governance; flows of people (including migrants); and environmental spillovers.

China's presence in Africa is much more coordinated than that of previously dominant northern powers. Thus, whereas Western aid tends to be relatively distant from its commercial interests, in China's case there is less light showing between these two channels of interaction.

Complementary and Competitive Impacts

In each of these channels of interaction, we can observe a mix of complementary and competitive impacts. For example, with regard to trade, China may both provide cheap inputs and consumer goods to SSA, and be a market for SSA's exports. On the other hand, imports into SSA from China can readily displace local producers. Another example is FDI. China may be a direct source of inward FDI into SSA and perhaps crowd-in FDI into SSA from third countries as parts of extended global value chains. These are complementary impacts. But China may also compete with other economies for global FDI.

The key element of these interactions is the "for whom" component. Countries may be affected differentially—in some economies, for example, imports of fabrics from China may feed productively into a vibrant clothing and textile value chain; in other cases, it may displace a country's exports and production for the domestic market. But these effects are not just felt at the national and economy-wide level. They affect groups within countries differentially. For example, cheap clothing imports from China may displace clothing and textile workers, but cheapen wage goods and hence reduce wage costs for producers in other sectors (which is indeed what has been occurring in many high income economies during the early years of the twenty-first century). These impacts on a complementary-competitive axis may also change over time, and most importantly, they will vary for different classes, regions, and groups within economies.

Channel	Impacts			
	Complementary		Competitive	
	Direct	Indirect	Direct	Indirect
Trade				
Investment				
Aid				
Global governance				
Migrants				
Environment				

Figure 6.3 A framework for assessing the impact of China on SSA

Direct and Indirect Effects

The complementary-competitive axis of impacts is readily comprehended and widely recognized. Less widely acknowledged is the distinction between direct and indirect impacts. In part this is because the indirect impacts are difficult to measure. However, indirect impacts are often more significant than direct impacts. Indirect impacts occur in third country markets and institutions. For example, China's trade with the United States may open or foreclose the opportunities for SSA economies to export into that market. Similarly, China's high savings rate has had the effect of lowering global interest rates, indirectly facilitating investment in SSA. China's participation in International Financial Institutions may change the conditionality of much of the multilateral aid given to low income economies in general, including those in SSA.

As in the case of the complementary/competitive access, the impact of the direct and indirect impacts can be gauged either at the country level, or at intranational levels, for example, with regard to different regions, sectors, classes, and genders.

Figure 6.3 summarizes this framework for assessing the impact of China on SSA.

The Rise of China and the Impact on the Terms of Trade

Although figure 6.3 charts a number of complex interacting modalities of China's impacts on SSA, in this chapter I will focus on the trade vector and the implications that these developments have for SSA development trajectories. In pursuing this discussion I will focus on the impact of China's growing external trade on the terms of trade that, as we saw in section 2 above, has played a formative role in the strategic choice of development strategy on the African continent (and, indeed, elsewhere, see Hogenboom and Yusuf, this volume).

As we are in the twenty-first century, there is reason to question the conventional wisdom of the terms of trade turning in favor of manufactures and against commodities. As Asia in general (and China in particular) participates much more actively in global product markets, historic patterns of relative price movements (as reflected in terms of trade) have begun to alter.

Much of the second half of the twentieth century was a period of inflation in the global economy. Prices of most commodities rose, although (as we have seen in figure 6.1) the price rise was faster for manufactures than for primary products. By the 1990s, most economies had begun to get on top of high rates of inflation and for the OECD (Organization for Economic Cooperation and Development) economies as a whole the rate of inflation at the turn of the millennium was less than 3 percent. What followed was a period of price deflation in manufactures, beginning with a slowdown of the rate of inflation in the late 1980s, and then after 1998, in absolute nominal prices (figure 6.4).

Figure 6.5 shows the impact of China's outward oriented industrial growth on this downward trend in the global prices of manufactures. It reports the proportion of the sectors for which the unit price of imports into the EU from different income groups (and China) fell between 1988 and 2001. The prices of products exported into the EU by China and low income economies were more likely to decline than the prices of the same products groupings sourced from other high income economies.

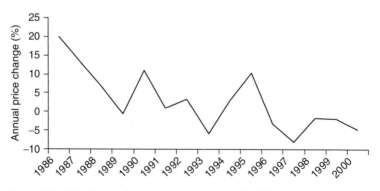

Figure 6.4 World manufacturing export price, 1986–2000

Source: IMF, World Economic Outlook Database, September 2003.

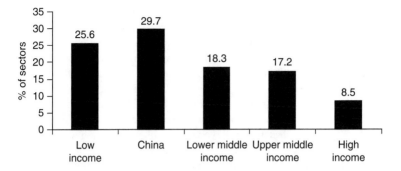

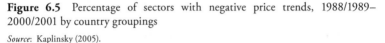

Figure 6.5 Percentage of sectors with negative price trends, 1988/1989–2000/2001 by country groupings

Source: Kaplinsky (2005).

At the same time that manufacturing prices were falling toward the end of the 1990s, commodity prices began to rise. This involves all three of the major components of the commodity sector—the "hard commodities" (minerals, metals, and precious stones); fuels (oil, gas, and coal); and the "soft commodities," including both food products and primary products feeding into industrial products (e.g., cotton, timber, and palm oil). A key driver in all of these rising commodity prices was demand from China.

Focusing on basic metals, China's demand for imports has been fueled by three factors. The first has been the rapid growth of domestic demand for household consumer goods and autos (see Gallagher, this volume). Second, there has been very substantial investment in infrastructure, both in the public and private sector, and this has been particularly basic metal–intensive. And, third, many of China's exports have been of metal-based products. Consequently, China's share in global steel production has grown from less than 10 percent in 1990 to 32 percent in 2006, equivalent to three times that of Japan, and more than either the EU or the United States. Between 2000 and 2006, China's share of the growth in global demand for steel, aluminium, copper, and nickel was 62 percent, 58 percent, 84.3 percent, and 64.3 percent respectively, and in 2005 alone, China accounted for 66 percent and 25 percent of growth in demand for copper and nickel respectively (UNCTAD 2007:89). It is projected that utilization of these basic metals is likely to grow even further in the future, in part because of China's relatively low per capita consumption of these materials (Kaplinsky 2005, IMF 2006). Bear in mind, China accounts for more than 20 percent of global population, and it is inevitable that as incomes grow and the minerals-intensive consumption grows as it has in other countries, this will continue to lead to rising demand for imported materials.

This expansion in Chinese commodity imports has been closely reflected in the global prices of many hard commodities. For example, between 2002 and 2007, the price of hot-rolled coil steel rose from around US$140/ton to more than US$600/ton,[4] much higher than the previous postwar peak of US$400/ton in 1994. Between 2001 and 2007, copper prices have more than trebled from around US$1,577/ton to US$7,117/ton, exceeding the previous postwar peak of US$2,846/ton in 1989.

The impact of China on commodity prices also extends to the energy sector. In 2007, China became the largest emitter of greenhouse gases and has a rapidly growing demand for energy (see Gallagher, this volume). Each year it adds to its capacity a demand that is greater than the total annual electricity generation of South Africa, Africa's largest consumer of electricity and one of the most energy-intensive economies in the world. Much of this demand for energy is met through coal-based generating plants, but some of this energy demand is also reflected in China's imports of hydrocarbons, particularly to power its burgeoning stock of autos. Prices of Australian thermal coal leapt from US$27/ton to US$70/ton between 2002 and 2007[5] higher than the previous postwar peak of 1981. Hard-coking coal prices doubled from US$50/ton to more than US$100/ton between 2002 and 2004, a postwar high. China's thirst for energy was one of the major reasons underlying the rapid rise in global energy prices in 2007, and indeed its demand for hydrocarbons is a major reason underlying China's growing presence in key oil-exporting economies in SSA, notably Angola, Sudan, and Nigeria.

The impact of Chinese demand on minerals began to be felt in the late 1990s. However, the impact on agricultural commodities has been more recent, but has been no less significant. Two China-related factors began to drive up the price of soft commodities in the new millennium. The first was the indirect impact of its thirst for energy. This played an important role in spurring the drive toward biofuels (both grains and starch-based feedstock for ethanol, and oil-based feedstocks for diesel), placing major demands on a variety of agricultural products such as corn, sugar, and palm oil. Second, rapid income growth in China has led to a changing pattern of food consumption, with growing demand for animal feeds, affecting the price of grains and vegetable oil crops. Prices of many agricultural products consequently jumped. Wheat, soya, palm oil, and rubber prices all trebled between 2000 and 2007.

Although the collective force of these price impacts has been severe, and significantly higher than previous price hikes in the 1920s, 1950s, and 1970s, the issue remains whether these changing terms of trade are likely to be sustained. After all, in each of the previous eras of price rises, the relative prices of manufactures and commodities rapidly returned to their long-term trends, generally within a period of 5–7 years. However, this time round, there are reasons to suggest that the change in relative prices will be sustained for a much longer period.

On the manufactures side of the terms of trade equation, there have been, and will continue to be, inflationary pressures in China (as well as an appreciating exchange rate). But, despite this, not only has the impact on the global price of manufactures been muted, but there is significant production capacity in Asia (including in the Chinese interior, as well as in India, Indonesia, Thailand, Vietnam, and other low cost East Asian economies) to suggest that the prices of manufactures will continue to be muted for some years to come.

By contrast, on the commodities side, there are a number of factors that suggest that prices will continue to be firm and to rise for some time ahead. First, insofar as minerals and metals are concerned, prices have already shown an upward surge for more than five years and most observers in the metals and mineral sector—including those scarred by the optimism of rising commodity prices in earlier eras—are predicting sustained price pressure until at least 2010. Second, pricing pressures on agricultural commodities are predicted to remain until at least 2016, particularly for grains, starches, and vegetable oils (FAO 2007). Third, during previous price spikes, the source of upward pricing pressure lay in interruptions to supply, such as droughts, frost, or wars. However, where price increases arose from augmented demand, they endured for much longer periods (Cashin, Liong, and McDermott 2000). Chinese demand for many commodities is still, as we have seen, at an early stage of the cycle and is unlikely to peter out soon; Indian demand lies around the corner.

The Challenge to Development Strategy in SSA

We can already see the consequences of these changing relative prices on economic performance in SSA. This impact is observable on both the manufactures and commodities side of the terms of trade equation.

Beginning with manufactures, the impact has been felt in production for the domestic market. Take two basic industries, footwear and clothing, as an example. In Ethiopia, competition from Chinese shoe imports has had a negative impact on employment and domestic output although it has led simultaneously to an upgrading of processes and design by many domestic firms. A study of 96 micro, small, and medium domestic producers reported that as a consequence of Chinese competition, 28 percent were forced into bankruptcy, and 32 percent downsized activity. The average size of micro enterprises fell from 7 to 4.8 percent employees, and of SMEs, from 41 to 17 percent (Tegegne 2006). In South Africa, imports from China grew from 16.5 percent of total apparel imports in 1995 to 74.2 percent in 2005 (all data in this and the following paragraph from Morris 2007). Including imports from Hong Kong, China-sourced apparel was 78.8 percent of total apparel imports in 2005. The expansion of apparel imports was associated with a period of rapid decline in formal sector manufacturing in both clothing and textiles. In apparel, employment fell from 97,958 in 2004 to 78,694 in 2006, and in textiles from 21,380 in 2003 to 16,800 in 2005. Morris cautions that this overestimates the extent of employment loss, since at the same time there is evidence that the informal apparel sector grew rapidly. However, wages and job security in the informal sector are much inferior to the formal sector, suggesting a period of wage compression during this period of import expansion from China. In Zambia, an embarrassing incident during President Hu Jintao's visit to Zambia as part of his tour around SSA in early 2007 was the closure of the Mulungushi textile factory and the loss of more than 1,000 jobs. This was a direct result of competitive imports from China, and, ironically, led to the closure of a textiles factory that the Chinese had built and supported with great fanfare in the 1970s.

But the negative impact of Chinese competition can also be observed on the export front, this time the effect being indirect in nature. Between 2000 and 2006, six SSA economies (Kenya, Lesotho, Madagascar, Mauritius, South Africa, and Swaziland) expanded their apparel exports to the United States to significant volumes, taking advantage of the African Growth and Opportunity Act (AGOA) preferences. In 2005, Kenya's clothing exports to the United States were in excess of US$300 million; for Lesotho, the figure was just over US$400 million. Here, SSA economies were favored not just by quantitative quotas on Chinese exports to the United States, but also by tariff preferences. With the ending of the Multifibers Agreement at the end of 2004, SSA apparel exporters were subject to intensified competition from China and other Asian economies in that the quota controls were removed. And despite the fact that they continued to benefit from tariff preferences, their exports were severely hit. In the first two years, total SSA clothing exports to the United States fell by 26 percent; during the same period, Chinese clothing exports of the same product groups rose by 71 percent. In Lesotho, this led to the loss of 29 percent of apparel jobs— bear in mind that apparel exports were manufactured exports (Lesotho having no other manufactures to sell abroad) and that Lesotho is one of the poorest countries in the world with few other employment opportunities available. In neighboring Swaziland, almost as dependent on apparel exports as Lesotho, employment fell by 56 percent. The wider significance of these developments should not be overlooked, since excluding South Africa, apparel accounted for more than half of all SSA manufactured exports in 2006. Of course, the impact of Chinese exports of manufactures to SSA was not all negative. The apparel exports of Kenya, Lesotho, and Swaziland—all least developed countries—were dependent on the incorporation of Chinese fabrics (an option not open to the higher income South African, Mauritian, and Madagasy economies). An increasing share of SSA's machinery and equipment is also being sourced from China, often at a much lower price, and being more appropriate in nature to competitive products previously sourced from high income economies. But it is the consumer who has been most favored by Chinese manufactured exports to SSA. In South Africa, for example, while the overall price index increased by 30 percent between 2000 and 2005, that of clothing fell by 5 percent. Significantly, as in the case of the Ethiopian shoe industry, some of this price decline was due to lower cost imports from China but competition from Chinese manufactures also forced local manufacturers to upgrade their competitiveness (Morris 2007).

On the commodities side, rising prices have had a positive impact, but on a smaller group of countries. High energy prices have meant that five economies have gained significantly—Angola, Nigeria, Equatorial Guinea, The Congo, and Sudan. On the other hand, oil-importing countries—the majority of SSA economies—have been hard hit, so much so that the rise in oil prices exceeded the total inflow of aid and debt forgiveness in 2007. On the minerals and metals side, the country distribution of gains has been somewhat more widespread, but even then only 12 countries accounted for more than 90 percent of all SSA's metals and minerals exports. Agricultural commodities show the greatest potential for beneficial spread effects from rising primary product prices, with 23 (out of 51) SSA economies accounting for more than 90 percent of total exports (figure 6.6).

Politics and Economics Interact

So far I have addressed the impact of China on the global terms of trade as an issue affecting the choice of an optimum strategy of economic development. I have argued that these China-induced changes in relative prices undermine the feasibility of industrial development in an open economy. Without protection and other state measures designed to foster the industrial sector (such as cross-sector measures designed to compensate for market failures, sector-specific support to promote capability growth and

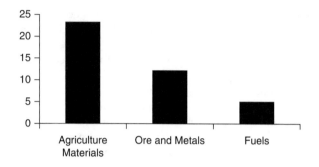

Figure 6.6   Number of countries accounting for 90 percent of SSA Exports (excl SA)

Source: Calculated from COMTRADE data, accessed January 15, 2008.

dynamic comparative advantage and region-specific support to strengthen spatial clusters) SSA will be driven even further backward into a commodity specialization.

Within this, while the continent does have valuable resources in fuels and minerals and metals, its geology and climate are not particularly favorable for agriculture (Bloom et al. 1998). Moreover, only five countries account for 90 percent of all fuel exports, and 12 countries for 90 percent of all metals and minerals exports. Thus, the country distribution of the benefits from the commodity boom is likely to be limited in nature, unless there are significant intraregional spillovers from commodity-exporting economies (about which we currently know very little).

However, as observed in the opening remarks to this chapter, there is a danger of reducing this analysis to the realm of rational economic choice. In fact, there are a series of very important social, political, and environmental characteristics of mineral-producing economies that feed into wider political processes. Here we can identify two groups of such impacts—those affecting what are called "point commodities," that is, commodities such as fuels, metals, and minerals that are located under the ground and are immovable in nature, and "diffuse commodities" such as coffee and cocoa that can be produced in a wide range of places (Auty 2004).

Before considering each of these commodity groups, it is helpful to begin with a brief characterization of the manufacturing sector. In the early stages of the development strategy debate in the 1950s, 1960s, and 1970s, it was common to characterize manufacturing as being capital- and skill-intensive, creating few jobs and with few spillovers and therefore being undesirable in comparison to the agricultural sector. However, the global fragmentation of value chains during the 1980s and 1990s led to the outsourcing of the labor-intensive and unskilled stages of production to the developing world, so that manufacturing—particularly export-oriented manufacturing—has increasingly been seen as being employment intensive and developmentally beneficial in nature.

Instead, it is the point commodities sector that displays many of the negative social and economic characteristics previously attributed to the manufacturing sector. Mines and oil fields are highly capital- and skill-intensive in nature. They employ few people, many of whom are expatriates. They involve very large agglomerations of financial capital, thus almost always either involving foreign ownership or domestic ownership by wealthy individuals and corporations. They are thus supportive—indeed generative—of very high levels of inequality. Moreover, because the revenue generated by most point commodities is highly concentrated (i.e., limited payments of large sums of capital), they are ideally suited to appropriation by individuals or small groups of people. In the case of precious stones and metals, the output is also easy to conceal. The capital-intensive nature of their production systems involves large contracts that are favorable to corrupt sourcing decisions. It is therefore not surprising that in most of SSA (and indeed in many other economies), point commodities are closely associated with corruption and violent conflict. It doesn't take too long to scan SSA economies and see how tight this association has been. Add to this negative environmental spillovers, and there are further reasons to be concerned about the developmental impact (as opposed to the economic impact) of a deepening of point commodity specialization in SSA.

Point commodities therefore are associated with particular forms of political coalitions. This may involve relatively stable democratic structures with deeply embedded inequality (South Africa, with a wide portfolio of point commodities, is probably the best example), systems that are relatively stable but are deeply undemocratic, unequal, and corrupt (Equatorial Guinea and oil) or those that are highly unstable, unequal, and corrupt and are associated with frequent military coups (Nigeria) and wars (Sierra Leone, DRC).

By contrast, the diffuse commodities are often associated with less developmentally malign patterns of political coalitions. They may often incorporate small and medium scale producers, both in crop production and crop processing. They also involve more elaborate value chains, either because of the spoilage of untreated crops such as sugar, or because of weight or volume loss in processing (timber). But while a specialization in these diffuse agricultural commodities may have better spread effects, here too SSA producers face challenges. First, as noted earlier, the geology and climate in SSA is not generally conducive to their production, and many SSA countries may become net importers rather than net exporters of foodstuffs, thus suffering additionally from changing terms of trade. Urban consumers will be particularly badly hit. Second, insofar as these agricultural commodities are being exported to markets in high income countries, they are increasingly subject to standards (such as environmental and labor standards) and, by their nature, these standards are often exclusive of small-scale producers (Kaplinsky and Morris 2002). And, third, the prices of diffused commodities are often highly volatile in nature, since they are subject to changing climatic conditions. In an era of rapid climate change and increasing climate variability, these adverse factors may be deleterious to welfare.

One final factor takes us squarely into the political domain. The point commodities—the primary beneficiaries so far of the changing terms of trade—are highly capital-intensive and an economic specialization in these sectors is likely to be associated with high levels of unemployment. In the early years of the twenty-first century, for the first time more than half of the world's population lived in cities (UN-Habitat 2003), and urban poverty has been growing much more rapidly than rural poverty (Chen and Ravallion 2007). Whereas the cities of earlier centuries have been places of industry, modern cities have become dumping grounds for the dispossessed and marginalized. As a consequence, urban politics has moved from class-based allegiances to premodernist, millenarian, and faith-based affiliations—the religious right of the north, fundamentalist Islam and Judaism in the Middle East and Asia, and Pentecostal churches in Latin America and Africa (Davis 2004). In many respects they represent the politics of the dispossessed, excluded from the fruits of the commodity boom.

In moving beyond an exclusive focus on the economic impact of the commodity boom, we do not only face the danger of defining a narrow and technicist agenda, making policy recommendations in an apolitical vacuum, and therefore frequently being surprised when they are not implemented. We also face the additional danger of reading-off political events from economic and technological determinants, a direction of analytical causality that privileges the technical over the social and political. Politics in SSA are not just a consequence of external factors (including prices); it has its own dynamics so that commodity specializations are often a reflection both of external determinants and internal political processes. Which commodities are exploited, in which regions, and with which ownership structures reflects domestic politics and has a dynamic of its own, notwithstanding the impact of external factors.

But, whatever this direction of causality may be, there can be little doubt that SSA political economies may be in for a rocky ride. Many opportunities are opened by the rise of the Asian Drivers in general, and China in particular. But the challenges are manifest, complex, and significant.

Notes

I am grateful to Masuma Farooki for her assistance in updating the data in this chapter.

1. The lower income elasticity of demand for commodities means that as their incomes grow, consumers tend to spend a greater proportion on manufactures than on commodities. The higher price elasticity of demand for commodities means that for a given increase in prices, demand is likely to fall more for commodities than for manufactures.
2. IMF Balance of Payments Statistics. http://www.imfstatistics.org/BOP (accessed June 24, 2008).
3. Ramo argued that the distinctive features of the Beijing Consensus is that each country should follow its own route, and that reform should be staged, rather than occur in a single burst. From the perspective of SSA countries, the key element of the Beijing Consensus is that there is no consensus, that is, a rejection of the World Bank-IMF formulaic Washington Consensus policy agenda.
4. MEPS. World Carbon Steel Prices with Individual Product Forecasts. http://www.meps.co.uk/World%20Carbon%20Price.htm (accessed May 8, 2008).
5. IMF Primary Commodity Prices. http://www.imf.org/external/np/res/commod/index.asp (accessed May 8, 2008).

References

Auty, Richard. 2004. Natural Resources and Civil Strife: A Two-Stage Process. *Geopolitics* 9(1): 29–49.

Bloom, David E., Jeffrey D. Sachs, Paul Collier, and Christopher Udry. 1998. Geography, Demography and Economic Growth in Africa. *Brookings Papers on Economic Activity* 29(2): 207–295.

Cashin, Paul, Hong Liang, and C. John McDermott. 2000. How Persistent Are Shocks to World Commodity Prices? *IMF Staff Papers* 47(2): 177–217.

Chen, Shaohua and Martin Ravallion. 2007. Absolute Poverty Measures for the Developing World, 1981–2004. *PNAS* 104(43): 16757–16762.

Davis, Mike. 2004. Planet of Slums: Urban Involution and the Informal Proletariat. *New Left Review* 26: 5–34.

FAO (Food and Agriculture Organization of the United Nations). 2007. Implications for World Agricultural Commodity Markets and Trade of Rapid

Economic Growth in China and India. Committee on Commodity Problems, Session 66. Rome (Italy), April 23–25.

Gu, Jing, John Humphrey, and Dirk Messner. 2008. Global Governance and Developing Countries: The Implications of the Rise of China. *World Development* 36(2): 274–292.

IMF (International Monetary Fund). 2006. *World Economic Outlook: Globalization and Inflation*. Washington, DC: International Monetary Fund.

Kaplinsky, Raphael. 2005. *Globalization, Poverty and Inequality: Between a Rock and a Hard Place*. Cambridge: Polity Press.

Kaplinsky, Raphael, Dorothy McCormick, and Mike Morris. 2008. The Impact of China on SSA, Agenda-Setting. Paper prepared for DFID, IDS Working Paper Brighton, Institute of Development Studies.

Kaplinsky, Raphael and Mike Morris. 2002. *A Handbook for Value Chain Research*. University of Sussex: Institute of Development Studies.

Keeley, James and James Wilsdon. 2007. *China: The Next Science Superpower*. London: Demos.

Morris, Mike. 2007. The Rapid Increase of Chinese Imports: How Do We Assess the Industrial, Labour and Socio-Economic Implications? Paper delivered at the 20th Annual Labour Law Conference. Sandton Convention Centre, July 4–6.

Nolan, Peter. 2005. *Transforming China: Globalization, Transition and Development*. London: Anthem Press.

Prebisch, Raúl. 1950. *The Economic Development of Latin America and Its Principal Problems*. New York: United Nations.

Ramo, Joshua Cooper. 2004. *The Beijing Consensus*. London: Foreign Policy Centre.

Shenkar, Oded. 2005. *The Chinese Century: The Rising Chinese Economy and Its Impact on the Global Economy, the Balance of Power and Your Job*. Upper Saddle, NJ: Pearson Education.

Singer, H.W. 1950. The Distribution of Gains between Investing and Borrowing Countries. *American Economic Review* 40(2): 473–485.

Tegegne, Gebre-Egziabher. 2006. Asian Imports and Coping Strategies of Medium, Small and Micro Firms: The Case of Footwear Sector in Ethiopia. Mimeo. Addis Ababa: Addis Ababa University.

Tull, Denis M. 2006. China's Engagement in Africa: Scope, Significance and Consequences. *Journal of Modern African Studies* 44(3): 459–479.

UN-Habitat. 2003. *The Challenge of the Slums: Global Report on Human Settlements 2003*. London: James/Earthscan.

UNCTAD (United Nations Conference on Trade and Development). 2007. *World Investment Report 2007*. New York and Geneva: United Nations.

World Bank. 2002. Globalization, Growth, and Poverty: Building an Inclusive World Economy. Policy Research Report, Washington, DC: World Bank and Oxford: Oxford University Press.

Chapter 7

Latin America and the Rise of China: Possibilities and Obstacles for Development

Barbara Hogenboom

At first glance, China's expansion is a very positive development for Latin America and the Caribbean, as trade figures show steep rises. Several countries greatly benefit from China's enormous demand for energy, minerals, and other primary commodities. Yet to other countries the "China effect" is mainly trade competition in local and global markets. With respect to foreign investment the effects of China's expansion are diverse, too, involving competition for MNC investment, but also new Chinese joint ventures, especially in the exploitation of Latin America's natural resources. However, the contrast between China's rise and Latin America's low and volatile growth figures leads to the question of what Latin America can learn from the People's Republic of China (PRC). In particular, this contrast stresses the crucial role of the state in developing countries to maintain or broaden their economies' position in global markets. Also for Latin America the issue of the Chinese miracle is about 'the future "spaces" open for the development of industrial exports in a liberalized world in which the PRC is preempting many markets for products that developing countries can export' (Lall and Weiss 2004:23).

The rapid liberalization and globalization of the 1980s and 1990s have not only had a major impact on the economies of developing countries, they have profoundly changed South-South relations. The relations between China and Latin America serve as an interesting case of the complex shifts within the "Global South." The end of the Cold War and of China's Maoism has eased the relations between Latin America and the People's Republic of China as well as the latter's relations with other developing countries. These new South-South relations became particularly clear during the 2003 summit of the World Trade Organization (WTO) in Cancún. Although China had only entered into the organization in December of 2001, it joined Brazil, India, South Africa, and the other developing countries of the G-20 in a successful attempt to change global politics and policies. For the first time since the start of the debt crisis in the 1980s there was genuine South-South cooperation, resulting in a deadlock in international trade negotiations that has still not been resolved.

This chapter studies the great economic and political importance of the rise of China for Latin America. With respect to recent economic effects, the region has both winners and losers. These different economic experiences partly explain the differences in political relations between Latin American countries and China, but geopolitical factors play a role too. It is important for Latin America that China has been supporting the growing influence of the "Global South" in international relations. It may help Latin America to limit U.S. influence in the region, allowing for more political space and for development policies that no longer follow the Washington Consensus of free markets and a small state. While both China and Latin America have profoundly liberalized their economies since the 1980s, the contrast between China's economic successes and Latin America's crises and stagnation stresses the need for reconsidering the role of the state in economic development.

In this chapter I first review China's miraculous growth and globalization, and aspects of the new political relations between China and Latin America. These economic and political dimensions are then used to analyze the complex links between the rise of China and the prospects for development of Latin America. Finally, in the conclusions, I discuss the need for regional cooperation and integration policies for Latin America.

Complementarity and Competition in Globalized Production

The rapid growth and globalization of China's economy has become a major global phenomenon that has affected Latin America in several ways. Due to its extensive industrialization China is importing increasingly larger volumes of primary commodities, and thereby pushing up their world market prices (see Kaplinsky, this volume). As shown in figure 7.1, resource rich Latin American countries are profiting from these higher international prices and Chinese imports as well as from the growing direct investments by Chinese companies in exploring and exploiting Latin American mines and oil fields. To Latin America's manufacturing sector, however, China's success poses serious problems of competition: Chinese products compete with Latin American products in local and third markets; and China competes with Latin America in attracting investment by multinational companies. The cases of Brazil, Chile, and Mexico clearly demonstrate the very different outcomes of these parallel economic processes, which helps explain the differences in the relations of Latin American countries with China.

China proved to be the absolute winner of economic globalization in the era of neoliberalism. From 1985 to 2000 it achieved the highest average annual export growth of 4.5 percent, while the second most successful country in this respect was the United States, which achieved no more than 1.8 percent. At a time when the economies of developing countries in general only at 3 percent a year, China's annual average growth of real Gross Domestic Product (GDP) from 1980 to 2000 was on average 10 percent. Since 2000 China has been able to maintain this high economic growth. While the average GDP growth of low and middle income countries increased substantially to 6.0 percent in 2005–2006, the 10.1 percent of China (classified by the World Bank as lower middle income country) remains exceptional. As a result, China has become the

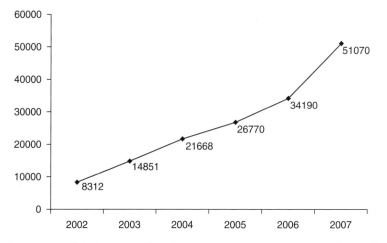

Figure 7.1 China's imports from Latin America, 2002–2007 (in millions of U.S. dollars)

Source: CEPAL (2005b) and MofCom (2008).

third largest importing as well as exporting country, the fourth economy in the world, and one of the top three destinations of foreign direct investment (UNCTAD 2006, 2005, 2004, 2003, World Bank 2007). The fact that China has become a central place for production, investment, imports, and exports is closely linked to China's role as "the factory to the world." Between 1980 and 2003, China's share in world trade increased more than fivefold: its exports rose from 0.9 to 5.8 percent and its imports from 1.0 to 5.4 percent (UNCTAD 2005:133). With its rapid economic growth and expanding export production, China has become a major consumer of natural resources and commodities, many of which originate from other developing countries. Internationally, it is the second largest consumer of energy, and the largest importer of several important commodities, such as iron ore. In 2004, China consumed 40 percent of the world's coal, 25 percent of the nickel, and 14 percent of the aluminum. This massive Chinese demand has contributed to rising commodity prices, which is beneficial to exporting developing countries that suffered from years of low world prices and related worsening terms of trade. The price level for metals, for instance, was about twice as high in 2006 as the average price level of the 1980s and 1990s (IMF 2006:54–63).

The rapid growth of China and some other (emerging) economies in the East and the South is creating a new global economic outlook for all developing countries, including those of Latin America. Although for China the trade relations with Latin America and the Caribbean are relatively modest (compared to Chinese trade with Asia or the United States), its imports from Latin America have grown substantially since the mid-1990s, and especially since 2000 (see table 7.1). In 2000, the region's exports to China were US$5.4 billion, and in 2005 they had more than tripled to

Table 7.1   Trade of Brazil, Chile, and Mexico with China, 1995–2004 (in millions of U.S. dollars)

	Brazil		Chile		Mexico	
	Export	Import	Export	Import	Export	Import
1995	1,204	418	287	390	37	520
2000	1,085	1,222	902	949	217	2,880
2004	5,442	3,710	3,212	1,847	474	14,373
2005	6,835	5,355	4,390	2,541	1,136	17,696
2006	8,402	7,989	4,942	3,483	1,688	24,438
2007	10,749	12,618	n/a	n/a	1,899	29,792

n/a: not available
Source: UN Comtrade 2008.

US$18.6 billion. Latin American exports consist mainly of primary products and manufactures based on natural resources, which represented 46 and 30 percent of the exports, respectively, in 2004. China depends on Latin America for products like sugar and fruits, soy (beans and oil, in particular from Argentina and Brazil), minerals (Brazil), and copper (Chile). In 2005, nearly 40 percent of the imports came from Brazil; other important countries were Chile (17 percent), Argentina (15 percent), Mexico (10 percent) and Peru (7 percent). China's exports to Latin America are strong in low technology products (e.g., clothing and footwear). These Chinese imports threaten local production. Moreover, low Chinese production costs in these sectors are harming Latin America's chances for export production for the U.S. and European markets, as will be discussed later (CEPAL 2005b, 2007).

Although Latin America competes with China in attracting international capital, several Latin American countries are profiting from China's increasing investments abroad. Primarily driven by its growing demand for natural resources, China has become the world's sixth largest foreign investor in developing countries, with its direct investments reaching US$21 billion in 2006. Of the top 50 nonfinancial multinational companies from developing countries, in 2005 7 were Chinese. These Chinese multinationals are generally controlled by the state and their rise is the result of the government's determination to create China's own "global champions," which are internationally competitive while operating under state control (Jiang 2007, *The Economist* 2005, UNCTAD 2007).

Both Latin America and China are important recipients of foreign direct investment. As the number one destination for FDI to developing countries, China received US$69.5 billion in 2006, whereas the whole Latin American and Caribbean region received US$83.8 billion (figure 7.2). The abundance of low cost labor is China's largest competitive advantage: it possesses a labor market of over 700 million workers who, on average, cost US$0.61 per hour compared to, for instance, the US$2 in Mexico. In the manufacturing sector labor costs in China are 3.7 times lower than in South America's poorest country, Bolivia, and 12.5 times lower than in Chile. The Chinese economy also better matches the preferences of MNCs than most Latin American countries due to its large internal market and the major public sector investments in infrastructure and high technology development. As a result, China is competing favorably with Latin America in the labor-intensive segments of the international markets (CEPAL 2004 and 2005a, Gutiérrez 2003, Shafaeddin 2002, UNCTAD 2007).

Nonetheless these regional trade and investment figures hide the large differences among Latin American countries. For instance, Peru has one

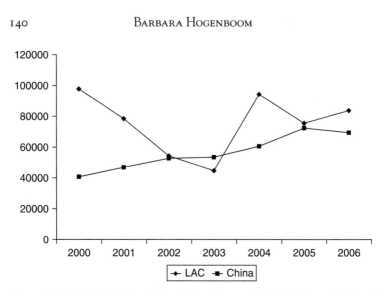

Figure 7.2   Net FDI inflows in Latin American and the Caribbean (LAC) and China, 2000–2006 (in millions of U.S. dollars)

Source: FDI STAT (2008).

of the region's highest percentages of exports to China (10.7 percent in 2005, including fish meal, copper, and iron), but to its neighbor Bolivia the Chinese market is marginal (0.7 percent of Bolivia's total exports in 2005) (CEPAL 2006b). The following short comparative overview of Brazil, Chile, and Mexico demonstrates the diversity of China relations in the region (see also table 7.1).

Brazil

Since 2000 Brazil's trade with China has increased rapidly. Already in 2002 Brazil exported more soy (31 percent) and iron (22 percent) to China than to any other country. Although considerably less than its exports to its number one export market, the United States, in 2007 Brazil's exports to China were US$10.7 billion. For some years after 2000 Brazil had a trade surplus with China, but this trend was reversed in 2007 when Brazil's imports from China reached US$12.6 billion. Brazil's imports from China are mainly electronic and chemical products. The dominance of electronic and communication technologies in these imports is related to the global production strategies of vertical specialization that are used by MNCs in this sector. Companies like Philips have some of their production processes in China, then send parts for assembly to their Brazilian factories, and either sell the end products in Brazil, or reexport them to other markets in the region (UN Comtrade 2008, Mesquita Machado and Tinoco Ferraz 2005, CEPAL 2006b).

Chile

Chile has benefited greatly from China's growing demand as well as from the related rise of world prices, as its economy is basically complementary to China's economy. Chile imports Chinese manufactures like textiles, clothes, footwear, toys, and electronic products, and exports primary commodities like agro products, cellulose, marine products, chemicals, but most of all copper to China. China has turned into Chile's second trading partner (after the United States); above traditionally important trade partners like Argentina, Japan, and Brazil. With Chile's exports to China of US$4,942 million and China's exports to Chile of US$3,483 million, in 2006 Chile's trade surplus with China equaled US$1,459 million. This trade surplus has much to do with China being the world's largest copper importer, consuming 20 percent of this mineral's global trade, and Chile being the world's main producer and exporter (León 2005).

Mexico

The economic relations between Mexico and China are mostly about competition. China became Mexico's second largest trade partner in 2003, but mainly due to massive Mexican imports of Chinese goods. These imports are partly products for Mexican consumers, but a substantial share consists of parts and semi-manufactures to be further processed in Mexico into export products, especially for the U.S. market. In 2007, Mexico's exports to China valued only US$1,896 million whereas its imports from China valued US$29,792 million, which is more than 15 (!) times as much (UN Tradecom 2008). Evidently, this very unbalanced trade relation gives way to a huge Mexican trade deficit. In addition to the large flows of legal imports, there are many illegal imports: possibly over half the garment consumption in Mexico is of illegally imported products, mostly from China. Even more problematic to Mexico is the strong Chinese competition in the exports of manufactured goods to the United States, especially in textiles and electronics. As we will see further along, China's trade and investment competition is highly problematic for Mexico's competitiveness in the context of globalized markets.

Interests and Politics in Globalized Markets

The relations between China and Latin America in general have significantly improved and strengthened since the 1990s. Still, there is a wide variation in the nature and quality of bilateral relations as a result of the difference in economic and political interests. China's integration into the global economy, including its accession to the WTO, was a key motivation for its government to establish good relations with as many countries as possible. In addition to trade benefits and Chinese rewards for supporting the country's WTO ambitions, some Latin American countries have been interested in China as a partner in broader South-South cooperation. Others have kept a distance because of China's competitiveness or their relations with Taiwan. Overall, however, Latin America's economic and political relations have intensified rapidly, as exemplified by the Chile-China free trade agreement of 2005, and the strategic alliance between Brazil and China that has fed the effective resistance of the G-20 in the WTO against the trade agenda of the United States and the European Union.

In 1986, the People's Republic of China solicited admission to GATT, which started a process of 15 years of multilateral and bilateral negotiations that ended in 2001 with the entry of China into GATT's successor: the WTO. In the multilateral negotiations the totality of GATT/WTO members, including the Latin American and Caribbean countries, determined the terms and conditions of the accession of China. In the bilateral negotiations China had to negotiate the conditions and compromises of mutual market access with each of the members. Government officials discussed the tariffs on industrial and agricultural products, and the obligations that China had to meet with respect to its internal market and access by foreign service providers. Later on the bilateral negotiations were "protocolized" and "multilateralized," enabling China to be recognized as "most favored nation." This whole process culminated at the WTO Ministerial Conference in Doha, Qatar, on November 10, 2001, when the member states approved the terms of China's accession.

China's active pursuit of closer diplomatic relations with Latin America since the early 1990s in the context of the WTO negotiations stands in stark contrast with China's previous international isolation and its ideologically based support for liberation movements in the 1960s. Now economic interests and pragmatism prevail. Since 1990 China has attended the annual meetings with foreign affairs ministers of the countries of the Group of Rio (a permanent regional consultation mechanism), mainly to search for joint positions in international institutions. In 1991, China became a permanent observer of the InterAmerican Development Bank, and in 1994 of the Latin American Integration Association ALADI. In 1998, the People's Bank of China became a member of the Caribbean Development Bank. Moreover, China has established mechanisms of permanent dialogue with MERCOSUR and with the Caribbean Community and Common Market (CARICOM), and in 2004 it became a permanent observer of the Organization of American States (OAS) and of the Latin American Parliament. In addition, China signed more than 100 agreements with Latin American countries on scientific and technological cooperation, ranging from satellites industry to agriculture (Cornejo 2005, Gutiérrez 2003:23).

Chile

Due to China's rapidly increasing economic importance, many Latin American countries have intensified their relations with the People's Republic of China. The Chile-China relations are friendly, due to the economic complementarity between the two countries, and both have cooperated in international institutions such as the UN and the APEC. In line with its strategy of dynamic "open regionalism," Chile accepted the accession of China into the WTO relatively early, in 1999. Since then, Chile has aimed to achieve a privileged position in attracting Chinese FDI, in particular in its mining sector. In 2002, China proposed to Chile to extend their economic relations and they started preparing the so-called third generation agreement, including not only trade and investment but also educational, environmental, and cultural accords. In 2005, the free trade agreement between Chile and China was signed. That same year a leading Chinese metal company, Minmetals Non-ferrous Metal Co., and the world's largest producer of copper, Chile's state company CODELCO, established a strategic alliance to meet the growing Chinese need for this mineral and exploit the Chilean reserves.

Brazil

China's most privileged Latin American associate is Brazil. In 1993 the Chinese government defined its relations with Brazil as a strategic alliance, implying that through their bilateral relations they can achieve more just global trade rules, in particular improving developing economies' access to the U.S. and EU markets. Brazil supported China's entry into the WTO from early on because it was convinced that the economic benefits would involve investment and the opening of an important alternative market that could compensate for the negative effects of U.S. and European protectionism. Of all Latin America countries Brazil has put the most efforts into intensifying its relations with China and the two countries have been cooperating in several high technology fields. Still, the main component of the bilateral relations of Brazil and China remain commodities. Among other things, the mining company Vale do Rio Doce signed association agreements with Baoshan Iron and Steel and other Chinese companies to produce iron and aluminum in the North East of Brazil. With the Chinese firm Yanguang this Brazilian company agreed to invest in oil products for export to third markets. And the state companies Petrobras and Sinopec jointly explore and produce oil in Africa and the Middle East (CEPAL 2005a, Mesquita Machado and Tinoco Ferraz 2005).

Mexico

The relations between Mexico and China are difficult. Mexico faces strong Chinese competition on its main export market: the U.S. market for labor-intensive products. It was the last Latin American country to accept China's WTO membership, and since then Mexico has joined the United States in bringing complaints about illegal Chinese subsidies and tax breaks to the WTO. The conflicts over China's competition, Mexico's lining up with the United States vis-à-vis China, and limited Chinese interest to date to invest in Mexico have resulted in bilateral relations that are far from strategic and friendly.[1]

WTO and South-South Cooperation

Other Latin American countries have a more cooperative attitude toward China and its WTO membership, although the strong competition of Chinese products and the role of the state in China's economy are sometimes problematic to them, too. They have been supportive of China's goal to become officially recognized as a "Market Economy" by as many WTO members as possible. This status as Market Economy is very important for China as it limits antidumping conflicts over cheap Chinese exports.[2] Especially, the United States and the European Union claim that China is still not a market economy because of government assistance to its industries, and that they need to protect their industries against unfair Chinese competition. Mexico argues the same, but so far 15 Latin American and Caribbean countries have granted China the status of Market Economy, including Brazil, Chile, Argentina, Venezuela, and Peru.

This cooperative attitude is exemplary of the rise of new South-South relations in a (post–Cold War) multipolar world. President Lula Da Silva's foreign policies have sought intensified and influential relations of Brazil with countries like China—but also India and South Africa. Both Brazil and China aim to improve their economies' added value and the international prices for primary and manufactured products, prioritizing investments that involve technology transfers. Their collaboration in the G-20 within the WTO has had important results in the last round of international trade negotiations, called the Doha Development Round, involving a broad agenda for global trade, investments, services (intellectual) property rights, and more. The G-20 now includes more than 20 developing countries of which more than half are from Latin America, including countries with very different political regimes (and different relations with China) such as Argentina, Bolivia, Chile, Cuba, Mexico, Paraguay, and Venezuela. In the G-20, Brazil, India, and China have played key roles in increasing developing countries' influence, in particular on agricultural issues. In the fifth ministerial summit of the WTO in Cancún (Mexico) in September of 2003, the G-20 rejected the joint proposal of the European Union and the United States, proposing instead to eliminate U.S. and EU agro-subsidies. Also in the WTO negotiations on services, intellectual property rights and investments Brazil and China have by and large had coinciding interests and agendas.

China's and Latin America's Development Models

During the last quarter of the twentieth century economic liberalization was the central element of the development model in both China and Latin America. Still there are some important differences between these two in the style and outcome of this liberalization, especially with respect to the role of the state. There is a major contrast between the Latin American model that aimed at a very limited economic role for the state, and the Chinese model in which the state has kept a key role in stimulating and facilitating economic processes, sectors, and actors. China's economic success raises questions about the appropriateness of Latin America's development model and the prospects for propoor growth in the long run.

In many Latin American countries, as in China, policies of economic opening were initiated by an authoritarian state that excluded any form of participation of civil society or political society. In Latin America, the economic liberalization reforms were largely "imported," with U.S.

government pressures followed by International Monetary Fund (IMF) and World Bank conditionalities during the debt crisis, and the so-called Washington Consensus. Since the late 1980s, processes of democratization allowed for the compatibility of neoliberalism with democratic political regimes. In the case of China, on the other hand, the initiative of economic reforms came from within; from 1978 onward the aim was to restructure the economy gradually under the control of the state party. Starting in 1992 the centrally planned economy became subordinated to market mechanisms as an instrument for assigning productive resources in the economic process. With these last reforms the political class of the Chinese state hoped to maintain its position (after the Tiananmen events of 1989), thus using the economic successes of China's capitalism to legitimize its monopolized control over the state and political processes.

As a result of these different trajectories of economic liberalization, the Chinese state still maintains the capacity to control and boost the process of globalization of China's economy, whereas in Latin America neoliberalization has basically left the state as subsidiary to economic globalization while the private sector has turned out to be not the powerful motor for economic modernization it was expected to be. Several Latin American analysts claim that the larger intervention capacity of the Chinese state in its economy's globalization is a weakness, hindering corporate governance and market discipline. Compared to the extensive financial liberalization in Latin American countries, for instance, the limited deregulation of China's financial sector is seen as negative for its access to credit (Lora 2005, Cornejo 2005). However, there is another side to this story. To accelerate its economic growth, China greatly diversified and expanded its export sectors. Evidently, transnational companies have gained terrain in China, but the Chinese government has vigorously promoted local companies, with massive public and public-private investments in industrial upgrading. The state has actively used diverse instruments to derive development benefits from foreign direct investment such as training local human resources, transfer of technology, and the development of production chains (see Yusuf, this volume).

In contrast to China's broad policy spectrum, in Latin America privatization was central to neoliberal restructuring. This gave way to a process of substantial economic concentration. For a short period of time, privatization attracted large sums of FDI and was profitable to both Latin American and transnational companies. But privatization together with liberalization and deregulation policies did not bring about the envisioned development and modernization of the region. This strategy failed because little was done to deal with Latin America's weaknesses in infrastructure, human resources, and technological development. Moreover, rather than stimulating entrepreneurship, the massive support of the public sector for "big business" and the close relations between technocrats and important entrepreneurs—during as well as after privatization—gave way to the creation of a new oligarchy. With their globalized assets and capital, this new oligarchy has limited interest in the development of the domestic economy. And with a generally small state, in many Latin American countries the public sector lacks the necessary capacity to enhance significantly its economy's modernization (Fernández Jilberto and Hogenboom 2007).

Despite these general Latin American weaknesses, Chile and Brazil have overall been quite successful in their strategies of insertion in global markets, and due to the complementarity of their economies with the Chinese economy they have mostly benefited from the rise of China. Chile is one of the most liberalized economies of Latin America and the model with which Chile has inserted itself in the global economy consists of an extreme form of "open regionalism." A free trade agreement with the United States, trade accords with the European Union, and numerous trade agreements with countries in Latin America and Asia have strengthened Chile's position as an exporter of goods and services, particularly natural resources. Although not without difficulties, Chile integrates its production according to the exigencies of dynamic transnational production, and together with the efficiency of its services and professionals Chile has turned into the commercial platform of South America (Fazio 1999, Ffrench-Davis and Stallings 2001). Brazil has followed another rather successful strategy of global economic reinsertion, using MERCOSUR as a regional platform to launch its economy. Simultaneously, Brazil furthers its economic as well as diplomatic relations with other large upcoming markets in order to improve bilateral exchange and advance the international development agenda of the Global South.

Pro-poor Growth for Latin America?

In Mexico as well as Central America and the Caribbean cheap Chinese products and aggressive Chinese policies to attract foreign investments have caused a process of industrial South-South relocalization that particularly harms *maquiladora* (assembly) industries. Heavily affected by the Chinese competition in the U.S. market, these countries are forced to reconsider their still rather new strategies for insertion into global production chains. Despite NAFTA, the free trade agreement between the United States, Central America, and the Dominican Republic (DR-CAFTA), and U.S. policies of limited taxation that have favored imports from these countries, China has become the world's number one in the production chain from yarn to textile to garment (YTG). China's textile capacity is 10 times bigger than Mexico's, and in terms of jobs its YTG chain is almost 40 times bigger than that of Mexico. In China this chain has been stimulated by a mix of economic liberalization and high state subsidies, resulting in a coordination of companies based on public-private interests.

Computers are another important export product for Mexico in which China is a direct competitor. While 90 percent of the PCs produced in Mexico go to the United States, China is increasingly replacing Mexico in this market. Chinese exports and the number of companies are growing as a result of government policies that have promoted high tech innovation since 1984. China's five-year development plan for 2001–2005 considered the high tech sector as strategic, focusing public sector efforts on stimulating industry, higher education, and high tech industrial parks, and providing a series of grants, credits, and tax advantages (Dussel Peters 2005).

In addition to the negative effects of China's successes, Mexico's neoliberal economic model with privatization and North American regional integration as central elements is part of the problem. As in most of Latin America, and many other parts of the world, after more than 20 years of neoliberal policies Mexico has experienced that economic growth based on free market principles is lower and more volatile than anticipated, and unsuccessful in producing the social progress that followed the mixed economy policies of import substituting industrialization. This is reflected, above all, in the employment situation. Liberalization and privatization have resulted in a wide and structural gap between formal jobs and employable persons. Almost half of Mexico's population is engaged in one or several informal economic activities, and some 40 percent of GDP is in this informal sector.

Apart from Mexico and Central America that focus on assembly industries for export to the U.S. market, other Latin American countries have to reconsider their model of development too. South American countries like Brazil, Chile, and Argentina that have expanding resource based industry tend to make these activities more capital-intensive without providing many additional jobs. "Both types of activities have relatively low domestic-value-added content, and neither provides the kind of transformation of the domestic production and export pattern that would allow trade to become an engine of growth" (UNCTAD 2003:141). From Mexico's recent problems one might easily conclude that maquiladoras are not the road to modernization, at least not in a liberalized world economy in which China is able to offer massive amounts of similar products at a lower price. However, the economic growth achieved by some other Latin American countries largely based on providing primary products may not bring about much propoor development either.

Even countries that so far have not been threatened by the "China effect" may well face some serious problems in the longer term, as future efforts for technological upgrading are likely to meet a major competitive threat by China. Compared to China, Latin America and the Caribbean will remain a high wage region, which can only be offset by high levels of technological competence or skill. Together with the relatively weak position of Latin America's global production networks (except for Mexico and Central America) there is thus reason for concern about the region's competitive position in the world economy.

Conclusions

The rise of China involves possibilities as well as obstacles for Latin America's development. On the one hand, Chinese competition is of great concern to Latin American countries with a substantial manufacturing sector. In addition, dependency on exporting primary commodities can also have adverse effects on development (see Kaplinsky, this volume). And China's success in becoming the "factory of the world" in the era of open markets confronts the whole of Latin America with the dilemma of how to modernize their economy. On the other hand, several countries have been profiting from rising exports, commodity prices, and investments, or hope to do so in the future. China's rise and the more general growth of the Asian economy also help Latin America to diversify its international trade and investment relations, thereby diminishing the subcontinent's dependence on the U.S. and EU economies. Simultaneously, the bilateral political relations between Latin American countries and the People's Republic of China have overall improved, and feed South-South cooperation in international political arenas.

Apart from setting an example for alternative development strategies, China's recent global economic influence encourages such alternatives for developing countries in several ways. By joining the G-20 in the WTO's Doha Development Round, China has been of support in advancing the interests of developing regions in global politics and the world market. Meanwhile, as a new export market and an emerging source of foreign investment, the "China effect" is indirectly political too. Economic growth in Latin American countries that are benefiting from the commodity boom diminishes these countries' dependency on international financial institutions and their policies (Weisbrot 2006). It needs to be remembered, however, that China's global agenda is clearly based on its economic interests. While China can be expected to enhance the South-South agenda and support international demands of developing countries, it may also enhance a globalization that seriously neglects human rights and environmental degradation, while making it very hard for Latin American manufacturing to survive and modernize.

Since the years of economic wonders in Latin America (1940s–1960s), the puzzle of how to enhance industrialization and achieve sustainable high rates of propoor growth has not been solved. Rather than bringing quick and easy solutions to this puzzle, China's ongoing economic miracle is forcing Latin America to have an open-minded regional debate on the possibilities for development in a context of globalization and liberalized markets. Central issues are national economic policies, regional integration, and the international rules for the global economic system. The apparent paradox of China is that economic liberalization has been as central to its miraculous growth as the strong state. China's rise shows developing countries that there is a viable alternative to free markets policies. Interestingly, this comes at a time of economic and political circumstances that have rendered Latin America open to discussing its development model and integration in the global economy. For two decades since the 1980s, the mixture of debt crisis, low growth, technocratic dominance, and Washington Consensus meant almost an end to Latin America's development debate, but recently the weak economic and negative social results of this period have contributed to a surprising political shift in Latin America while the extension of South-South trade and cooperation offers possibilities for a new development agenda of the Global South.

The big challenge for Latin America is to achieve the high level of regional (economic and political) cooperation that will be necessary to initiate new development strategies and make them viable in a world of fierce global competition. Regional cooperation and integration are crucial if Latin America wants to survive the Chinese competition in manufacturing and make sure that the short-term returns of the commodity boom are invested in economic modernization for the long term. For reaching this level of regional cooperation and integration several high hurdles need to be overcome, requiring considerable political willingness and governmental efforts of all countries.

A first hurdle is recognizing that profound regional cooperation is possible and indispensable. For this it is important to counter the tendency of an increasing economic and (geo)political North-South division within the region between Mexico and Central America that have become part of the North American free trade area, and the rest of Latin America. A second hurdle is recognizing that Latin America's integration has to move quickly beyond current initiatives for regional infrastructure (e.g., IIRSA, Plan Puebla-Panama, and PetroAmérica), and has to equally invest substantial time and money in political, institutional, and social integration. By doing so the construction of roads, canals, pipelines, and so on can become part of a regional program for sustainable and propoor development. A third hurdle is recognizing the need for a minimal regional consensus on a new development model, in particular with respect to the roles of the state and the private sector (MNCs as well as local companies). Assessing and discussing Latin America's historical development phases and experiences of China and other parts of the Global South may contribute to the development of a genuine "Latin America Consensus".

Notes

This chapter is part of a research project of the author with Alex E. Fernández Jilberto; they are the editors of *Latin America Facing China: South-South Relations beyond the Washington Consensus* (Leiden: Brill 2009).

1. For some Central American countries and Paraguay their diplomatic relations with the Taiwan issue stand in the way of good relations with Beijing. In 1990, Nicaragua ended its diplomatic relations with China and, in 2006, it signed a free trade agreement with Taiwan. Costa Rica, however, decided in 2007 to recognize China, and ended its relations with Taiwan.

2. The status of Market Economy allows China to use the Chinese domestic price of the product as the fair measure of the price of the exported good. Countries that do not grant China the Market Economy Status are entitled by the WTO to use the Non-Market Economy (NME) methodology toward Chinese products until 2016. When a country accuses China of dumping a product on its market, this methodology allows the country to calculate the real price of the product (by referring to an analogue market, for instance, Brazil or the United States).

References

CEPAL (Economic Commission for Latin America and Caribbean). 2004. *Panorama de la Inserción Internacional de América Latina y el Caribe 2002–2003*. Santiago: Naciones Unidas.

———. 2005a. *La Inversión Extranjera Directa en América Latina y el Caribe 2004*. Santiago: Naciones Unidas.

———. 2005b. *Latin America and the Caribbean in the World Economy, 2005 Trends*. Santiago: United Nations.

———. 2006a. *Foreign Investment in Latin America and the Caribbean, 2005*. Santiago: United Nations.

CEPAL (Economic Commission for Latin America and Caribbean). 2006b. *Panorama de la Inserción Internacional de América Latina y el Caribe 2005–2006*. Santiago: Naciones Unidas.

———. 2007. *Latin America and the Caribbean in the World Economy, 2007* Trends Santiago: United Nations.

Cornejo, Romer. 2005. América Latina en la perspectiva de China. In *Política exterior de China. La diplomacia de una potencia emergente*, ed. Xulio Rios. Barcelona: Ediciones Bellaterra.

Dussel Peters, Enrique. 2005. Economic Opportunities and Challenges Posed by China for Mexico and Central America. DIE Studies 8. Deutsches Institut für Entwicklungspolitik.

The Economist. 2005. The Myth of China Inc. September 3, pp. 53–54.

Fazio, Hugo. 1999. *El "Tigre" Chileno y la Crisis de los "Dragones Asiáticos."* Santiago: Editorial LOM.

Fernández Jilberto, E. Alex, and Barbara Hogenboom. 2007. Latin American Conglomerates in the Neoliberal Era: The Politics of Economic Concentration in Chile and Mexico. In *Big Business and Economic Development: Conglomerates and Economic Groups in Developing Countries and Transition Economies under Globalisation*, ed. Alex E. Fernández Jilberto and Barbara Hogenboom. London and New York: Routledge.

Ffrench-Davis, Ricardo y Barbara Stallings. 2001. *Reformas, Crecimiento y Políticas sociales en Chile desde 1973*. Santiago: CEPAL/Lom.

Gutiérrez, Hernán. 2003. *Oportunidades y desafíos de los vínculos económicos de China y América Latina el Caribe* . Serie Comercio Internacional 42, Santiago: CEPAL.

IMF (International Monetary Fund). 2006. *World Economic Outlook: Globalization and Inflation*. Washington, DC: International Monetary Fund.

Jiang, Wei. 2007. Outward FDI Hits $21.16b for 2006. *China Daily* September 15. http://www.chinadaily.com.cn/china/2007-09/15/content_6109739.htm (accessed August 25, 2008).

Lall, Sanjaya and John Weiss. 2004. People's Republic of China's Competitive Threat to Latin America: An Analysis for 1990–2002. ADB Institute Discussion Paper No. 14, Tokyo: Asian Development Bank Institute.

León, José Luis. 2005. La Relación Económica China-América Latina. Expresiones y Causas de dos Trayectorias Distintas. VI Reunión de la Red de Estudios de América Latina y el Caribe sobre Asia-Pacífico, Buenos Aires: Redealap/Banco Interamericano de Desarrollo.

Lora, Eduardo. 2005. Debe América Latina Temerle a La China? Departamento de Investigación, Documento de Trabajo 536, Banco Interamericano de Desarrollo, Washington, DC.

Mesquita Machado, João Bosco, and Galeano Tinoco Ferraz. 2005. *Comércio Externo da China e Efeitos sobre as Exportações Brasileiras*. Brazil: CEPAL/IPEA.

Shafaeddin, S.M. 2002. The Impact of China's Accession to WTO on the Exports of Developing Countries. New York and Geneva: United Nations Conference on Trade and Development, UNCTAD Discussion Papers. No. 160.

UN Comtrade. 2008. http://comtrade.un.org (accessed 25 August, 2008).

UNCTAD (United Nations Conference on Trade and Development). 2003. *Trade and Development Report 2003*. New York and Geneva: United Nations.

———. 2004. *Trade and Development Report 2004*. New York and Geneva: United Nations.

———. 2005. *Trade and Development Report 2005*. New York and Geneva: United Nations.

———. 2006. *World Investment Report 2006*. New York and Geneva: United Nations.

———. 2007. *World Investment Report 2007*. New York and Geneva: United Nations.

Weisbrot, Mark. 2006. Latin America: The End of an Era. *International Journal of Health Services* 36(4): 477–500.

World Bank. 2007. *World Development Report 2007*. Washington, DC: World Bank.

Chapter 8

How China Is Reshaping
the Industrial Geography of
Southeast Asia

Shahid Yusuf

Competition and Coexistence

The variety of channels through which China's growing economic and political weight has begun impinging upon other countries has aroused intense interest and not a little concern. Nowhere is this interest—and concern—stronger than in China's Southeast Asian neighborhood. The economies in this region are feeling the sharp edge of competition from Chinese products in their shared export markets. They also are benefiting from China's swelling appetite for imports fueled by growth of Gross Domestic Product (GDP) averaging close to 10 percent per annum between 2001 and 2007. Southeast Asian countries can see the positive and negative sides of the trade ledger, and they are reassured that in the medium term, China's rapid development is likely to be a plus. It has provided new and fast growing markets for their exports and opportunities for investment by Southeast Asian firms. Although a substantial volume of foreign capital is now heading toward China, enough is still flowing into Southeast Asia, which soothes nerves. Moreover, governments in Southeast Asian countries believe that their business environment, manufacturing capabilities, and the skills of their workforce provide them with a competitive edge. They also derive some comfort from the rising wages in China's coastal cities that they hope will contain a widening of the cost advantage in China's favor.[1] Even if China squeezes Southeast Asian producers out of the markets for low tech, labor intensive, "commodified" manufactures, countries such as Malaysia and Thailand see opportunities in moving up the value chain and of diversifying into profitable niches via technological upgrading and innovation. Policymakers throughout the region and around the Pacific Rim console themselves that the laws of trade theory are firmly on their side. In a globalizing and growing world economy, a country, even a very large one, cannot have an absolute advantage in all products and services (Yusuf, Nabeshima, and Perkins 2007).

This is where matters rest. Across Southeast Asia there is wariness over China's economic muscle and export competitiveness but no sense of panic. However, there is also a realization that market conditions have changed irrevocably; competition is much fiercer and survival will depend on more determined efforts to increase efficiency, to move up the technology ladder, to innovate and to diversify into products and services that promise to generate higher profits. Against this backdrop, the chapter addresses three questions: Do recent trends in trade and Foreign Direct Investment (FDI) point to the emergence of a symbiotic relationship between China and the economies of Southeast Asia, with a mutually advantageous division of labor whereby China assembles and exports mainly final products and buys many of the components and other imports from its Asian neighbors? If, in fact, there is the likelihood of much greater competition in existing product categories, what are the options for Southeast Asia? Are economies such as Malaysia and Thailand developing the capabilities that will enable them to thrive and grow in an international market environment within which China and later India are two of the most dynamic players?

The chapter focuses on Malaysia and Thailand because these two countries are charter members of the club of fast growing East Asian tiger economies. They are two, representative, mid-sized, middle income, industrializing countries that rely substantially on exports for their economic performance and are increasingly subject to pressures from Chinese producers and to the pull of the Chinese market. The findings in this chapter indicate that although interregional trade with China is on the rise, ongoing backward integration into component manufacturing could reduce China's import of components from Southeast Asia. Malaysia and Thailand are not making sufficient progress in diversifying and in moving up the product value chain even though they continue to attract a large volume of FDI. This may have to do with the limited technological spillovers and linkages from MNC operations. More likely, it is the result of weaknesses in the innovation systems in these countries. To sustain growth, Southeast Asia's leading economies will need to invest more in innovation capability with an emphasis on the quality of science and engineering education, basic research in universities, R&D by firms, and in the hard infrastructure of labs and ICT to support a move upstream into new products and services.

The balance of the chapter is divided as follows: I describe and assess the challenges posed by China for Southeast Asia in the next section. The succeeding sections discuss how Malaysia and Thailand are affected by the "China factor." In the final section, *Two Scenarios for South East Asia*, I sum up the findings and present two scenarios on future outcomes and examine their implications.

How China's Development Affects Southeast Asia

From the perspective of growth and industrial change in Southeast Asia, four aspects of China's development are of most relevance. First is China's extraordinarily high growth rate that has averaged close to 10 percent per annum between 1994 and 2007. Although a weakening of the U.S. economy in 2008–2009 and China's own efforts at dampening domestic demand so as to ease inflationary pressures could lead to a temporary slowdown, the likely persistence of the current levels of investment, expansion of the urban workforce, and increase in total factor productivity (TFP),[2] should enable GDP to continue growing at between 8 and 9 percent per annum for the next decade or more.[3] Such economic performance will generate strong demand for imports that would favor China's trading partners in Asia.

A second aspect is the growth of China's exports, the composition of these exports, and their competitiveness. For China's Southeast Asian competitors, what matters is the overlap between their exports and those of China; the relative price competitiveness that affects export shares for individual products; the quality of specific exports that determines the prices these products command and the profits accruing to sellers; and movements up the value chain in existing product categories as well as diversification into new product categories higher on the technological scale and that embody greater domestic added value. When China's exports overlap substantially with those of one of its competitors, when Chinese firms can quote lower prices and equivalent or better delivery schedules, and when they can ramp up production faster to meet demand, and when Chinese firms are able to meet the component needs of MNCs worldwide, the advantage resides with China. If China's revealed comparative advantage

(RCA)[4] increasingly is in higher value and technologically more sophisticated products, producers in Southeast Asia have a harder time entering these markets and if they do, they face more intense competition. Similarly, if Chinese firms are quicker at raising the quality of products, the unit values of their exports will rise along with the profits, which advantage these firms relative to their competitors. With China rapidly raising domestic R&D, absorbing technology from abroad, and making haste to build a productive national innovation system, Southeast Asian countries are on notice that unless they move quickly, their options for maintaining growth by diversifying into higher tech products could be constrained by China's capacity to not only dominate the low tech end of the product spectrum but also to acquire an innovation and competitive advantage in the more lucrative, technologically advanced products.

A third aspect of relevance is China's manufacturing capability, and how quickly the country is moving up the value chain. This has important implications for China's foreign suppliers. The current division of labor between China and countries in Southeast Asia is that Chinese firms mainly concentrate on the final assembly of consumer electronics products, autos, and various kinds of engineering products while importing many of the parts that go into these products from overseas. However, backward integration by Chinese manufacturers into components especially for products with long, nonmodular, and complex value chains such as autos and some kinds of electronics will eat into the demand for imports. This is a logical step for Chinese producers as their manufacturing capability strengthens, because designing and producing components is more profitable. Furthermore, in some industries closer proximity among suppliers and assemblers assists in product development, reduces transport and inventory costs, and speeds up delivery. A shift of component production to China, which is happening, does not mean that intra-industry trade cannot continue to thrive; however, its growth can be diminished and competition can become more severe.

A fourth and final aspect is FDI. China, Malaysia, and Thailand have all benefited from foreign investment that has channeled capital into strategic export subsectors, transferred manufacturing know-how, developed local skills, and hooked the producers in these countries to global value chains.[5] In all three countries, foreign invested enterprises account for a large share of the exports and the bulk of the exports of the leading electronics industry.[6] So long as China was a closed economy isolated from the international trading system and capital flows, most of the FDI in manufacturing industries went to Southeast Asian countries. Since the mid-1990s, this has changed and China is now the principal destination for FDI among the developing countries. To the degree that it may be diverting capital that would otherwise have gone to Southeast Asia, China is affecting the growth, trade, and technology acquisition prospects of countries such as Malaysia and Thailand. And to the extent that China is pulling in a bigger share of the FDI in technologically higher end activities and in R&D activities, Southeast Asian economies will have to work harder and rely more on their domestic resources to diversify their industrial base and upgrade their exports.

These four are not the only avenues through which China's emergence as an economic powerhouse affects the Southeast Asian region, but they are surely among the leading ones. Looking ahead, China's own FDI in Southeast Asia and elsewhere, spearheaded by Chinese MNCs, will add another factor. However, the scale, direction, and consequences of such flows are difficult to gauge at this juncture.

In order to arrive at a better understanding of how the aspects of China's development enumerated above rub against the economies of the Southeast Asian region, some numerical estimates and the findings of modeling exercises can be helpful. These are presented below.

Partners and Competitors

China is not only one of the world's fastest growing economies, it is also remarkably trade oriented for a country of its size. The smaller open economies are in the forefront led by Malaysia and Thailand, with a trade to GDP ratio of 211 and 142 percent, respectively. But among the larger countries, China's trade to GDP ratio is conspicuous and has risen to over 50 percent since 1995. By this measure, China is more than twice as open as the U.S. (28 percent) and Japan (32 percent). Openness has also been promoted by a drastic reduction in China's nominal tariffs that have fallen from 20 percent in 1995 to about 5 percent in 2005. Imports, which were US$151.9 billion in 1995, reached US$953.9 billion in 2007, averaging a growth rate of 17.4 percent. More importantly, the import elasticity of GDP, which was 1.65 in the first half of the 1990s, had climbed to 2.21 in 2001–2006. In other words, China's propensity to import is high and the recent trend has been upward. This has been advantageous for its trading partners in the East Asian region, all of which have seen their exports to China expand at a rapid clip. In 2006, China ranked as Malaysia's second largest trading partner and the third most significant partner for Thailand. Exports of resource based products, such as palm oil and plywood from Malaysia in 1995, have been overshadowed by electronics in 2000 and in 2005, a positive development, except that local value added in Malaysia of these exports is no more than 23 percent. Similarly, Thailand has graduated from exports of agricultural commodities such as rice, cane sugar, and rubber sheets, to electronic products, auto parts, and metallic products. More striking than the change in composition of Southeast Asian exports to China is the transformation of China's exports to Malaysia, Indonesia, and Thailand. As a share of China's total exports, these rose from 0.9 percent in 1995 to about 1.4 percent in 2006 though in value terms they are expanding at between 20 and 40 percent. In the mid-1990s, China's exports to Southeast Asia were comprised mainly of processed light manufactures—metal products, silk, oil, and fabric. These have been displaced by electronics, machinery, transport equipment, and iron and steel products reflecting both greater diversity and on average, higher domestic added value.

By maintaining a high rate of GDP growth and an open trade regime, which has been cemented by a recent free trade agreement with ASEAN (Association of Southeast Asian Nations), China has thus, on balance, exerted a positive influence on the performance of the exporting industries in Southeast Asian countries.

Export Overlap

The overlap between China's exports and those of Southeast Asian economies during 1995–2005 is an indicator of the pressure China is exerting on other trading nations in third country markets. As China's manufacturing industry has modernized and expanded into the electronics, ICT and electrical engineering subsectors,[7] the overlap in terms of commodities has increased and is over 98 percent with both Malaysia and Thailand. In terms of trade values it rose sharply after 1995 for Malaysia and has since stabilized at 61 percent, whereas for Thailand it is still climbing beyond 71 percent. This raises the further question as to whether the Southeast Asian countries are responding by acquiring a comparative advantage in new export products and pushing up the unit value of their exports through improvements in quality.

Trade statistics show that China has enlarged the share of electronic and electrical products between 1995 and 2005, from about 10 percent of exports to nearly 30 percent, and that the country is now contesting the exports from Southeast Asia. The leading exports from China, Malaysia, and Thailand are in the electronics and engineering category. However, China is forging ahead much faster than the others. In response, Malaysia may have to rely more on primary products (e.g., palm oil and by-products) and Thailand more on engineering products. Undoubtedly, China has reduced the scope for further enlarging the shares of electronics in the exports of both Southeast Asian countries.

By estimating unit values for similar electronic components exported by China, Malaysia, and Thailand we can get a sense as to what is happening to the quality of the products. These estimates show that the movements in unit values for representative kinds of integrated circuits are unchanged or falling for Malaysia and Thailand but are slowly rising in China's case, pointing to greater success in upgrading the industrial product mix.[8] This is encouraging for China, but it is an unsettling development for Thailand and Malaysia that have been in the business of producing electronic components for much longer (Yusuf 2008).

Export Specialization and Diversification

Additional insight into the evolving relative competitiveness of the three countries can be gauged from a technique devised by Hausmann and Klinger (2006) to assess the degree of export specialization (i.e., a crude indicator of competitiveness) in specific product categories and show how readily a country can diversify into other products categories so as to deflect export competition.[9] An analysis of the data indicates that China is becoming more specialized in relatively high tech electronics and electrical engineering products and better placed to move upscale because "opportunities for diversification" are "closer" to what China currently produces. In contrast, both Malaysia and Thailand are lower on the scale of specialization, the former less so than the latter (Yusuf and Nabeshima 2008). On balance, they have more resources in mid- and low tech industries and their options for industrial diversification are more diffuse. The 10 estimates of revealed comparative advantage (RCA), in tables 8.1 and 8.2 provide additional evidence on this score. They show that China is moving more rapidly to stake out a comparative advantage in medium and high tech manufacturers.[10] In contrast, both Malaysia and Thailand have yet to graduate out of a comparative advantage in primary products and processed agricultural commodities.[11] These estimates of the RCA belie the countries' principal exports, which are electronics and petroleum products in the case of Malaysia and electronics, petroleum products, and automotive equipments in the case of Thailand.

Taken together these findings indicate that China's exports are growing faster than its competitors—from a large base—and that there is accumulating evidence of China specializing in higher tech products, and

Table 8.1 Top 10 commodities with highest RCA in Malaysia (p.c. GDP of US$4,360), 2005

Product	Product Name	RCA	PRODY	Technology Class
440331	Logs, Meranti red	63.5	2,287	RB1
851931	Turntables with record changing	55.9	15,997	MT3
440721	Specified tropical woods	52.5	3,667	RB1
900620	Cameras used for recording	51.6	4,723	HT2
851991	Sound reproducing apparatus	41.6	15,330	MT3
151329	Palm kernel or babassu oil	40.9	4,661	RB1
261220	Thorium ores and concentrates	40.7	13,865	RB2
151190	Palm oil or fractions simply refined	36.5	4,635	RB1
240290	Cigars, cigarillos, cigarettes	33.5	12,204	RB1
401519	Gloves of vulcanized rubber	32.1	8,173	LT1

Note: PP: Primary Products, RB1: Agro-Based, RB2: Other Resource-Based, LT1: Textile, garment & footwear, LT2: Other, Low-Technology, MT1: Automotive, MT2: Process, MT3: Engineering, HT1: Electronic & Electrical, and HT2: Other, High-Technology. Based on classification adopted in Lall (2000).
Source: UN Comtrade.

Table 8.2 Top 10 commodities with highest RCA in Thailand (p.c. GDP of US$2,494), 2005

Product	Product Name	RCA	PRODY	Technology Class
400129	Natural rubber in other forms	74.90	1,169	PP
110814	Manioc starch	70.10	8,693	RB2
400110	Natural rubber latex	64.75	1,169	PP
520615	Uncombed single cotton yarn	64.33	4,262	LT1
400121	Smoked sheets of natural rubber	59.31	1,169	PP
110230	Rice flour	52.26	4,753	RB1
845012	Washing machines of a dry linen cap	50.45	18,070	MT3
100640	Broken rice	44.91	4,455	PP
200820	Pineapples, prepared or preserved	40.49	9,337	RB1
160414	Prepared or preserved tuna	36.54	10,775	RB1

Source: UN Comtrade.

upgrading. Moreover, China's revealed comparative advantage has shifted toward medium and high tech products whereas that of Thailand and Malaysia remains more in resource based and processed commodities. Hence China's prospects of moving into new and higher value products are better than those of Malaysia and Thailand. In conjunction with the pressures arising from export overlap, and the changing composition of

China's exports, there is reason to believe that relative to China the com-petitive position of the Southeast Asian countries in the trade arena could be weakening, currently and prospectively.

Intercountry Trade in Electronics

The apparent strengthening of China's manufacturing capabilities but-tressed by continuing heavy investment that speeds up embodied tech-nological change and "learning" will enhance the competitiveness of China's current exports by raising productivity. It will also make it easier for Chinese firms to integrate backward and challenge the exports of elec-tronic components and auto parts from Southeast Asian economies.[12] This could upset the existing symbiosis and barring an upsurge of intra-industry trade, producers in Malaysia and Thailand would be faced with increasing hardship. Although the volume of exports to China has grown robustly, from the perspective of Southeast Asian countries, the trend in shares paints a bleaker picture. The share of China's electronics imports sourced from Malaysia rose between 1995 and 2000 but has declined since 2000. Thailand's share also increased after 1995 but stabilized after 2000. From 2000 onward, China has increased its imports from Korea and Japan, mainly of higher valued and sophisticated components and equipment.[13]

Meanwhile, the share of China's electronic exports to Malaysia has expanded steadily suggesting that MNCs assembling products in Penang, Kuala Lumpur, and Johor are relying more on parts from China, rather than sourcing them domestically. Exports to Thailand as a percentage of China's total rose between 1995 and 2000 and then shrank between 2000 and 2005. These developments underscore the point made earlier about the comparative advantages of the two Southeast Asian economies. Each has specialized to a lesser degree in electronics and, as a consequence, it is harder for them to diversify and upgrade their product lines and match the offerings of Korean and Japanese exporters to Chinese firms. Moreover, neither is integrating backward and Malaysia is becoming more dependent on China.

There is little evidence that MNCs and Southeast Asian firms are shutting down their component manufacturing plants in Thailand and Malaysia and moving production to China.[14] However, MNCs and con-tract manufacturers are unlikely to expand their "high volume, low mix" operations in these countries. Automotive companies are gravitating toward China because the market prospects there completely overshadow those in some of the Southeast Asian countries that are both smaller and in the case of Malaysia, close to saturation. According to some estimates, China's auto market could surpass that of the United States by 2015. In 2007, production of autos in China rose over 20 percent to reach 8.9 million and is likely to exceed 10 million in 2008 (UMTRI 2005).[15] Firms are not producing more high value items for export to China. Casual empiricism suggests that the big increase in capacity fueled by Chinese and MNC investment is in Mainland China. If so, some kinds of assembly, testing, and manufacturing activities in Southeast Asia are entering their twilight years and could migrate just as they did from Taiwan (China), Singapore, and earlier from Japan.

Innovating to Survive or to Grow

Sensing that the winds of trade are shifting and that competition from China calls for a fresh response, Southeast Asian countries are beginning to emphasize R&D and a development process that is knowledge based (World Bank 2008). Policymakers in both Malaysia and Thailand are realizing that sustaining growth momentum will depend upon innovation and productivity gains in their existing crop of industries and in acquiring the technological capability to diversify into other products and services. China is also committed to a similar strategy and is moving faster to create an effective national innovation system (Yusuf and Nabeshima 2008). Past experience suggests that the knowledge economy can expand to accommodate all comers by creating the demand for new products. If they can become successful product innovators, Malaysian firms could carve out markets alongside niches created by successful Chinese firms. Likewise, Thai or Chinese firms that succeed in introducing ingenious process innovations that raise productivity industry wide improve the industry's growth prospects overall. Innovation need not be a zero sum game. However, innovative firms can steal market share and even drive out others by becoming more competitive with respect to cost, quality, or design; or by developing variant products that eclipse rival products.

The race to become innovative is on and China is running harder than the Southeast Asian countries. There is no sure recipe to guide countries attempting to construct a productive national innovation system; however, all recipes include the following ingredients: (i) tax and other incentives to increase private expenditure on R&D, supplemented by direct public spending on upstream research; (ii) education policies to enhance the supply of tertiary level skills and their quality to meet the rising demand from the business sector; (iii) financial and institutional incentives so as to promote the entry of small firms in areas with better growth prospects; (iv) a more competitive market environment that induces larger firms to pursue innovation as a means of survival and to adopt an open innovation system (Liu and Lundin 2007). The size of a country helps but there are plenty of examples of innovative small countries that have succeeded through focused research effort, and an inspired combination of the other ingredients. Switzerland, Finland, Israel, the Netherlands, and Taiwan (China) come to mind.

By setting a crackling pace, China has raised the ante for countries in Southeast Asia that compete with China in electronics, auto parts, and biotechnology and engineering industries. Firms in most Southeast Asian countries have been notably laggard in using innovation as a means of deriving competition advantage. Their attitude has been passive and it is governments rather than firms that have begun to take the initiative (Williamson 2004, World Bank 2008). Singapore however, has responded to the pressure from China's exports by redoubling its efforts to diversify its comparative advantage through R&D, improving the education system to encourage creative thinking and entrepreneurship, and by enhancing further the attractiveness of the city state's business environment (Liu 2007). Between 1995 and 2006, China raised spending on R&D from 0.6 percent of GDP to 1.43 percent. In absolute terms this was a huge increase because GDP more than doubled during this interval. Measured with reference to purchasing power, China's research expenditure is second only to that of the United States. By comparison, R&D spending in Malaysia is less than 1 percent and in Thailand it is closer to 0.25 percent (see table 8.3). The correlation between R&D outlay and innovation, as proxied by patenting, suggests that this is likely to increase the production of ideas. With the right incentives, these ideas can stimulate commercial innovation. The speed at which patenting is on the rise in China suggests that the investment in research is beginning to pay off. Rates of patenting in Malaysia and Thailand are far lower and most of the patenting is by the MNCs (table 8.4). China has also moved with great speed to raise the output of graduates in science and engineering and laid the groundwork for world class universities so as to improve the quality of skills. Between 1995 and 2004, the number of S&E graduates increased from 396,405 to 1,019,638. The vast gulf that separates China from some of the Southeast Asian countries in this regard is apparent from table 8.4. To strengthen research skills and enhance the productivity of research, China has encouraged FDI in R&D centers and thus far, more than 300 foreign firms—many of which are among the most innovative in the world—have established research facilities in China. This will have spillover effects that will augment China's research capacity and encourage domestic firms to pursue innovation more aggressively. An open innovation system is being created through the efforts made to network with China's vast diaspora of knowledge workers overseas. It is encouraged also by the incentives for universities and research institutes to collaborate with business firms in conducting research and developing technologies with commercial potential. In a similar vein, state-owned enterprises as well as other firms are casting around widely for better technologies by setting up "sentinel" laboratories in the United States and Europe; through the acquisition of firms overseas; and through subcontracting arrangements that enable Chinese producers to improve their design capabilities and acquire the tacit knowledge that helps enhance and develop process technologies.

China's domestic market for most manufactures is highly competitive and barriers to imports have been steadily reduced. Such openness and competition from imports identifies profitable opportunities and induces local producers to acquire new technologies so as to achieve competitive parity.

Table 8.3 R&D spending as percent of GDP and total patents granted by USPTO, 1996–2006

Indicator	Year	China	Malaysia	Thailand
R&D Spending as % of GDP	1996	0.57	0.22	0.12
	2000	0.90	0.50	0.25
	2006	1.40	0.95	0.25*
Patents granted by USPTO	1996	62	7	8
	2000	119	42	15
	2006	661	113	31
	Total (1995–2006)	2699	556	230

Source: WDI; USPTO.

*Indicates data is for the year 2004.

Table 8.4 Science and engineering bachelor's degrees, by Malaysia, Thailand, and China, between 1990 and 2002

Country	1990	2002
Malaysia	3,400	4,800
Thailand	24,200	51,457*
China	268,400	533,600

*Denotes most recent data for Thailand is from 1998.

Source: National Science Foundation, Division of Science Resources Statistics (2007), and Office of the Permanent Secretary for University Affairs, Ministry of University Affairs, Thailand.

To facilitate the entry of firms in the more technologically dynamic areas, the government has increased the supply of venture capital from public providers and offered a range of incentives that have attracted private domestic and foreign venture capitalists. They draw encouragement from China's commitment to build world class research universities, and with the achievements to date of the leading tertiary level institutions not only in Beijing and Shanghai but also in places such as Chengdu, Xian, and Wuhan. Efforts by governments in Malaysia and Thailand, mainly spearheaded by publicly funded providers of venture capital, have yet to induce a significant deal flow or to stimulate interest in high tech activities by local entrepreneurs. Moreover, the leading public universities in Malaysia and Thailand have struggled unsuccessfully to raise the quality of S&E graduates and have been unable to build up substantial graduate programs in the sciences and to stimulate basic research.

The risk for the Southeast Asian countries is that China will pull ahead in the technological race and make it harder to find new technological niches further along the value chain. In failing to raise the caliber of their major universities, the Southeast Asian countries have weakened their capacity to engage in the technological arms race and to graduate out of the increasingly vulnerable low cost model of development into a knowledge-intensive one with better prospects.

Foreign Investment

Export-oriented manufacturing industries in Southeast Asia have relied heavily on FDI and the issue countries such as Malaysia and Thailand face is whether FDI will assist them in transitioning to a higher industrial plane. For these countries, two questions loom large. First, what is the likely scale of future FDI. There is a worry that the attraction of China's market and supply of skills will lure away some of the FDI that would come to Southeast Asia. Such diversion of flows has not been confirmed by research. In fact, China is pulling in FDI commensurate with its GDP and well below its neighbors to the south in per capita terms. Nonetheless, the perception lingers and Southeast Asian countries are anticipating a slower increase, if any.

A second question pertains to the distribution of FDI and to what degree FDI will assist Southeast Asian countries move up the innovation value chain. Undoubtedly, FDI has created manufacturing capacity in key industries and built manufacturing skills. However, technological spillovers and backward integration into higher value components are less apparent in Thailand and Malaysia although there is collaborating evidence from China. Foreign firms have viewed their operations in Southeast Asia mainly as production platforms and have not been active in encouraging innovation even of the incremental sort. Beyond local customization, they have done little to build design and applied research skills or to support the creation of local production capacity for increasingly sophisticated parts and components.

China appears to be a different story and not because the MNCs have been more proactive. In China's case technology transfer and industrial deepening through backward integration has been promoted in large part by incentives to and pressure upon MNCs to add value locally and transfer intangible technology capital while luring them with the potential of a large market. Enforcement of local sourcing rules by the Chinese government (unlike the case in Southeast Asia), strongly reaffirmed by the efforts of Chinese companies to internalize new technology, has been buttressed by MNCs' own sense of longer term opportunities in China with respect to markets for their products and the supply of skills for production and R&D (Sigurdson 2005).[16]

The activities of MNCs in China have induced local firms to compete by stepping up their own efforts at absorbing technology and by innovating, which explains the "great wall of patents" described by Hu and Jefferson (2006). Malaysian and Thai firms have demonstrated less initiative, and the virtual absence of domestic ODMs (own design manufacturers) and major contract manufacturers in the electronics sector suggests that entrepreneurship and innovativeness may be a factor, particularly in the 1990s when entry barriers were lower than they are now. China's attempts at catching up in the technological sense and to compete on the basis of innovation is aided by the maturing of state-owned enterprises into world class players such as CIMC, Lenovo, Shanghai Zhenhua Port Machinery (SZPM), Haier, SAIC, and TCL and the appearance of new firms such as Wanxiang, ZTE, and Huawei that have burst on the world stage and are investing heavily in research.[17]

In other words, FDI is contributing directly to technology transfer and industrial deepening in China. It is also contributing indirectly by stimulating a competitive response from local firms that are strategically disposed to harness innovation. This has significant longer term implications because it means that Chinese firms, aside from enjoying the advantages of low labor costs, could gain an additional edge over competitors elsewhere in the East Asian region via process innovation. Such innovation could help raise productivity and, combined with design or product innovation, would enable them to advantageously differentiate their products from those of their competitors. There are several large multinational Malaysian and Thai firms; however, none of these has responded to FDI by increasing R&D and adopting a focused competitive strategy that is based on innovation and the systematic upgrading of products. Firms like CP in Thailand have a large stake in food processing but are not attempting to compete with the Nestle's and Proctor and Gamble's of the world on the basis of innovation. Nor are firms such as Sime Darby in Malaysia moving into more technology-intensive activities.

There is another side to FDI that promises to gain in importance. This is FDI by Chinese companies in Southeast Asia and FDI by firms in Malaysia and Thailand.[18] In East Asia, such intraregional FDI among the industrializing economies has been ongoing for some time; but until the 1990s, it mainly took the form of first Japanese, then Korean, and later Taiwanese FDI.[19] Thailand, Malaysia, and China did not enter the fray until the mid-1990s, and then only on a small scale, although CP was already a major investor in China toward the end of the 1990s.

China now and in the future is likely to have an abundance of resources to invest overseas. To a lesser degree, so also will Malaysia and Thailand. The vehicles for this investment are companies and sovereign wealth funds. Chinese firms have begun investing in resource based activities in Southeast Asia, albeit on a small scale. They have also shifted some of their textile and light manufacturing operations to Vietnam. Likewise, firms from Southeast Asia have made small investments in China.

Is China likely to raise FDI in Southeast Asia? This looks unlikely in the medium term because opportunities for acquisitions are fairly sparse and there may be resistance to the takeover of larger firms. Assets in the United States and Europe, and resource development in Africa and in Latin America, appear more promising. Even if Chinese firms invest in Southeast Asia or vice versa, the technological spillovers are unlikely to be significant. Domestic effort will be critical to building innovation capability.

Two Scenarios for Southeast Asia

China's interaction with Southeast Asian economies has been expanding thus far to the mutual advantage of both parties. Trade has increased, other exchanges have grown, China is not absorbing a disproportionate volume of FDI, and the inevitable frictions between a more confident and assertive China and its neighbors have been kept in check through collective self-restraint. Barring unforeseen developments, this positive sum status quo can continue for some years. Thailand, Malaysia, and other Southeast Asian economies could well sustain GDP growth rates of 5–6 percent per annum for the next five years, with China averaging a rate of between 8 and 9 percent.

However, such equilibrium might not persist beyond the medium run. Two possible scenarios come to mind. One assumes that the Southeast Asian economies are slow in mounting a response to the challenge posed by China. The other assumes that they enjoy a measure of success in pro-actively upgrading and diversifying their industrial activities. In either scenario, the industrial geography of Southeast Asia will change. But in the second scenario the change will be far more benign and could become the basis for a new equipoise that could endure for decades into the future.

As noted above, Southeast Asian countries such as Malaysia and Thailand are increasingly reliant on the exports of a fairly narrow range of "commodified" manufacturers. In the case of Thailand, electronics, autos and auto parts, and food products account for 55 percent of total exports. Malaysia's exports of electronics and electrical engineering products and processed food products comprise 60 percent of the total. Both countries are now competing with China in some of these product categories. Continued backward integration in China in the electronics industry, which is in the cards, will intensify competition in standardized electronic components. China's lower wages[20] and strengthening manufacturing capabilities could begin to squeeze out exporters in Southeast Asia. China's auto components industry is maturing rapidly and is already a major exporter and at current rates of investment, its footprint in regional and international markets is sure to expand. Food processing is another industry where Chinese firms are aggressively expanding their overseas sales.[21] Although quality control issues remain, this is likely to become a hotly contested product category because it is large and lucrative and relatively immune to large business swings often seen in electronics and automotive products. Chinese producers of cut flowers are competing against those from Thailand.[22] In these three major product groups, China's advantage over Southeast Asian countries derives from the scale economies offered by the domestic market—whereas producers in Southeast Asia are more heavily dependent on exports—heavy investment in production capacity, intense efforts to upgrade technology, and the growing size and international reach of Chinese firms. In each of these sectors, profitability and even survival is dependent on a firm's ability to become a global supplier and to operate in multiple markets. Chinese firms clearly have global ambitions, are fast becoming multinationals and working hard to establish their brand names. Few firms in Southeast Asia have pursued such ambitions and the vast majority remains small.

Whereas in China local companies are expanding their presence in the electronic and automotive industries and dominate food processing, the electronics industry in both Thailand and Malaysia—not to mention the Philippines—is in the grip of foreign companies. The automotive sector in Thailand is centered on foreign assemblers and component manufacturers. Malaysia's auto industry is more homegrown, but inefficient and vulnerable to foreign competition. Although both countries have sizable food processing industries, most producers are small scale and the few large firms have yet to establish a regional brand reputation and become serious players in regional markets. Foreign firms have maintained production bases in Malaysia and Thailand in the interests of diversifying sources of supply and because a long history of production has generated local manufacturing capability, trust in the local labor force and suppliers, and familiarity with local conditions.

Increasing competition from Chinese firms could cause shrinkage of the electronics and automotive industries in Malaysia and Thailand. And as wage costs rise in Malaysia and Thailand, MNCs are likely to shift their labor-intensive assembly operations to China, Vietnam, and India, in particular. A gradual exodus of the low value added activities concentrated in Malaysia and Thailand may not be offset by expanding higher value and higher tech production because from the perspective of the MNCs, China and India are the preferred locations for technology development. China has the research and technical skills that the MNCs are seeking, Southeast Asia has been unable to accumulate these fast enough.

In this scenario, there is a risk that the industrial development of Malaysia and Thailand could stagnate and atrophy and growth eventually slow to a crawl. Unable to upgrade existing activities and to diversify, the Southeast Asian countries are undercut by lower cost producers in China and Vietnam. They have difficulty entering the markets for higher tech products because of insufficient human and R&D capital and also because firms in China and Korea are already entrenched. Southeast Asian economies that are forced into this situation would slide down the food chain, and have to compete in resource based low tech industries. A shrinkage and migration of the electronics and automotive industries in Southeast Asia would have profound consequences for the region. It would have knock-on effects that could constrain the development of ICT industries, software, metallurgy, biotechnology, and renewable energy, all of which share important boundaries with electronics and the automotive industries. Of course, the example of India shows that under special conditions, IT enabled services can flourish without electronics hardware production. But this is exceedingly rare. Moreover, there are now no examples of a biotech industry developing independently of a mature electronics/IT industry.

There is, in addition, a risk of Southeast Asia being reduced to a backwater not only because of the rise of China but more so because of a failure to complement manufacturing capability by climbing the innovation value chain, the latter being the ticket to industrial upgrading and diversification into new areas.

A second scenario projects a positive sum relationship between China and Southeast Asia and a comfortable coexistence a la Switzerland and Austria with Germany and France. This would require a deliberate effort at specialization and the cultivation of world class expertise in a few high value products and services by Malaysia and Thailand. These product categories may not be high tech items in the conventional meaning of the term; after all watches, chocolates, and cheeses are not in the same class as micro-processors, but it does not matter so long as they generate handsome profits (Porter 2008). If Thailand, for example, were to realize its ambition of becoming a "kitchen of the world" and a Thai firm were to become the world's leading producer of Asian foodstuffs with a strong focus on innovation, packaging, marketing, and multinational distribution, this would provide a building block for future prosperity.

Were Malaysia to emerge as a force in tree crops, cost-effective biofuels, and environmental technologies associated with intensive agriculture and tropical food products, these could very well become the cornerstone for its future development and the source of high value exports.

Observing Malaysia's and Thailand's struggle to try and deepen their electronics industries over 20 years makes one ask whether the industrial future for these countries might lie in their areas of traditional comparative advantage areas, which are not so intensely contested. Succeeding in these product categories will also require heavy expenditure on R&D in agricultural biotechnology, materials sciences, packaging, design, and other areas; however, both countries would be starting with a stronger hand and a clearer focus. Relative to China, neither Malaysia nor Thailand has much domestic innovation capability and worse their R&D is nonoptimally distributed among a variety of technological fields. Only a concerted effort on a narrower front has much chance of yielding commercial results within the decade's breathing space both countries have. If this strategy works and domestic firms are able to acquire a multinational presence, a downsizing of electronics, auto parts, and engineering industries would be offset by the expansion of agricultural, resource based and processing industries that rely on advanced research. In a warming and more populous world in which all natural resources may be under pressure, resource based products could enjoy stronger market demand and more favorable terms of trade.

In either scenario, there is high probability that countries with the per capita GDP of Malaysia or even Thailand will no longer remain competitive in assembly processing and testing activities associated with electronics, ICT, and the automotive sector where the value added is low. The competition from China, India, and other lower income countries will make it increasingly impracticable to sustain these industries. The shape of the industrial landscape to come in the next decade will depend upon the capacity of Southeast Asian countries to consolidate their core competitive advantage in resource based, processing industries and diversify along the innovation value chain. China's industrialization is likely to continue deepening in the coastal areas and spreading selectively to cities in the interior and its industry will cast a long shadow over the rest of East Asia and not just this region alone.

The competition between China and Southeast Asian economies in the Asian region and in Western markets is perhaps the major focus of medium term interest. However, over the longer term, China's ability to develop and to penetrate markets in Africa, South Asia, the Middle East, and Latin America could solidify its competitive advantage. This penetration will be assisted by three factors: one is the activities of China's construction companies that are helping build transport infrastructure and are ambassadors for China's products and services. Second, the activities of these companies and the economic footholds they help to create will not only support the entry of Chinese FDI. Chinese service providers working in myriad projects across the world will contribute to the emergence of China's "soft power," and the form it takes and how it is buoyed by China's exports of fashions, cultural products, and name brands, which will inevitably follow.[23]

A third factor is the aid China has begun to provide some countries that opens up economic pathways linking China to the aid recipients. It is impossible to say at this stage how China's relationships might evolve. However, China's entry into the club of aid giving countries will have long-term ramifications.

Unlike China, Southeast Asian countries have a low economic profile outside the region and are doing little to raise it. Their efforts at penetrating new markets overseas are meager and this could have serious long-term consequences. The globe bestriding MNCs of the future are not being nurtured in Southeast Asia. The region is not seen as the factory of the world, the way China is. Southeast Asia is not conspicuous in assisting other countries even in a token manner, and currently, it has no soft power at all.

Notes

1. See (Banister 2005) on wage trends in the 1990s and into the early 2000s and (Inagaki 2006) on labor shortages in the coastal areas starting around 2002. Also see "How Rising Wages Are Changing the Game in China." 2006. *BusinessWeek*, March 27. http://www.businessweek.com/magazine/content/06_13/b3977049.htm. Alongside wages, productivity is also increasing that contains unit costs, and China's overall employment in manufacturing is not on the rise.

2. See Bosworth and Collins (2007) and Kuijs (2006) on estimates of China's TFP. These range from 3 percent to 4 percent for the period 1993–2005.

3. China's goal is to quadruple per capita GDP between 2000 and 2020, which assumes a growth rate of 8 percent per annum. Given the scope for intersectoral shifts in the workforce, for interindustrial distribution of resources, technological upgrading, gains in allocation and organizational efficiencies and increase in human capital, such a goal would seem to be within reach (see Fogel 2006).

4. Revealed comparative advantage (RCA) is a measure of the export competitiveness of a country, in a particular commodity. It is calculated as the ratio of a country's market share in a specific commodity in the world export market, to the country's share of exports in overall world exports.

5. See http://www.globalvaluechains.org/concepts.html.

6. Nearly 58 percent of China's total exports and a higher percentage of electronic exports are by foreign invested companies. In the cases of Malaysia and Thailand, foreign companies are responsible for close to 90 percent of electronics exports.

7. The Chinese government identified electronics as a "pillar" industry in 1994 and thereafter, provided it with a variety of financial and other incentives, including encouragement to promote technological transfer. The result has been a rate of growth that is little short of explosive. The share of electronics in GDP and in manufacturing rose from 1 percent and 5 percent respectively in 1995 to 3.2 percent and 10.2 percent respectively in 2005 (Zhao and others 2007).

8. This is supported by observers of the industrial scene, who note the success of companies such as Huawei that produces mid-range routers and Mindray Medical that manufactures ultrasound imaging equipment and equipment for blood testing. See "China Rushes Upmarket." 2007. *BusinessWeek*, September 6. http://www.businessweek.com/magazine/content/07_38/b4050055.htm."

9. The idea behind this approach is that each commodity that a country produces creates different opportunities for future diversification (see Hausmann and Klinger 2006). That is, some products offer easier and multiple diversification paths to other related products while others do not. In general, primary and resource based products do not lead to many opportunities for diversification. By contrast, manufacturing goods such as electronics engage skills and assets that are similar to those required for the production of other manufacturing commodities, and hence are classified as high value products.

10. The measure used to assess if a country is exploiting its productive potential by focusing its efforts on high value goods is that of the potential diversification opportunities arising from each one of its exports. In particular, the density of each commodity gives the probability that a country will export a pair of goods conditional on it already exporting at least one of the goods. The more a country specializes in high value goods (in terms of highest densities), the greater is its potential for diversification into other high value products. For each product, a weighted average of the GDP per capita of countries exporting that product is calculated to assign a PRODY value, which is a proxy for the quality of a product. The weights denote the revealed comparative advantage of each country exporting the product. EXPY represents the level of sophistication of a country's overall export basket. It is calculated as the sum of the PRODY for each commodity in a country's export basket, weighted by its share. A positive value for (PRODY-EXPY) means "upgrading" in a sense of exporting more sophisticated commodities relative to the overall export basket.

11. In 1985, China's comparative advantage resided in primary products. This had been displaced by other products in 1992 (Hinloopen and Marrewijk 2004).

12. These are similar to the results arrived at by Haltmaier and others (2007).

13. Navarro (2007) finds that 19 percent of China's price advantage over its competitors derives from a networking effect arising from the clustering of assemblers and component suppliers—local and foreign. The importance of proximity could strongly promote backward integration. See "The China Price." 2004. *BusinessWeek*, December 6. http://www.businessweek.com/ magazine/content/04_49/b3911401.htm."

14. The increase in intra-industry trade between China on the one hand and Korea and Japan on the other has been analyzed by Kang and Lee (2007). They find that, although China relies on these two countries for higher level intermediate inputs and capital goods, the pattern is changing. In the case of Korea, China is importing fewer of the more highly valued intermediates and more of lower valued ones. Moreover, the unit values of China's own exports of intermediates to Japan and Korea is rising, which points to successful backward integration into higher value items.

15. Also see "China's Auto Production, Sales Hit Record High in 2007." 2008. *India eNews*, January 13. http://www.indiaenews.com/asia/20080113/91342. htm."

16. Also see "A Dragon in R&D," 2006. *BusinessWeek*, November 6. http://www. businessweek.com/magazine/content/06_45/b4008057.htm.

17. CIMC produces half of the world's shipping containers; and Shanghai Zhenhua has over half the world's market for port cranes.

18. Seventy percent of China's FDIs that amounted to US$40 billion in 2005 was in Asia (Fung, Liu, and Kao 2007, Morck, Yeung, and Zhao 2008, Wu 2005).

19. Taiwanese FDI has served to transplant first light industry and now medium and high tech industry to other Asian countries (see, for example, Thun 2001).

20. Navarro (2007) ascribes 39 percent of China's price competitiveness to lower wages.
21. See "China Deal Hurting Farm Sector." 2007. *Bangkok Post*, July 28. http://www.bilaterals.org/article.php3?id_article=9173.
22. See "Chinese Flower Power Hit Thai Growers." 2006. *Inter Press Service*, July 29. http://www.bilaterals.org/article.php3?id_article=5370.
23. China's soft power will depend upon the success of efforts to build upon the culture and linguistic affinities with countries in the Southeast Asian region, to encourage the more widespread use of the Chinese language, through appeals to Asian values and by increasing the enrollment of foreign students in Chinese universities. Their number had grown to 110,000 in 2004. Three-fourths of the students were from Asian countries (Saunders 2006).

References

Banister, Judith. 2005. Manufacturing Earnings and Compensation in China. *Monthly Labor Review* 128(8): 22–40.

Bosworth, Barry P. and Susan M. Collins. 2007. Accounting for Growth: Comparing China and India. NBER Working Paper 12943. Cambridge, MA: National Bureau of Economic Research.

Fogel, Robert W. 2006. Why China Is Likely to Achieve Its Growth Objectives. NBER Working Paper 12122. Cambridge, MA: National Bureau of Economic Research.

Fung, Hung-Gay, Qingfeng Wilson Liu, and Erin H.C. Kao. 2007. China's Outward Direct and Portfolio Investments. *China & World Economy* 15(6): 53–68.

Haltmaier, Jane T., Shaghil Ahmed, Brahima Coulibaly, Ross Knippenberg, Sylvain Leduc, Mario Marazzi, and Beth Anne Wilson. 2007. The Role of China in Asia: Engine, Conduit, or Steamroller? FRB International Finance Discussion Paper No. 904. Washington, DC: Board of Governors of the Federal Reserve System.

Hausmann, Ricardo and Bailey Klinger. 2006. Structural Transformation and Patterns of Comparative Advantage in the Product Space. CID Working Paper No. 128. Cambridge, MA: Harvard University.

Hinloopen, Jeroen and Charles van Marrewijk. 2004. Dynamics of Chinese Comparative Advantage. Tinbergen Institute Discussion Paper TI 2004-034/2. Amsterdam: University of Amsterdam.

Hu, Albert Guangzhou and Gary H. Jefferson. 2006. A Great Wall of Patents: What Is behind China's Recent Patent Explosion? Singapore and Waltham, MA: National University of Singapore and Brandeis University.

Inagaki, Hiroshi. 2006. South China's Labor Shortage—Will the Current Worker Shortage Escalate? Mizuho Research Paper 9.

Kang, Minsung and Jeong-Dong Lee. 2007. Evolutionary Characteristics of China's Intermediate Manufactures. *China & World Economy* 15(6): 1–21.

Kuijs, Louis. 2006. How Will China's Saving-Investment Balance Evolve? World Bank Policy Research Working Paper 3958. Washington, DC: World Bank.

Lall, Sanjaya. 2000. The Technological Structure and Performance of Developing Country Manufactured Exports, 1985–98. *Oxford Development Studies* 28(3): 337–369.

Liu, Xielin and Nannan Lundin. 2007. Toward a Market-Based Open Innovation System of China. Graduate University of Chinese Academy of Science, China; Research Institute of Industrial Economics, Sweden.

Liu, Yunhua. 2007. Facing the Challenge of Rising China: Singapore's Responses. *Journal of Policy Modeling* 29(3): 505–522.

Morck, Randall, Bernard Yeung, and Minyuan Zhao. 2008. Perspectives on China's Outward Foreign Direct Investment. *Journal of International Business Studies* 39(3): 337–350.

Navarro, Peter. 2007. Report of the China Price Project. Working Paper Merage School of Business, University of California-Irvine. http://works.bepress.com/peter_navarro/2.

Porter, Michael E. 2008. The Five Competitive Forces That Shape Strategy. *Harvard Business Review* 86(1): 78–93.

Saunders, Phillip C. 2006. China's Global Activism: Strategy, Drivers, and Tools. Institute for National Strategic Studies. Occasional Paper 4.

Sigurdson, Jon 2005. *Technological Superpower China*. Cheltenham, UK and Northampton, MA: Edward Elgar.

Thun, Eric. 2001. Growing Up and Moving Out: Globalization of "Traditional" Industries in Taiwan. MIT IPC Globalization Working Paper 00-004.

UMTRI (University of Michigan Transportation Research Institute). 2005. Picturing China's Automotive Future. *UMTRI Research Review* 36(4): 1–3.

Williamson, Peter J. 2004. *Winning in Asia: Strategies for Competing in the New Millennium*. Cambridge, MA: Harvard Business School Press.

World Bank. 2008. Towards a Knowledge Economy in Thailand. Bangkok: World Bank.

Wu, Friedrich. 2005. The Globalization of Corporate China. *NBR Analysis* 16(3), http://www.nbr.org/publications/analysis/pdf/vol16no3.pdf.

Yusuf, Shahid. 2008. *China and S.E. Asia: Economic Symbiosis and Competition. Processed*. Washington, DC: World Bank.

Yusuf, Shahid and Kaoru Nabeshima. 2008. Strengthening China's Technological Capability. In *Public Finance in China: Reform and Growth for a Harmonious Society*, ed. Jiwei Lou and Shuilin Wang. Washington, DC: World Bank.

Yusuf, Shahid, Kaoru Nabeshima, and Dwight H. Perkins. 2007. China and India Reshape Global Industrial Geography. In *Dancing with Giants: China, India, and the Global Economy*, ed. Alan L. Winters and Shahid Yusuf. Washington, DC: World Bank.

Zhao, Zhongxiu, Xiaoling Huang, Dongya Ye, and Paul Gentle. 2007. China's Industrial Policy in Relation to Electronics Manufacturing. *China & World Economy* 15(3): 33–51.

Part 4

The Rise of China: Geostrategic Implications

Chapter 9

Fueling the Dragon: China's Strategic Energy Dilemma

Michael T. Klare

As several of the chapters in this volume observe, China has enjoyed extraordinary economic growth over the past few decades and is expected to experience continuing high rates of growth for many years to come. According to the World Bank, China's Gross Domestic Product (GDP) grew by a factor of 10 between 1970 and 1990, reaching US$1.2 trillion at the end of that period; 5 years later, it had doubled again to US$2.3 trillion. Although most analysts believe that China will not be able to sustain double-digit rates of growth year after year in the future as it has in the past, it is still expected to outpace most other major economies. Indeed, a recent estimate by the U.S. Department of Energy places China's GDP in 2025 at US$7.1 trillion, putting it ahead of every other economy on the planet save that of the United States (DoE/EIA 2008:Table A4, p. 99).[1]

The rapid growth in China's economy is visible in all the ways that have captured international attention: the stunning expansion of Chinese cities (both horizontally and vertically); the nationwide expansion of infrastructure, encompassing roads, highways, bridges, railroads, subways, airports, stadiums, and so forth; and the massive acquisition of appliances and other consumer items by ordinary Chinese citizens. One way to appreciate this extraordinary boom is to gaze over central Shanghai, the country's great southern seaport and commercial hub, where some 4,000 new skyscrapers—almost double the number found in New York City—now occupy a crowded horizon. And the future promises more of the same: Another 1,000 skyscrapers, along with gargantuan apartment and shopping complexes, are slated to be built in Shanghai by 2010. Most of these buildings are cooled in summer by air-conditioning; and most house computers and other advanced electronic devices as well as a wide variety of modern appliances, all powered by a vast electrical grid. To transport Shanghai's estimated 13.5 million people to and from work, the city is constructing highways at a dizzying pace and adding new lines to its 310-mile subway system, already one of the world's largest (Barboza 2005).

Another image of the boom can be gleaned by visiting China's automobile showrooms, where newly affluent consumers are buying motor vehicles in unprecedented numbers. Until very recently, private automobiles were the exclusive prerogative of party functionaries and senior managers; now, ordinary middle-class citizens are lining up to buy cars of their own. "Our living standard has improved to the point where we think it's time to buy a nice car," said Sang Guodong, the owner of a small clothing factory, while examining new models in a Beijing dealership.[2] In 2005, customers like Mr. Sang purchased a record 5.9 million private vehicles, pushing China ahead of Germany and Japan to become the world's second largest automobile market after the United States. With China's average income (when measured in purchasing power parity) now exceeding US$6,000 per year—the level at which consumers in other developing countries have turned in their bicycles and scooters for private cars—hundreds of millions of Chinese citizens are poised to join the ranks of automobile owners. According to some projections, the number of automobiles clogging China's overtaxed highway system will increase tenfold over the next 25 years, to about 130 million vehicles; some forecasts put the number even higher.[3]

To accommodate all of these new private vehicles, China is building new highways at a frenetic pace. Under current plans, it is adding approximately 2,000 miles of expressway a year to an existing grid of about 20,000 miles—a project that will endow China with a superhighway network larger than the existing U.S. interstate highway system. Local governments in the major cities are also adding highways, tunnels, bridges, and new parking lots and garages for all those added cars, trucks, and vans. And, to transport all those Chinese who do not yet own private vehicles, China is constructing 3,500 miles of high-speed rail lines in the country while also refurbishing some 25,000 miles of its existing rail network (*The Economist* 2006:69, 2003:53–54, Khan 2003).

All of these objects—the skyscrapers, highways, subways, automobiles, and electrical appliances—have one thing in common: all rely on a vast hoard of raw materials for their construction, operation, and upkeep. Every large building requires tons of steel and concrete, along with plywood, glass, and copper (for electrical wiring); every highway line needs huge supplies of concrete and asphalt; every car needs steel, chromium, aluminum, and glass, plus oil for propulsion; every appliance needs a reliable flow of electricity. The vast expansion of China's infrastructure has been made possible, in other words, by a colossal increase in the production and procurement of basic commodities, especially iron ore, copper, aluminum, lead, tin, cement, timber, oil, coal, uranium, and natural gas. Without a steady and ever-growing supply of these materials, none of the impressive gains described above could have been achieved.

To fully appreciate the scope and magnitude of China's exploding resource use, it is helpful to examine some of the data on the consumption of particular materials. The production of raw steel in China, for example, rose from 66.1 million metric tons in 1990 to 220.1 million tons in 2002—an extraordinary increase not matched by any other country. At the start of this extraordinary surge in output, China trailed Japan, the United States, and the former Soviet Union in steel production; at the end, it towered over all the others. The same pattern is evident for copper and aluminum. In 1990, Chinese refineries produced 560,000 metric tons of copper; by 2003, they were supplying 1.8 million tons; over the same period, China's production of aluminum rose from 850,000 to 5.5 million metric tons.[4] (A metric ton is equal to 1000 kilograms or approximately 1.1 American ton.)

It is in the consumption of energy, however, that China's economic growth has had its greatest impact. As recently as 1990, China consumed a mere 27 quadrillion British thermal units (BTUs) of energy per year, representing but 7.8 percent of world energy usage (at a time when its citizenry constituted 22 percent of the world's population). Between 1990 and 2005, however, China's energy demand grew so rapidly that its net consumption reached 67.1 quadrillion BTUs at the end of this period, or nearly 14.5 percent of world energy use. The net increase in Chinese energy consumption over these 15 years, 40.1 quadrillion BTUs, was far greater than that posted by any other country.[5]

This spurt in China's energy usage required a corresponding increase in the consumption of all major sources of energy: coal, oil, natural gas, nuclear energy, and hydropower. According to the U.S. Department of Energy (DoE), China's consumption of coal rose by 131 percent between 1990 and 2005, from 20.3 quadrillion BTUs energy equivalent to 46.9 quadrillion; of oil, by 191 percent, from 2.3 million barrels per day to 6.7 million barrels; of natural gas, by 240 percent, from 0.5 trillion cubic feet to 1.7 trillion; of nuclear energy, from 0 to 50 billion kilowatt hours; and of hydropower (and other sources of renewable energy), by 208 percent, from 1.3 to 4.0 quadrillion BTUs.[6] These spurts in usage have naturally raised China's international profile in each of these commodities: with respect to coal, for example, China is by far the world's leading consumer; in 2003, it surpassed Japan to be the world's number two consumer of oil, exceeded only by the United States (IEA 2008b:243–421).

But it is China's *future* consumption of energy that will have the greatest significance for the international community. Between 2005 and 2030, China's net energy use is projected to increase by 131 percent, rising from 67.1 to 155.2 quadrillion BTUs—a far bigger gain than that expected for any other country. Over the course of this period, China's share of world energy usage will jump from 14.5 to 22.3 percent—three times what it was in 1990. Even more significant, China is expected to overtake the United States to be the world's leading consumer of energy (although U.S. citizens will continue to use more energy on a per capita basis than their Chinese counterparts).[7] As in previous decades, this will translate into a rise in the consumption of all primary fuels: an estimated 83 percent increase in coal consumption; a 134 percent increase in oil; a 277 percent increase in natural gas; and a 720 percent increase in nuclear power.[8] (See table 9.1.)

All of these energy surges will generate international issues and problems of one sort or another. China's projected increase in the use of coal, for example, will result in increased emissions of noxious pollutants and climate-altering "greenhouse gases" (GHGs), significantly affecting Beijing's ties with neighboring states like Japan and complicating efforts to establish a new regime for controlling the global buildup of GHGs (see Gallagher, this volume). The completion of the Three Gorges Dam, along

Table 9.1   Energy profile of China

Category	History		Projections	
	1990	2005	2020	2030
Primary energy consumption (quadrillion BTUs)	27.0	67.1	120.6	155.2
Oil consumption (mbd)	2.3	6.7	11.7	15.7
Oil Production (mbd)	2.8	3.7	4.0	4.1
Oil imports (mbd)	−0.5	3.0	7.7	11.6
Natural gas consumption (tcf)	0.5	1.7	5.0	6.4
Coal consumption (quad BTUs)	20.3	46.9	82.5	103.4
Nuclear energy consumption (billion kilowatt hours)	0	50	267	410
Hydrolectricity & other renewable energy (quadrillion BTUs)	1.3	4.0	5.5	8.1

Note: BTUs = British thermal units; mbd = million barrels per day; tcf = trillion cubic feet.
Source: U.S. Department of Energy, *International Energy Outlook 2008* (Washington, DC, 2008), 95, 100–104, 199.

with plans for additional dams on the Mekong and the construction of dams on the Nu (Salween) River, have raised questions among environmentalists about the safety of such massive barriers, the quality of downstream water flows, the relocation of affected populations, and the destruction of unique ecological habitats. Likewise, China's plans to increase its reliance on nuclear power raises questions about reactor safety, the storage of radioactive wastes, and the proliferation of fissile materials.

Reliance on Imported Energy

By far, however, the greatest international challenges are raised by China's growing consumption of oil and natural gas. Consider that coal, which provides about 70 percent of China's net energy, is largely obtained from domestic sources of supply. Hydroelectricity, which provides another 6 percent, is derived entirely from Chinese rivers. Nuclear power does require some imported uranium, but at this point provides only a very small percentage of China's net energy supply so is not yet a significant factor in its foreign policy. This leaves oil, which provides 20 percent of China's energy, and natural gas, which provides 3 percent now and is expected to rise much higher in the years ahead; neither can be satisfied with domestic supplies alone and so must be supplemented with substantial imports (BP 2008).[9] And because the rise in Chinese oil and gas consumption is coinciding with a slowdown in the growth of global supply, China's growing reliance on imports has become a matter of international concern.

Historically, Chinese officials have sought to rely as much as possible on domestic sources of energy (and other vital materials) to satisfy the nation's basic requirements. This outlook was adopted during the early years of Communist rule to immunize the country as much as possible from the effects of economic and trade sanctions—like those imposed by the United States on Cuba after the rise of Fidel Castro—and to minimize expenditure on imported commodities. This approach succeeded for a time, thanks to the presence of large domestic deposits of oil, coal, and other key minerals. But China's domestic supplies of oil, gas, and uranium are no longer sufficient to satisfy the country's swelling needs, and so ever-growing quantities of these materials will have to be imported.

China was once self-sufficient in petroleum: as recently as 1993, it produced and consumed approximately 3 million barrels per day. But Chinese oil output has increased only slightly—reaching 3.7 million barrels per day in 2007—while consumption has soared. As a result, the gap between production and consumption has grown larger every year, and the only way

Beijing has been able to fill that yawning gap has been through increased imports of foreign oil. In 2007, with China's total oil usage at 7.8 million barrels per day, imports had risen to 4.1 million barrels, or 52 percent of total consumption; by 2030, its import requirement is expected to reach 11.6 million barrels (out of total consumption of 15.7 million barrels), representing 74 percent of consumption.[10]

A similar picture prevails in the case of natural gas. In 2007, China produced all of the natural gas it consumed, about 2.4 trillion cubic feet. By 2030, however, China's principal domestic gas fields are expected to be in decline and so it will have to import a large share of its supplies, either by pipeline from Russia and Central Asia or in the form of liquefied natural gas (LNG) from Russia, Indonesia, Africa, and the Middle East.[11]

Obtaining all of this additional oil and natural gas will constitute one of the most formidable challenges facing the Chinese leadership in the years ahead. Without more energy—and lots of it—China will not be able to sustain the high rates of growth that it has achieved in the past. Every gain in factory output, ground and air transport, petrochemical production, and consumer lifestyle enhancement will entail the consumption of additional oil and gas. To put this in perspective, the additional 7.9 million barrels of oil per day that will be needed to reach China's projected daily consumption of 15.8 million barrels in 2030 is equivalent to the combined consumption in 2007 of Britain, France, Germany, and Italy. Securing these added millions of barrels per day—plus the additional trillions of cubic feet of gas—will prove a Herculean task that will make or break the Chinese economic miracle and play a decisive role in the global competition for access to vital energy resources.

China's Energy Policy

Theoretically, responsibility for decisions regarding the acquisition and utilization of raw materials in China rests with the management of individual firms and enterprises—not central planners in Beijing, as was the case during the Maoist era. Nevertheless, senior party and government officials continue to exercise considerable control over such endeavors. At the pinnacle of political and economic power in Beijing is the senior leadership of the Chinese Communist Party (CCP), concentrated in the Politburo and its executive arm, the Politburo Standing Committee. As general secretary of the CCP (since November 2002) and head of state (since March 2003), President Hu Jintao is the nation's paramount leader; day-to-day management of government ministries is overseen by Premier (Prime Minister)

Wen Jiabao, in office since March 2003. Considerable power is also wielded by Ma Kai, the chief minister of the National Development and Reform Commission (NDRC)—a sort of super-ministry for economic affairs. The management of energy-related affairs has been delegated to various bodies over the years; since 1993, however, ultimate control over energy matters has been exercised by the NDRC (DoE 2006:11–12).

It can be difficult for outsiders to monitor the activities of these various bodies, but the broad outlines of Chinese energy policy can be deduced from occasional policy statements and the actions of top officials. As noted, this policy places particular emphasis on the development of domestic sources of energy, especially coal and hydropower; but because these are plainly insufficient to meet the nation's ballooning requirements, the acquisition of imported oil, natural gas, and uranium has received special attention. This means, to begin with, obtaining *sufficient* quantities of imported energy to satisfy the country's needs. But obtaining sufficient volumes of supply is not the only objective of Chinese energy policy: the government also seeks to *diversify* the nation's foreign sources of energy, so as to minimize reliance on any individual source, and, to the degree possible, to acquire a degree of *control* over its foreign sources of energy, notably through the direct ownership of oil and gas reserves. To what extent these objectives are spelled out in formal government directives is not known, but it is clear that China has been proceeding along these lines since the late 1990s.[12]

The government's desire to diversify its foreign sources of energy is especially evident in the acquisition of petroleum supplies. As recently as 1996, China obtained over two-thirds of its imported petroleum from just three countries: Indonesia, Oman, and Yemen; at present, however, it obtains oil from a relatively large pool of producers, including Saudi Arabia (supplying 16.8 percent of China's imports in 2003), Iran (13.8 percent), Angola (11.2 percent), and Sudan (4.7 percent) in addition to the three countries it had relied on before (DoE 2006:22). The Chinese are also attempting to reduce their dependence on Middle Eastern producers by increasing oil imports from other potential suppliers, including Angola, Kazakhstan, Kenya, Libya, Russia, and Venezuela. Beijing also seeks diversity in another sense: by increasing the *types* of energy it imports. In recent years, it has sought to offset its heavy reliance on oil imports by seeking increased quantities of natural gas as well as uranium, for use in nuclear reactors.

In their avid pursuit of energy diversification, the Chinese have left no continent or region untouched. Moving outward from Beijing's long-standing ties to oil providers in Southeast Asia and the Middle East, they have courted potential suppliers in Africa, Latin America, and Central Asia—and even in

Canada, traditionally a major supplier to the United States. All of these areas have received close attention from government officials and the executives of China's major energy firms. To a considerable extent, Beijing has relied on the power of its purse to acquire the resources it seeks from foreign suppliers. It has spent vast sums—in the many billions of dollars—on imported oil and natural gas, substantially increasing thereby the global market price for these commodities. But Chinese officials also seek to ensure their long-term access to energy supplies by obtaining ownership rights over promising reserves of oil and gas.[13]

In most cases, China's efforts to diversify its foreign sources of energy and to acquire assets abroad are spearheaded by the country's major energy firms, especially the China National Petroleum Corporation (CNPC), the China National Petrochemical Corporation (Sinopec), and the China National Offshore Oil Corporation (CNOOC). Supposedly, these firms have a free hand to seek out and make investments whenever and wherever promising opportunities arise. It is clear, however, that the government sets the overarching objectives of Chinese energy policy and guides these firms' efforts to acquire foreign assets. It does so in several ways: by setting the broad political and economic parameters in which all state-controlled firms must operate; by selecting (and, when deemed necessary, removing) the chief executives of these firms; by reviewing and voting on major acquisitions; and by making available low cost loans from state-owned banks.[14]

The pivotal role played by China's government in the pursuit of key national objectives is especially evident in the overseas energy diplomacy conducted by President Hu Jintao and Premier Wen Jiabao since their ascendancy to high office in March 2003. Both have traveled to energy providers abroad, extolling the virtues of trade with China and promising diplomatic favors of one sort or another; they have also invited their counterparts from these countries to visit Beijing for lavish state visits. These encounters have led to the signing of numerous supply agreements and technical protocols over the past few years, in most cases intended to increase the flow of energy to China and to facilitate the involvement of Chinese firms in the development of foreign oil and gas reserves.[15]

Hu has made many such trips since assuming office in 2003, carrying him to most of the world's major oil- and gas-producing nations. At the height of the 2005 dispute over CNOOC's bid for the Unocal Corporation, for example, he traveled to Russia, Canada, and Latin America—in each case, touting the benefits of increased cooperation in the energy field. In Russia, he proposed the construction of new oil pipelines from Siberia to northern China; in Canada, he discussed possible Chinese involvement in the development of Alberta's petroleum-rich tar sands. He has also wooed the leaders of Kazakhstan and Saudi Arabia, seeking fresh opportunities for investment by Chinese energy firms. Indeed, no region of the world has escaped his attention: Africa, for example, has been a frequent destination for both Hu and Wen, and leaders of the continent's major oil-producing countries have been invited to Beijing for numerous visits of their own.[16]

Intensified Energy Competition and Its Geopolitical Implications

That China is vigorously seeking to enhance its access to foreign sources of energy is not, in itself, a source of friction in international relations. After all, the United States, Britain, France, Japan, and other Western oil-importing countries have long competed among themselves for drilling rights in overseas producing areas and have managed to divide up the available supplies in a (relatively) amicable fashion. China may be a newcomer to this contest, but is not behaving noticeably different from the other oil-seeking nations. Indeed, the National Energy Policy (NEP) announced by President George W. Bush on May 17, 2001 calls for U.S. officials to conduct the same sort of diplomatic quest in pursuit of foreign energy as that now being undertaken by Chinese officials. Speaking of Africa, for example, the NEP calls on the president to "direct the Secretaries of State, Energy, and Commerce to deepen bilateral and multilateral engagement to promote a more receptive environment for U.S. oil and gas trade, investment, and operations" (NEPDG 2001).[17] In a world of ever-expanding petroleum supplies, China would simply squeeze itself into this oil-seeking competition and use its abundant stockpiles of cash to buy up whatever energy it required.

But there are two major problems with this picture: first, there are growing indications that global oil supplies are not expanding fast enough to satisfy both the existing needs of the older industrial powers and the soaring demand from China and other rising economic dynamos like India; and second, many of the most prolific remaining sources of supply are already controlled by Western energy firms or by producer-owned national oil companies like Saudi Aramco, forcing China to seek development opportunities in marginal areas or "pariah" states shunned by the other major importers, often producing political and military friction with the West.

For decades, the world supply of petroleum has grown in tandem with the steady rise in international demand. In retrospect, this can be viewed as a major miracle that made possible the great worldwide prosperity of the past several decades along with the rise of China, India, and newly industrialized powers. But since the start of this century there have been growing signs that the industry is no longer capable of keeping pace with the surge in demand. Global output is still growing, but it is not rising *fast enough* to keep pace with rising world demand, thereby producing a condition of de facto insufficiency—with resulting supply anxieties, competitive pressures, and ever-mounting prices.

Many forces are contributing to the slowdown in the growth of world petroleum output, but the basic, underlying dilemma is that the industry as a whole has reached a mature stage in which many of the world's large and easy-to-exploit fields have already been substantially depleted, while those yet to be fully developed are, on average, smaller, more remote, and harder to bring into operation (whether for political, environmental, or technical reasons). Various techniques have been developed by the industry to prolong this stage of its existence, for example, through the employment of "enhanced oil recovery" (EOR) methods to (temporarily) maintain high levels of output at fields that are beginning to show signs of imminent or accelerating decline. Likewise, offshore drilling has moved into ever deeper waters in the search for promising deposits. But, by and large, these efforts cannot compensate for the systemic exhaustion of the major fields that have largely sustained global consumption for the past half-century.[18]

The magnitude of this conundrum is suggested by how reliant we have become on a relatively small number of giant fields that satisfy the bulk of global requirements. Although the world currently harbors tens of thousands of producing oil fields, only 116 of these, each pumping more than 100,000 barrels per day, provide nearly 50 percent of the world's daily petroleum intake. Of these, all but four were discovered more than a quarter of a century ago, and many of them are showing signs of diminished capacity (Bahorich 2006:30, King and Fritsch 2008). In August 2008, for example, the Mexican state oil company Pemex announced that output at Cantarell—Mexico's biggest field and one of the world's largest—had declined by 36 percent since the previous year, an astonishing plunge in such a short amount of time (Black 2008). Russian and Norwegian oil officials have also announced declines in output from some of their major fields.

Looking into the future, the decline of older fields is expected to accelerate. In its *Medium-Term Oil Market Report* for 2008, the International Energy Agency (IEA) revealed that it had raised its estimate of decline rates at mature fields around the world to 5.2 percent a year, up from 4.0 percent in the 2007 edition of this annual study. As the report's authors ominously note, this means adding 3.5 million barrels per day in added capacity every year *just to hold world production steady*. Put another way, it means that the global oil industry has to generate 24.7 million barrels per day in additional capacity between 2008 and 2013 in order to reach the target of 94.1 million barrels per day in anticipated worldwide demand at the end of this period (IEA 2008a). This is an enormous—and, many would contend, nearly impossible—task to achieve.

Just exactly why it will prove so difficult to achieve this ambitious goal is plainly evident in the pages of the 2008 IEA report. Although the major oil companies are naturally eager to bring new projects online, they are finding it increasingly difficult to complete major undertakings. This is a natural result of the aging of the industry and the disappearance of prolific fields in easily accessible locations; all that remains are the "tough oil" options—smaller and less-productive fields in remote locations, deep offshore waters, politically inhospitable countries, or areas of strife and rebellion. These options cost more, take longer to complete, and require costly, complex technologies. As noted by the IEA, "Project delays remain a major factor in supply-side underperformance, with slippage estimated at up to twelve months on average for the large projects surveyed, alongside an estimated doubling of costs" (IEA 2008a).

Under these circumstances, the major companies appear increasingly reluctant to invest many billions of dollars in risky new projects. Although a number of major projects that were undertaken in the late 1990s and early 2000s will finally come on stream in 2009 and 2010, there are very few waiting in line behind them, and so the IEA predicts a sharp fall-off in new capacity addition in 2011 and the years that follow—just when demand from China, India, and other developing countries will take off in earnest. The result, almost certainly, will be a perception of extreme scarcity accompanied by a sharp run-up in prices.

It is impossible, at this point in time, to predict exactly how much oil will actually be available in the decades ahead to meet the anticipated surge in global demand. The U.S. Department of Energy comfortably predicts that in 2030 there will be sufficient supply in the market to satisfy projected demand of 112.5 million barrels per day—an increase of 27 million barrels over current levels of output. If this projection proves accurate, there will be sufficient oil to meet China's projected demand of 15.7 million barrels as well as the 22.3 million barrels sought by the United States, the 16.0 million needed by Western Europe, the 4.9 million by Japan, and so forth. Under this comfortable scenario, prices will remain relatively stable and severe energy shortages will be averted. But, given the concerns raised by the IEA and other organizations, we can have no confidence that this scenario will prevail. Indeed, it would be safer to conclude that global supplies will *not* expand sufficiently to satisfy anticipated demand, that prices will rise significantly, and that the competition for whatever supplies *are* available will grow far more intense and fractious. It is in this context that China's efforts to secure rising Chinese demand must be viewed.

How, exactly, this will play itself out cannot be foreseen. But we already have some early indications. One is price: with China becoming an ever more significant player in a very crowded energy market, oil prices have risen much faster than expected even one year ago. In January 2005, for example, the DoE projected that prices would hover in the US$30–US$35 per barrel range during the period between 2005 and 2025; in February 2008, prices rose over US$100 for the first time in history and climbed to US$140 before falling back.

Even more significant, perhaps, was the hysterical reaction of the U.S. Congress to CNOOC's June 2005 effort to purchase the Unocal Corporation, a mid-sized American oil and gas producer. Although CNOOC's bid for Unocal was US$2 billion higher than that proffered by Chevron, U.S. lawmakers were so incensed about the possibility that a Chinese company might gain control of American energy assets that they voted in August 2005 to place insurmountable obstacles in the way of CNOOC's purchase; CNOOC then withdrew its offer. The fact that Unocal's oil and gas reserves were mostly located in Asia to begin with and played a negligible role in satisfying U.S. demand made little difference to those who voted against CNOOC.[19]

The Unocal affair did not, in the end, produce a significant breach in U.S.-China relations but did hint at the potential for future friction and conflict between Washington and Beijing over the pursuit of vital energy supplies. Indeed, one outcome of the Unocal affair was an amendment to the Energy Policy Act of 2005, mandating a "National Security Review of International Energy Requirements" that would focus in particular on "the growing energy requirements of the People's Republic of China and the implications of such growth on the interests of the United States." The resulting study examined some of the same issues raised in this chapter, and while generally moderate in tone, concluded that China's stepped-up efforts to acquire foreign energy supplies "have an impact on strategic U.S. interests" (DoE/EIA 2008:17).

The potential for friction arising from an increasingly competitive search for diminishing supplies of oil is made more severe by the second factor in this equation: the fact that many of the world's most prolific fields are controlled by the major Western oil firms or the producing countries' state-owned firms, such as Saudi Aramco and the Kuwait Petroleum Corporation. The state-owned firms dominate production in most of Latin America and the Middle East, while the Western firms have established a commanding position in such other producing areas as sub-Saharan Africa and the Caspian Sea basin. Chinese energy officials would no doubt like to obtain a foothold in these areas, but have often been frustrated by the well-established presence there of these competing firms. For example, when CNOOC and Sinopec jointly sought to purchase a one-sixth stake in the consortium developing the large Kashagan reservoir in the Caspian Sea, the original members of the consortium, including Exxon Mobil, Royal Dutch Shell, and ConocoPhilips, exercised their "right of first refusal" to exclude the Chinese and acquire the stake for themselves (Saigol and Roberts 2003).

Having been excluded in this manner from many of the more attractive producing areas, the Chinese have opted for the only path seemingly open to them: the pursuit of reserves in marginal producing areas and "pariah" states like Iran, Myanmar, Sudan, and Uzbekistan that have largely been shunned by firms from the United States and its allies. "Chinese companies are prepared to go to countries that may be considered risky to major Western oil companies," the DoE noted in the report mandated by Congress in 2005. "This is due, in part, to the fact that there are few untapped areas for petroleum investment left in the world that are available to foreign investors and, as a latecomer, China seems pushed to invest in areas where other oil companies cannot or will not go" (DoE/EIA 2008:32). China's position in Sudan is particularly noteworthy: CNPC currently holds a 40 percent stake in the Greater Nile Petroleum Operation Company, the leading producer in Sudan, and a substantial stake in other Sudanese energy consortia; it also built a 930-mile pipeline from southern Sudan to Port Sudan on the Red Sea and a refinery in Khartoum.[20] In Iran, Sinopec has helped construct a pipeline from the Caspian Sea to Tehran and is involved in the development of natural gas reserves.[21]

The fact that China has established such close ties to countries considered unfriendly to the United States is seen in Washington as provocation enough. But, in its efforts to cement its relations with these suppliers, it has also provided them with military and diplomatic aid, further provoking ire in Washington. Sudan and Uzbekistan, for example, have become a major recipient of Chinese arms and military training; Iran has been the recipient of Chinese missiles and missile technology.[22] "In countries like Uzbekistan, Sudan, and Burma, China has openly supported regimes whose human rights violations, support for terrorism, or proliferation activities have engendered worldwide opposition," the DoE observed. "As a long-term trend, China's behavior in this respect runs counter to key strategic goals of the United States" (DoE/EIA 2008:29).

The seriousness with which top U.S. officials view these activities was noticeably evident in Pentagon's 2005 report on Chinese strategy and capabilities, *The Military Power of the People's Republic of China*, which for the first time highlighted energy competition as a significant factor in the U.S.-Chinese security affairs. In a section on "Resource Demands as a Driver of Strategy," the report observed, "Beijing's belief that it requires such special relationships in order to secure its energy access could shape its defense strategy and force planning"—thus, presumably, posing a potential threat to U.S. national security (DoD 2005:10). Subsequent editions of this annual report have continued to highlight this threat, and it was given heightened attention in 2008. Although Taiwan remains a major "driver" of Chinese planning, the report notes, "analysis of China's military acquisitions and strategic thinking suggests Beijing is also developing capabilities for use in other contingencies, such as conflict over resources..." (DoD 2005:1). This threat has also been cited in various Pentagon documents calling for an expansion of U.S. naval capabilities, so as to offset anticipated gains in China's own naval forces (Klare 2008a).

These concerns, it should be noted, are being expressed at a time when China is importing only about 4 million barrels of oil per day, or about one-third of the current U.S. oil-import tally; imagine the degree of alarm we might expect in 2030, when China's oil imports are expected to rise to nearly 12 million barrels per day, representing approximately two-thirds of America's projected import requirement. Although it is impossible to predict the future course of U.S.-China relations, it appears safe to assume that disputes arising from the competitive pursuit of foreign oil will play an increasingly critical—and divisive—role in the relationship, possibly eclipsing such other concerns as the status of Taiwan and two-way trade imbalances.

The Struggle for Natural Gas

So far, we have largely examined issues arising from China's growing thirst for petroleum. As time goes on, however, China will also need an expanded supply of natural gas—and this, too, could produce significant friction in international affairs.

At present, China consumes a relatively small quantity of natural gas, about 2.3 trillion cubic feet per year—a mere 10 percent of the amount consumed in the United States. But China is expected to consume far more natural gas in the future, mostly to fuel electrical power plants but also as a source for fertilizer, hydrogen, and assorted petrochemicals. As Beijing's awareness of the environmental dangers of overreliance on coal grows, moreover, it is likely to depend increasingly on natural gas to generate electricity, further ramping up demand. As a result, China's gas consumption is expected to grow by 5.5 percent per year—the highest rate of any large economy.[23] Much as in the case of China's growing petroleum demand, supplying all of this additional natural gas will prove a major challenge for the government.

Chinese officials would prefer to rely on domestic sources for as large a share of the needed gas as possible, and so has invested considerable funds in efforts to develop promising fields of the Tarim Basin of Western China and to transport this gas to energy-starved areas on the coast.[24] But these sources are not sufficient to satisfy China's growing needs, and so Beijing has had to look elsewhere for additional supplies—here again, as in the case of oil, generating various forms of friction in international affairs.

The world's largest reservoirs of natural gas are found in Iran and the former Soviet Union, and China has sought supplies from both—causing problems with the United States in the case of the former and with Japan in the case of the latter. In October 2004, Sinopec signed a 25-year, US$100 billion contract with Tehran for the production and export of up to 10 million tons of liquefied natural gas to China and for participation in the construction of a refinery for natural gas condensates. Although details of this plan are still being worked out, it could result in a major infusion of new capital into Iran, thus frustrating U.S. efforts to isolate that country and thereby impede its efforts to acquire nuclear weapons.[25]

The problem with Japan over Russian gas is of a different character, entailing competition over the ultimate destination of gas supplies discovered off the coast of Sakhalin Island, in Russia's Far East. Japanese firms have provided much of the capital and technology for development of these fields, and Tokyo has always assumed that the resulting output would be carried southward by pipeline to Japan. Recently, however, Chinese officials have been negotiating with the Sakhalin consortium for a substantial share of the field's gas supplies and for the construction of a pipeline heading westward, to China. Although the Russian government and its corporate partners in the Sakhalin project have yet to decide on the ultimate destination of this gas, the very fact that China has swooped in and attempted to capture a large share of it has produced considerable dismay in Japan (Brooke 2004).

An even more serious dispute with Japan has arisen over the development of offshore gas fields in contested waters of the East China Sea. Chinese and Japanese geologists believe that considerable gas lies in the Xihu Trough, a deep undersea region located midway between China's East Coast and Japan's southernmost islands. Citing provisions of the United Nations Convention on the Law of the Sea (UNCLOS), Japan claims that its offshore boundary lies at the median line between the Chinese and Japanese coasts, putting it directly over the Xihu Trough; China, citing an older rule, insists that its outer maritime boundary extends to the edge of the continental shelf, much further to the east. Recently, CNOOC and

Sinopec have been drilling right at the edge of the median line claimed by Japan, sucking up gas from what Tokyo believes is Japanese territory (but China claims is its own). Both sides have periodically deployed warships in the area, provoking a series of threatening naval encounters—none of which has yet entailed actual gunfire, but has every potential for doing so. The gas dispute has also helped stoke rising anti-Chinese hostility in Japan and anti-Japanese hostility in China, complicating efforts to resolve the dispute peacefully.[26] (The May 2008 meeting between Chinese President Hu Jintao and then Japanese Prime Minister Yasuo Fukuda was to initiate a fresh round of negotiations, but Fukuda's resignation on September 1, 2008 puts this into limbo.)

It's Not China's Problem Alone

Most of the disputes and other issues discussed above derive from a complex but interrelated set of problems: China seeks more imported energy to sustain its economic growth and satisfy the aspirations of its increasingly affluent citizens, and must do so in a world in which many of the most prolific sources of energy are already owned by or earmarked for the older industrial powers. Of course, in a globalized world economy, China can seek to buy what it needs on the open market, using its abundant reserves of cash. But, like many of its competitors in the energy marketplace, China seeks ever increasing supplies of oil and natural gas at a time when the global supply of hydrocarbons is not growing fast enough to satisfy anticipated international demand, often putting it into conflict with other energy-seeking powers. As demonstrated by the Unocal affair, this can complicate China's ties with these countries and provoke an antagonistic reaction with national security overtones. With China's need for imported energy sure to grow, and the future availability of abundant oil increasingly in doubt, the danger of international tension and conflict over vital resources will become increasingly severe.

Viewed in this manner, the risk of friction and conflict over energy is not a "China problem" but a global dilemma. Unless the world's existing powers are prepared to descend into the sort of resource-driven geopolitical competition that resulted in World War I and many subsequent conflicts, they must make room at the table for an energy-hungry China. Efforts to exclude China from promising energy deals, like the Kashagan field in the Caspian and the Unocal sale, will only inflame tensions and drive Beijing to pursue more risky arrangements, with unpleasant international repercussions. At the same time, the eventual peaking of oil and the environmental consequences of our shared reliance on fossil fuels can only be addressed on the international level, involving close cooperation among all key parties, including China. It is essential, then, that the international community view China's strategic energy dilemma in a sympathetic manner and work with Beijing to diversify its sources of energy and accelerate the development of environmentally friendly energy alternatives, such as clean-coal technologies, advanced biofuels (i.e., those not derived from edible plants), wind, solar, geothermal, and hydrogen.

The United States could and should facilitate such efforts by cooperating with China in the development of energy alternatives. If managed in a prudent manner, such cooperation would be beneficial to both countries by reducing their respective needs for imported fuels and thereby reducing the risk of costly and dangerous friction between them.[27] Indeed, senior officials of both countries have endorsed collaborative ventures of this sort for precisely these reasons. "The issues of energy security and environmental sustainability are vitally important to both of our nations," U.S. Treasury Secretary Henry M. Paulson Jr. declared at the conclusion of a December 2007 meeting of Chinese and American energy and economic officials to arrange cooperation in this field. "I find it an exciting prospect that we will set out to a long-term strategic plan for working together toward progress in these important areas."[28]

Assuming that leaders of both countries agree to adopt such plans in earnest, there are several areas where cooperation would appear to make particular sense. These include the development of liquid transportation fuels from coal and natural gas (coal-to-liquids, CTL, and gas-to-liquids, GTL); the development of advanced biofuels; the development of advanced fuel-cells powered by hydrogen; and the design of advanced motor engines using less fuel.[29] (In the case of CTL, it is also essential to develop coal technologies that separate carbon from the fuel mix before processing and sequester it underground.) Other technologies may also appear attractive, but the important point here is to reverse the trend toward increased international competition and conflict over inadequate supplies of oil and gas and instead emphasize cooperation in the development of climate-friendly alternatives.

Notes

1. World Bank data secured at http://www.worldbank.org/ (accessed August 24, 2008).
2. As quoted in Erik Eckholm, "Emerging Middle Class Hits the Road in China." *New York Times*, October 7, 2001.

3. See "Auto Sales Expected to Climb 12 Percent." *China Daily*, February 4, 2006. http://service.china.org.cn on (accessed March 13, 2006). The prediction of 130 million vehicles by 2030 is from the statement of E. Anthony Wayne, assistant secretary of states for economic and business affairs, before the Senate Foreign Relations Committee on July 26, 2005. http://foreign.senate.gov (accessed April 30, 2006).

4. USGS (U.S. Geological Survey), *Minerals Yearbook 1994* Vol. 1 and *Minerals Yearbook 2003* Vol. 1. http://www.usgs.gov (accessed April 30, 2006).

5. DoE/EIA (2008:Table A1, p. 95).

6. Ibid., Tables A5–A9, pp. 100–104.

7. Ibid., Table A1, p. 95.

8. Ibid., Tables A5–A9, pp. 100–104.

9. Ibid., pp. 8, 11, 24, 27, 41.

10. Data for 2007: BP (2008:8, 11). Projections for 2030: DoE/EIA (2008:Tables A5, G1, pp. 100, 199).

11. For background and discussion, see IEA (2008b:328–334).

12. For discussion and background, see DoE (2006:16–32, Andrews-Speed et al. 2002, Downs 2000, Lieberthal and Herberg 2006).

13. For an inventory of China's foreign oil and gas acquisitions through January 2006, see DoE (2006:24–28). For background and discussion, see Klare (2008b) especially pp. 73–77, 132–137, 164–171, 194–201.

14. For discussion, see DoE (2006:14–15, 31–32).

15. For background and discussion, see DoE (2006:33–34).

16. On Chinese oil diplomacy in the Middle East and Africa, see Klare (2008b:165–170, 197–198).

17. Chapter 8, p. 11.

18. For background and discussion, see Deffeyes (2001), Goodstein (2004), Roberts (2004).

19. For background on this incident, see Klare (2008b:1–6).

20. DoE/EIA (2007). Country Analysis Briefs—Sudan. http://www.eia.doe.gov/emeu/cabs/ (accessed September 1, 2008).

21. DoE/EIA (2007). Country Analysis Briefs—Iran. http://www.eia.doe.gov/emeu/cabs/ (accessed September 1, 2008).

22. For background and details, see Klare (2008b:167, 198–199, 215–216).

23. DoE/EIA (2008:Table A6, p. 101).

24. DoE/EIA (2006). Country Analysis Briefs—China. http://www.eia.doe.gov/emeu/cabs/ (accessed September 2, 2008).

25. For background and discussion, see Klare (2008b:195–199).

26. Ibid., 221–224).

27. The author first argued this point in Klare (2008b:238–249).

28. Transcript of U.S. Delegation Press Conference, Third Meeting of the U.S.-China Strategic Economic Dialogue, Xianghe, China, December 13, 2007. http://www.treasury.gov (accessed December 22, 2007).

29. For further discussion of these and other candidate technologies, see Klare (2008b:249–258).

References

Andrews-Speed, Philip, Xuanli Liao, and Roland Dannreuther. 2002. *The Strategic Implications of China's Energy Needs.* London: International Institute of Strategic Studies.

Bahorich, Mike. 2006. End of Oil? No, It's a New Day Dawning. *Oil & Gas Journal* 104(31): 30–34.

Barboza, David. 2005. China Builds Its Dreams and Some Fear a Bubble. *New York Times* October 18.

Black, Thomas. 2008. Pemex Cantarell to Stabilize at 500,000 Barrels a Day. *Bloomberg News* August 28. http://www.bloomberg.com (accessed September 1, 2008).

BP. [British Petroleum] 2008. BP Statistical Review of World Energy June 2008. London: BP.

Brooke, James. 2004. China and Japan Jockey for Share of Russian Gas. *New York Times* November 3.

Deffeyes, Kenneth S. 2001. *Hubbert's Peak: The Impending World Oil Shortage.* Princeton, NJ: Princeton University Press.

DoD (U.S. Department of Defense). 2005. The Military Power of the People's Republic of China 2005. Annual Report to Congress. http://www.dod.mil/news/Jul2005/d20050719china.pdf.

DoE (U.S. Department of Energy). 2006. Energy Policy Act of 2005, Section 1837: National Security Review of International Energy Requirements. Washington. DC: DoE.

DoE/EIA (U.S. Department of Energy, Energy Information Administration). 2008. International Energy Outlook 2008. Washington, DC: Department of Energy.

Downs, Erica Strecker. 2000. *China's Quest for Energy Security.* Santa Monica: RAND Corporation.

Eckholm, Erik. 2001. Emerging Middle Class Hits the Road in China. *New York Times*, October 7.

Goodstein, David. 2004. *Out of Gas: The End of the Age of Oil.* New York: W.W. Norton.

IEA (International Energy Agency). 2008a. *Medium-Term Oil Market Report.* Paris: IEA.

———. 2008b. *World Energy Outlook.* Paris: IEA.

Khan, Joseph. 2003. China Gambles on Big Projects for Stability. *New York Times* January 13.

King, Neil Jr. and Peter Fritsch. 2008. Energy Watchdog Warns of Oil-Production Crunch. *Wall Street Journal* May 22.

Klare, Michael T. 2008a. The New Geopolitics of Energy. *Nation* May 19.

———. 2008b. *Rising Powers, Shrinking Planet: The New Geopolitics of Energy.* New York: Metropolitan Books.

Lieberthal, Kenneth and Mikkal Herberg. 2006. China's Search for Energy Security: Implications for U.S. Policy. *NBR Analysis* 17(1): 5–42.

NEPDG (National Energy Policy Development Group). 2001. National Energy Policy: Report of the NEPDG. Washington, DC: White House.

Roberts, Paul. 2004. *The End of Oil: On the Edge of a Perilous New World.* Boston and New York: Houghton Mifflin.

Saigol, Lina and Dan Roberts. 2003. Partners Move to Block Chinese. *Financial Times* May 10.

The Economist. 2003. The Great Leap Forward. February 1.

———. 2006. A New Train Set. March 25.

Chapter 10

China's Domestic Insecurity and Its International Consequences

Susan L. Shirk

China is reemerging as a major power after 150 years after being a weak player on the world stage.[1] History teaches us that rising powers are likely to provoke war. The ancient historian Thucydides indentified the fear that a rising Athens inspired in other states as the cause of the Peloponnesian War. In the twentieth century, rising powers Germany and Japan were the cause of two devastating world wars. Are China and America doomed to become enemies in the twenty-first century? Inevitably, as China moves up the economic and technological ladder, it will compete with the United States and expand its global reach. But a much graver danger is that as China rises in power, the United States will misread and mishandle it, so that we find ourselves embroiled in a new Cold War or an actual military confrontation.

Our best chance of avoiding a hostile relationship with China is to open up the black box of Chinese domestic politics, look inside, and figure out what makes China act as it does on the world stage. We find a society drastically changed by economic reforms and opening to the world. China no longer resembles the bleak People's Republic of the Mao Zedong era that was the object of our Cold War fears. The China of today looks more benign and familiar. It is less totalitarian and more capitalist, less mono-lithic and more diverse, less drab and more colorful, less isolated and more globalized. Although the transformations underway inside China give it a greater stake in international peace, they also make it more dangerous as its Communist leaders struggle to maintain political control. China's leaders face a troubling paradox. The more developed and prosperous a country becomes, the more insecure and threatened it feels. The PRC (People's Republic of China) today is a brittle, authoritarian regime that fears its own citizens and can only bend so far to accommodate the demands of foreign governments.

As I was writing a book about Chinese domestic politics and foreign policy called *China: Fragile Superpower*, I discussed its title with friends and colleagues in the United States and China. The Americans were puzzled by the term "fragile" and asked what I meant by it. But every Chinese with whom I spoke asked, "What do you mean by 'superpower'?" The Chinese reaction is telling: People in China do not yet think of their country as powerful. And no one questions the premise that China is internally fragile.

China is stronger economically and more secure internationally than it has been since the nineteenth century, but paradoxically, its leaders have an acute sense of domestic insecurity. To Americans, China's leaders look like giants because of the country's growing economic might. But in their own minds, these leaders have a very different self-image. They feel like scared children struggling to stay on top of a society roiled by economic change. It is China's internal fragility, not its economic or military strength that presents the greatest danger to us. Unless the United States begins to understand the fears that motivate China's leaders, we face the possibility of conflict with it.

The Belgrade Embassy Bombing

China's internal fragility came through vividly to me during a traumatic experience I had while serving as Deputy Assistant Secretary of State with responsibility for China in the Clinton administration. One evening in May 1999 as I drove home from the State Department I received a phone call informing me that a U.S. B-52 flying as part of a NATO mission in Yugoslavia had struck the Chinese Embassy with a number of bombs. As I turned around and rushed back to the State Department, I decided that it must be a case of "collateral damage" caused by stray fragments from a nearby target. But I soon learned that in fact the plane had targeted this building, mistakenly identifying it as a Yugoslav military facility. The plane had directly hit the building with five JDAM (Joint Direct Attack Munition) bombs, killing 3 Chinese journalists and injuring 20 others.

I was the U.S. official responsible for coordinating American efforts to defuse the crisis and salvage our relations with China. My first instinct was to have the United States apologize profusely. The Chinese people would never forgive us, or let us forget it, if they felt our apologies were inadequate, just as they have never stopped pressing the Japanese for a proper apology for the atrocities committed during their occupation of China during World War II. Therefore, President Clinton telephoned President Jiang Zemin, but Jiang refused to accept the call. Clinton sent an apology through American Ambassador James Sasser instead. The president also apologized on television, spoke by telephone with President Jiang a few days later, and signed the condolence book from the Chinese Embassy in Washington. The night after the bombing, Secretary of State Madeleine Albright visited the Chinese Embassy to apologize to Ambassador Li Zhaoxing and on her way out was jostled by a crowd of shouting, fist-waving Chinese journalists who had been invited in by the ambassador.

We adjusted the air traffic around Belgrade to enable a Chinese plane to retrieve the remains of the dead and evacuate the injured. Ambassador Sasser asked permission to attend the airport ceremony when the plane landed, but the Chinese government turned him down. We sought to send a high level envoy to Beijing right away but the Chinese government said to wait. Our embassy in Beijing and our consulates in other Chinese cities flew their flags at half mast. In every way we could think of, we sought to express our genuine remorse to the Chinese government and the Chinese people.

But much to our frustration, these efforts to communicate American regret had no effect on the Chinese reactions. The streets of Beijing soon were filled with the largest mass demonstration since the 1989 prodemocracy protests in Beijing's Tiananmen Square. Tens of thousands of young people, mostly students, protested outside the U.S. Embassy in Beijing and the consulates in Guangzhou and Chengdu. The demonstrators shouted anti-American slogans and threw bricks and Molotov cocktails while the police stood by. Protestors burned the consul general's residence in Chengdu.

From the first public report of the incident, China's official media described it as intentional, a "brazen" and "barbarian" act. The media delayed reporting the apologies from the U.S. president, secretary of state, and other senior officials, but did report favorably on the demonstrations as expressions of youthful patriotism. At government request, the universities provided the buses that transported the students to demonstrate outside the American Embassy and consulates. President Jiang Zemin avoided the limelight but sent Vice President Hu Jintao to appear on television to express the government's support for the protestors but to warn them not to go too far, "to conduct all activities in good order and according to law."

Why did the Chinese government risk a major confrontation with the much more powerful United States by allowing student protestors to trash the American missions? A Chinese study of the crisis explains: "Facing heavy pressure, the government and university administrations had to allow students and civilians to protest. President Jiang Zemin later told American officials that 'It is unstoppable when 1.2 billion people are angry" (Wu 2005).

We need to put ourselves in the shoes of China's leaders to understand their reaction. The timing of the accident triggered the leaders' defensive reflexes. The bombing occurred on May 8. Two weeks before in late April, Jiang Zemin and the other Chinese leaders had awakened one morning to the alarming sight of more than 10,000 adherents of a spiritual sect called the Falun Gong sitting silently on the pavement surrounding Zhongnanhai, the compound where the leaders work and live. The Falun Gong is an organization of people who practice a type of traditional Chinese breathing exercises called *qigong* that they believe are beneficial for their health. The group, using cell phones and the Internet, had stealthily organized the sit-in to petition the party for recognition as a legitimate organization. The public security police had given no forewarning. Needless to say, the leaders, particularly Jiang Zemin, were very alarmed. One political insider told me that the night after the Belgrade Embassy bombing, Jiang Zemin stayed up late writing a long memo, not on how to handle the crisis with the United States, but on how to crush the Falun Gong.

Several major anniversaries of historical events fell during 1999, and past anniversary gatherings had snowballed into mass protest. In spring 1999, the Chinese Communist Party was anxiously preparing for two anniversaries of historical protests that might bring students out on the streets against the government again: the eightieth anniversary of the May 4, 1919, demonstrations against the Republican government's concessions to Japan, and the tenth anniversary of the June 4, 1989, prodemocracy demonstrations in Beijing's Tiananmen Square and more than 130 others cities in China. When the Belgrade Embassy bombing occurred, the leaders anticipated that students might march to Tiananmen or Zhongnanhai a few weeks early because they blamed their own government for being so weak that the Americans would believe they could get away with bombing the Chinese Embassy. The government provided the buses to make sure that the students targeted the U.S. missions rather than the Chinese leadership. The larger import of this incident is that China's leaders were willing to risk a confrontation with the United States in order to protect themselves from domestic attacks.

The 2005 Anti-Japan Protests

In April 2005, students used cell phone text messaging and the Internet to organize large and sometimes violent protests against Japan in more than 25 Chinese cities. The United Nations was considering Japan's application to become a permanent member of the Security Council. Japanese Prime Minister Junichiro Koizumi, despite criticism from China and South Korea persisted in visiting the Yasukuni Shrine in Tokyo that honors Japanese war dead, including 14 war criminals. And the Japanese government had recently approved a new textbook that glossed over the slaughter of civilians in the infamous Nanjing Massacre of 1937 and denied Japan's responsibility for its wartime aggression in China. The number of anti-Japan demonstrators was even larger than the protests after the Belgrade Embassy bombing.

In a manner reminiscent of its stance toward the anti-American protests in 1999, the Chinese government signaled a permissive attitude toward the anti-Japanese activism. An online petition initiated by Chinese people living abroad, urging the Chinese government not to support Japan's application for Security Council membership until it properly acknowledged its historical crimes, was prominently publicized on the main officially guided Internet news sites, a clear sign of official sanction. People in Chinese offices and factories rounded up signatures, with no hint of disapproval from party authorities. The Foreign Ministry spokesman defended the petition in a press briefing. The police allowed the students to trash the Japanese Embassy, shops selling Japanese goods, and Japanese restaurants, just as they had tolerated the anti-American actions in 1999.

Anxious to avoid becoming the target of the nationalist protests, the party leaders identified themselves with the protestors by publicly criticizing Japan and announcing that China would not support Japan's membership in the Security Council. After two weeks of snowballing protests, they became alarmed that the unrest was threatening stability—a number of large-scale protests related to domestic problems were happening at the same time. They brought the demonstrations to a close with a *People's Daily* commentary on April 16 praising young people's patriotism but urging them to "cherish social stability" and express their patriotism rationally through their studies and jobs. The public security officials also sent text messages to cellular telephone subscribers to inform them that public demonstrations against Japan would no longer be allowed.

The 2008 Tibet Protests

A more recent example of Chinese leaders' willingness to take international risks for domestic self-preservation occurred in March 2008 when they were caught by surprise by demonstrations in Tibet and the Tibetan communities of Western China. The Tibetan protests turned into a violent ethnic riot—the Tibetans attacked Chinese shops and shopkeepers in Lhasa—and Chinese Netizens reacted with outrage. Online critics railed not just against the protestors' violent attacks on innocent Chinese, but also against the weak response of the government to the violence.

Chinese leaders defended themselves by getting out in front of this upsurge of nationalism. Encouraged by the propaganda authorities, the Chinese media vilified the Dalai Lama with inflamed rhetoric of the sort that hadn't been heard in China since the Cultural Revolution. They called the Tibetan spiritual leader a "wolf in monk's robes," "a devil with a human face but the heart of a beast," and the struggle against him a "life-and-death battle." Government spokespeople also endorsed the criticisms that had appeared on the Internet against CNN and other Western media for anti-Chinese bias in their reporting of the Tibet story. And when the public became aroused by the roughing up of Olympic torch carriers by anti-Chinese demonstrators in Paris, the government facilitated an online petition against the French superstore Carrefours that led to demonstrations against Carrefours stores in China. Beijing's anti-Western stance played well with the Chinese public but put it at odds with the rest of the world just months before international visitors—including those CNN journalists—were due to arrive for the Olympics.

In all three of these cases, the fears of Chinese leaders that an international crisis might spark a domestic insurgency caused them to take foreign policy risks.

Why Are China's Leaders so Worried?

Insecurity and paranoia are occupational diseases of leaders in all authoritarian regimes. Politicians in authoritarian systems never know when their political rivals might conspire to depose them or when mass demonstrations might snowball into a successful revolt. Chinese leaders have been particularly insecure since the Tiananmen protests in 1989. At that time, the political system was shaken to its roots by nationwide student demonstrations that evoked broad public support and by the split in the leadership over how to handle the demonstrations. If the military had refused to obey Deng Xiaoping's orders to forcibly put down the demonstrations, Chinese Communist Party rule might have ended in 1989. In the very same year, the Berlin Wall fell and Communist governments in the Soviet Union and Eastern Europe started to collapse. The coincidence of the Tiananmen protests and the beginning of the end of Communist rule in Russia and Eastern Europe explains why China's leaders since 1989 have worried that their own days in power are numbered.

China's leaders of today also know that they lack the prestige and personal following of China's previous leaders, Mao Zedong and Deng Xiaoping, who were members of the PRC's founding generation. Hu Jintao, the current political leader, and his predecessor, Jiang Zemin, are colorless technocrats and organization men without much charisma. Their authority derives from the positions they hold—General Secretary of the Chinese Communist Party (CCP), Chairman of the Central Military Commission, and President—not from their personal popularity.

China's leaders also recognize that three decades of economic reform and opening to the world have turned Chinese society upside down and created latent political challenges to Communist rule. China today is a very different country than it was in the Mao era before the economic transformation began. The Communist Party can no longer keep track of the population, much less control it. In a historic exodus of urbanization, 150–200 million farmers have moved from the countryside to the city. Three-quarters of the work force are employed outside the state sector where they experience only minimal political constraints on their lives. Tens of millions of Chinese travel abroad every year.[2]

China also has experienced an information revolution that makes it increasingly difficult for the government to keep the public ignorant of events inside and outside the country. Market-oriented tabloid newspapers, cable television stations, and Internet news sites compete to attract audiences by publishing exciting news stories. The CCP invests much effort to censor the contents of the media, but media organizations have a commercial incentive to push the limits of that censorship. As a result, people in China have much more information than they did in the past. The main news source for the majority of Chinese is television, but newspapers, magazines, and Internet news sites are also important sources of international and domestic news.

The advent of the Internet further multiplies the volume of information. As of August 2008, China has more Internet users—over 250 million— than any other country in the world. Virtually all college educated people have access to the Internet and most of them use the Internet to learn about news events. Despite the Communist Party's advanced filtering and blocking technologies and the thousands of Internet "nannies" the CCP recruits to monitor Websites and blogs, the so-called Great Firewall of China is porous. Internet users learn about events in Tokyo, Taipei, or Washington, DC, as well as in other regions of China. This information has the potential to stimulate new demands on government and to become the focus of collective action against the government.

Party leaders make no secret of their anxieties about how long Communist Party rule can last. At his annual news conference following the 2006 National People's Congress, Premier Wen Jiabao stated, "To think about why danger looms will ensure one's security. To think about why chaos occurs will ensure one's peace. To think about why a country falls will ensure one's survival."[3] Official statements and media talk incessantly about "social stability" in a euphemistic effort to persuade people that without the Communist Party in charge, the country would fall into chaos and civil war. This term "social stability" has been used with increasing frequency over the past several decades since 1989 (Shirk 2008:55). During 2005, Hu Jintao instructed universities and think tanks to analyze the causes of the so-called color revolutions[4] that had brought down authoritarian governments in Serbia (2000), Georgia (2003), Ukraine (2004), and Kyrgyzstan (2005).

The Lessons of Tiananmen

In the aftermath of the 1989 Tiananmen crisis, Deng Xiaoping did a postmortem that highlighted the imperative of preserving political stability: "Of all China's problems, the one that trumps everything is the need for stability...And we can't care what foreigners say...We will use severe measures to stamp out the first signs of turmoil as soon as they appear. This will show that we won't put up with foreign interference and will protect our national sovereignty" (Nathan and Link 2001:423). Based on what they learned from the 1989 crisis, the CCP leaders have devised an implicit formula for maintaining stability:

- Avoid public leadership splits;
- Prevent large-scale social unrest;
- Keep the military loyal to the CCP.

The three guidelines are interconnected. If the leadership group remains cohesive despite the competition that inevitably arises within it, then the Communist Party and public security police can manage social unrest and keep it from spreading out of control. Unless people receive some signal of "permission" from the top, protests are likely to fizzle out before they threaten CCP rule. But if the divisions among the top leaders come into the open as they did in 1989, people may take to the streets with little fear of punishment.[5] Then if the military splits too, or abandons the incumbent leaders, the entire regime could collapse.

Avoid Public Leadership Splits

The leaders of authoritarian political systems face two interrelated dilemmas. First, they want to prevent any individual leader from accumulating so much power in his own hands that he becomes a dictator. A dictator who is completely unconstrained by others might act imprudently or unwisely—running off "half-cocked," so to speak—and thereby endanger the entire regime, as Mao Zedong did in the Cultural Revolution. The other risk to the regime is that the competition that inevitably exists among the leaders might spill out beyond the inner circle to draw in ordinary party members or even the public, causing the entire regime to collapse.

Collectively, Chinese leaders have worked hard to prevent public leadership splits that could destabilize the regime. If they don't hang together, they could hang separately, as the Western saying goes. Yet each individual politician has moments of temptation, when an interest in acquiring more power for himself might lead him to exploit a crisis situation and reach out beyond the elite to mobilize a mass following, as Zhao Ziyang, then CCP general secretary, attempted to do during the Tiananmen crisis. Large protests increase the risk of a split by revealing that a following is in place and forcing leaders to take a stand on the protests. In that way, social unrest actually can create schisms at the top. The danger is built into the structure of Communist system. The commercialization of the mass media and emergence of the Internet further heighten the risk that the public might be drawn into elite disagreements. Leadership splits telegraphed to the public over the Internet have triggered revolutionary upheavals in other authoritarian countries. How long will it be before a Chinese leader announces his defection from an unpopular decision and tries to win a mass following by posting a manifesto on the Internet?

Beginning with Deng Xiaoping, CCP leaders have tried to reduce the risk of destabilizing leadership splits by regularizing leadership competition. They introduced fixed terms of office, term limits, and a mandatory retirement age. Greater institutionalization also reduced the risk of the rise of another Mao Zedong. Both post-Deng leaders (Jiang Zemin and

Hu Jintao) have been only first among equals in an oligarchic system of collective rule.

Managing a smooth political succession from one leader to another is the greatest challenge facing any authoritarian system. When Jiang Zemin, having reached the age of 77, retired from the positions of CCP general secretary (2002) and president (2003), it was the first time that a leader of a large Communist country had ever peacefully handed down power to a successor when still alive. As the price of retirement—Jiang was no more willing to step down than are politicians in other countries—the Chinese leader was allowed to keep his job as head of the Central Military Commission that had no formal retirement age. But without the powers of the top party post, Jiang's influence began to wane, and two years later in September 2004, he retired from the military commission position. Anxious to avoid a publicly divided leadership, senior and retired leaders had reportedly convinced Jiang that the best way to preserve his legacy was to retire completely.[6]

At the Seventeenth National Congress of the CCP in 2007, midway in the two five-year terms that President Hu Jintao was expected to serve, the leaders had to identify a successor who could be readied to take over as number one in 2012. To maintain unity and prevent Hu Jintao from aggrandizing too much power, the oligarchy rejected Hu's own favorite, Li Keqiang, and instead chose Xi Jinping, who is not closely connected with any incumbent leader. Xi is keeping a low profile to avoid attacks from rivals and maintain a proper deference to Hu. But the Chinese elite recognizes the continuing risk that a rival might spark a public leadership split by challenging Xi's succession between now and 2012.

Prevent Large-Scale Social Unrest

China's leaders are constantly nervous about the possibility of protest activity that threatens the regime, perhaps more nervous than they need to be. According to police statistics, the numbers of civil society protests rose rapidly from 8,700 in 1993 to 74,000 in 2004.[7] "Mass incidents have become a major problem for social stability," Public Security Minister Zhou Yongkang said in July 2005. "Their number is on the increase and their scale is constantly expanding the trend toward greater organization is clear."[8] Demonstrations by laid-off workers, dissatisfied farmers, urban migrants, Muslim extremists, ordinary urban residents, and retired People's Liberation Army veterans have become a frequent occurrence. Chinese students protested not just in 1989, but also in 1985, 1986–1987, 1999, and

2005. All this churning has occurred in the period since 1978 that might be considered China's most politically stable time in more than a century.

Yet most protests remain small scale and focused on local issues rather than opposing the Communist Party or central government. When protests by workers, farmers, or residents break out, the central government publicly sympathizes with the protestors and blames local officials for causing the problems; then, after perfunctory trials, it throws the protest leaders in jail. The party's effort to identify with the protestors and avoid becoming their target has reached the point that remarkably senior government ministers now hail rural protests as a sign of democracy and praise the farmers' awareness of how to protect their rights.[9]

The fears of Communist autocrats about large-scale demonstrations that could threaten party rule make them hypersensitive to the public mood. Their anxiety was on full display during the massive snow blizzards that struck China in winter 2008 on the eve of the Chinese New Year holiday. Millions of people attempting to travel back to their hometowns to visit their families were stranded by the storm without power or heat. The several hundred thousand frustrated people packed into the Guangzhou railroad station could have become an angry, violent mob if they blamed the government instead of the weather. Premier Wen Jiabao ran madly all around the country, including Guangzhou, with the television cameras following him, making speeches and apologizing to the people for the disruption to transportation and the difficulty they were having getting home. Six months later, Wen Jiabao was on the move and well-televised again, as the face of the Chinese government's impressively well-organized response to the devastating Sichuan earthquake that killed more than 70,000 people and left millions homeless.

On the economic front, the leaders place high priority on maintaining support by keeping growth rates high. By sustaining economic growth, China's leaders create new jobs and reduce the risk of unemployed workers who might go to the barricades. Annual growth rates of at least 7 percent are considered a political imperative.

China's leaders know that the greatest political risk lying ahead of them is the possibility of an economic crash that throws millions of workers out of their jobs or sends millions of depositors to withdraw their savings from the shaky banking system. A massive environmental or public health disaster also could trigger regime collapse, especially if people's lives are endangered by a media cover-up imposed by party authorities. Nationwide rebellion becomes a real possibility when large numbers of people are upset about the same issue at the same time.

China's officials do a lot of public hand-wringing about growing social inequality and its potential to spark instability. To head-off unrest and maintain popular support for Communist Party rule, China's current leaders strive to demonstrate that they identify with the have-nots. Their populist rhetoric and policy platform of narrowing economic gaps represent a kind of "compassionate communism." By raising the inequality issue themselves and channeling resources to rural needs, they hope to dampen unrest while sidestepping the underlying systemic causes of illegitimate wealth.

Nationalism and Unrest

What Chinese leaders fear most is a national opposition movement that fuses various discontented groups such as unemployed workers, farmers, and students, under the banner of nationalism. The lessons of Chinese history are very much on their minds. The previous two dynasties, the Ch'ing dynasty that fell in 1911 and the Republican government that was defeated by the Communists in 1949, were overturned by such movements. Nationalism is a powerful emotional force that can unite different groups against the government if they perceive it as too weak in the face of foreign pressure.

Yet the Chinese Communist Party itself bears some responsibility for the resurgence of nationalism over the past two decades. Following Tiananmen, the CCP launched a nationwide "patriotic education campaign" in schools and the mass media as a way to build popular support for the party now that Communist ideals had lost their luster. Beginning in 1994, schools added new courses to stimulate patriotic loyalty, and students won awards for reading the 100 patriotic books and viewing the 100 patriotic movies chosen by the party. School tours crowded historical sites now renamed "patriotic education bases," for example, the Museum of Testimony to the Crimes of Japanese Army Unit 731, the Japanese unit that experimented with chemical weapons on Chinese citizens, located in the northeastern city of Harbin.

Nationalism did not have to be entirely "constructed" by the state (Anderson 1991).[10] As China revived its economic and military might, nationalist emotions were spontaneously bubbling up in the popular psyche. All the school curriculum, media, and billboards had to do was reinforce these emotions by attaching them to the common script of China's triumph under Communist leadership after the "century of humiliation" at the hands of foreign enemies. The main themes of the story are the atrocities committed by Japan during its occupation of China, the loss of Taiwan inflicted by Japanese and American militaries, and America's hegemonic interest in keeping China weak and overthrowing the Communist government through "peaceful evolution." Patriotic education nurtured popular resentments against Japan and America and an expectation that Taiwan would soon be reunified.

China's press is not yet entirely free, but it is market driven and pushing the limits of party censorship, and the Internet amplifies its impact on public opinion. The media, competing to attract audiences, publish a lot of reporting about Japan, Taiwan, and the United States, the relationships that are the objects of intense interest and attention. By shining the light of publicity on these "hot button" issues, the media make it harder for decision makers not to treat foreign policy in these three issue areas as domestic politics Chinese officials read the tabloids and the Internet to find out what the public is really thinking, and come away with the impression that nationalism is sweeping the country. They feel under public pressure to take tough stands toward Japan, Taiwan, and the United States because what they are reading is highly skewed in the nationalist direction.

Keep the Military Loyal

The People's Liberation Army (PLA) has been a key player in Chinese politics since before the founding of the People's Republic in 1949. During the Revolution, the PLA and the Chinese Communist Party were practically merged. In the Mao era, the PLA was held up as a model of ideological commitment and public service. Its mission was to "serve the people" by building roads and irrigation, running state farms, preserving internal order, and preparing to defend the country in people's war, although it also saw combat in Korea, Vietnam, and elsewhere. The huge people's army consisted mostly of conscripted peasant youth eager to escape the hardships of rural life, garbed in baggy fatigues and sneakers, and equipped with antiquated weapons and the "spiritual atom bomb" of Mao Zedong thought.

Today this people's army has become a professional modern force that according to Pentagon reports has capabilities that "pose a credible threat to other modern militaries operating in the region" (DoD 2005:executive summary). and "put regional military balances at risk" (DoD 2006). The Pentagon also envisions China as the power with "the greatest potential to compete militarily with the U.S." (ibid.). Although most observers stress the international motivations for China's military modernization program, in particular its priority on preventing Taiwan independence and discouraging the United States from intervening to defend Taiwan, domestic motivations also should be factored in.

Assuring that the PLA is loyal to the CCP—and to him personally—is a high priority for China's top leader. If the political system is threatened by large-scale demonstrations and disagreements among the leaders about how to respond to them, then the military would form the last line of defense.

When Deng Xiaoping, a former PLA political commissar, led China he was so confident of the loyalty of the PLA that he squeezed it financially in order to concentrate on the modernization of the civilian economy. By cutting the size of the military from 4.5 million (1981) to 2.31 million (2001), China was able to enhance its capabilities to some extent. But military units had to earn a portion of their own funding by running businesses.

Under Jiang Zemin and Hu Jintao, the first Chinese leaders not to have served in the military and who cannot count on its loyalty, the PLA has enjoyed bigger government budgets and no longer has to earn its own income. Defense spending has risen in real terms and as a percentage of GNP since 1999. Official military spending has increased at double-digit rates throughout the decade and up to the present.

Chinese increases in military spending, although a significant trend, do not match the all-out military buildups that occurred in early twentieth-century Germany and Japan and led them into war. The 2005 official military budget was only 1.34 percent of China's total domestic product and 7.34 percent of total government expenditure (compared to 17.8 percent of total government expenditure of the United States, 11.4 percent of France, and 9.25 percent of Germany, according to Chinese calculations).[11] Even if China's actual military spending is two or three times the official number as many experts believe, then its total expenditure amounts to US\$60–US\$90 billion, comparable to Russia (US\$65 billion), but far behind the U.S. military budget of over US\$500 billion.[12]

Still, thanks to the generous financial support of Jiang Zemin and Hu Jintao, the PLA is becoming a modern force with the capability to pose problems for the United States and Asian countries if it chose to do so.

Domestic Fragility and Foreign Policy

When China's leaders make foreign policy, they have to keep in mind the reactions of the groups upon whom their political power depends—the mass public, other leaders, and the military. Their anxieties about domestic challenges to their power motivate them to use their power in two very different ways. First, China generally behaves like a cautious, responsible power preoccupied with its own domestic problems and intent on avoiding conflicts that would disrupt economic growth and social stability. Keeping the economy growing by at least 7 percent per year is considered politically essential to create jobs and prevent the widespread unemployment that could lead to large-scale unrest. Chinese businesses and local governments have a stake in keeping foreign trade and investment flowing. By cooperating with its neighbors, Chinese creates a good environment for economic growth and suppresses ethnic and religious unrest in Tibet, Xinjiang, and Inner Mongolia.

Acutely conscious that its rapid rise leads other countries to view it as a threat, China's diplomats have worked hard since the 1990s to build its reputation as a good global citizen and regional neighbor. China has become a staunch supporter of the World Trade Organization and the Nonproliferation Treaty, and it demonstrates its acceptance of the international status quo by participating in many more multilateral organizations than we would expect at its level of development (Johnston 2003:14). Seeking to reassure its Asian neighbors about its benign intentions, China has resolved almost all its border disputes, proffered free trade agreements to Southeast Asia, South Korea, and Japan, and established new forums for regional cooperation. China also has agreed to abide by a code of conduct with the Southeast Asian countries to prevent conflict over the contested territory of the Chinese China Sea, and signed a tripartite agreement with Vietnam and the Philippines to prospect jointly for oil and gas there. Most strikingly, it has stepped forward to mediate the dangerous standoff between the United States and North Korea over North Korea's nuclear weapons program and joined with other United Nations Security Council members to impose economic sanctions on North Korea after it tested a nuclear bomb. All of this cooperative behavior boosts China's international influence and is rooted in the leaders' interest in achieving a peaceful international environment to sustain economic growth and prevent social unrest.

But when dealing with Japan, Taiwan or the United States, the foreign policy issues that attract a lot of public attention and emotion, China shows a different, more assertive face. These issues are treated symbolically, as questions of principle instead of problems to be solved: the principle that Japan must atone for its historical sins, the "one China" principle that Taiwan must accept, and the principle of opposition to American hegemonism. Communist Party leaders, as well as their ambitious subordinates hoping for promotions, show their strength by taking a firm stand on principle. Swimming against this powerful current of political correctness on Japan, Taiwan, and the United States takes unusual bravery.

In the words of one policy advisor, "In China, when foreign policy is made by a handful of leaders, they make the right call, flexible and pragmatic. When it involves a larger group they tend to be more rigid and tough." This more emotionally volatile side of China's split personality, we might call it China's "id," could drive China into a military confrontation if its leaders make a threat and then feel they can't back down for fear of a public backlash that could sweep them out of power.

China's leaders are undoubtedly sincere when they state their intention for the country to rise peacefully. They have genuine economic and political motivations to be accepted as a responsible power—a term originally used in speeches by officials during the Clinton administration that has now been appropriated by China. Much of Chinese foreign policy is accommodating, flexible, and pragmatic.

But will China's leaders be able to sustain this constructive stance toward the world domestically in the face of increasing mass protests, intensifying nationalism, and news about what is going on outside China now reaching the Chinese public? Americans need to be aware of China's fragility when we make our own policies toward China. Everything Americans say and do regarding China reverberates through Chinese domestic politics. By keeping in mind how our words and actions resonate inside China we can enable China's leaders to behave like the responsible power they claim they are instead of being driven by their domestic insecurity into belligerent behavior.

Notes

Paragraphs (around 2000 words) from various parts of the chapter have been taken from *China: Fragile Superpower* by Shirk, Susan (2007). By permission of Oxford University Press.

1. This chapter draws from my book, *China: Fragile Superpower* (New York: Oxford University Press, 2007).
2. Approximately 30 million traveled abroad in 2007 (http://www.chinadaily. com.cn/bizchina/2007-10/31/content_6219496.htm).
3. PRC Premier Wen Jiabao News Conference, March 14, 2006, CCTV-1, CPP20060314070002.
4. The "color revolutions" refer to the nonviolent revolutions taking a color or flower as their symbol that toppled post-Communist authoritarian governments in Eastern Europe and Central Asia.
5. Douglas McAdam (1999) says that a protest movement only develops when there is a "political opportunity structure."
6. *Straits Times*, September 21, 2004.

7. *South China Morning Post*, July 7, 2005. The police released a statistic of 87,000 "public order disturbances" during 2005, a number that Western journalists use as a measure of the increase in protest activity. The category "public order disturbances" (*raoluan gonggong zhixu*), however, is not the same as the previously used category "mass incidents" (*qunti xing shijian*) according to political scientist and well-known china expert, Dr. Murray Scott Tanner (personal communication).

8. Public Security Minister Zhou Yongkang's report to the Chinese People's Political Consultative Congress, quoted in *Ta Kung Pao* (Hong Kong) and reported in Reuters, July 27, 2005.

9. *South China Morning Post*, July 4, 2005.

10. The nationalist sentiments expressed by Chinese living abroad, for example, during the tour of the Olympic torch in 2008, are evidence that not all contemporary Chinese nationalism is engineered by the CCP.

11. Xinhua, March 5, 2006.

12. Ibid.

References

Anderson, Benedict. 1991. *Imagined Communities: Reflections on the Origin and Spread of Nationalism*. London: Verso.

DoD (U.S. Department of Defense). 2005. The Military Power of the People's Republic of China 2005. Annual Report to Congress. http://www.dod.mil/news/Jul2005/d20050719china.pdf.

———. 2006. Quadrennial Defense Review Report. http://www.defenselink.mil/pubs/pdfs/QDR20060203.pdf.

Johnston, Alastair Iain. 2003. Is China a Status Quo Power. *International Security* 27(4): 5–56.

McAdam, Douglas. 1999. *Political Process and the Development of Black Insurgency 1930–1970*. Chicago: University of Chicago Press.

Nathan, Andrew J. and Perry Link, eds. 2001. *The Tiananmen Papers* (Compiled by Zhang Liang). New York: PublicAffairs.

Shirk, Susan L. 2008. *Fragile Superpower*. New York and Oxford: Oxford University Press.

Wu Baiyi. 2005. China's Crisis Management during the Incident of "Embassy Bombing."

World Economics and Politics 3.

Chapter 11

Would There Be Two Tigers Living in the Same Mountain? The Geostrategic Implications of China's Rise for U.S.-China Relations

Zhang Ruizhuang

In the past three decades China has sustained an economic growth with a speed and scale unprecedented in human history. This has sounded an alarm and caused concerns among many Americans who are worried about the prospect that China will one day rise to a superpower and be a threat to the United States. China is anticipated to pose a threat to the United States in two ways: first, China may challenge specific U.S. security or other vital national interests, and second, over the long term, China may eventually rival the United States for world dominance. China's rise as a superpower therefore depends on the probabilities of three subevents: the sustainability of China's current growth, the potential for conflicts of interests between the two countries, and China's intention to challenge the U.S. hegemony. This chapter tries to evaluate the prospect of China's anticipated threat to the United States by examining the likelihood of each subevent and the factors that influence their respective probability. Then, on the basis of such analysis, I will proceed to put forward policy recommendations for the United States that may help reduce the risk of the worst case scenario—facing a powerful, hostile, and revisionist China in the future.

I argue that—the key premise for gaining the capability both to inflict harm to the United States and to rival it for dominance—China's rise to superpower status still remains highly uncertain even though it has so far maintained its momentum of marvelous economic expansion. The enormous problems the country is facing on all fronts and the inherent weakness in its economic-social-political structure allows little optimism in the country's future in terms of political-social stability and sustainability of economic growth. China's military power lags behind not only the United States but also many secondary powers as well. Moreover, China's deficiency in soft power makes its becoming a true superpower even more uncertain. I further argue that even if, in the best case scenario, China should beat all the odds and reach superpower status; and even if, from a realist point of view, increased national strength and elevated power position enhance China's assertiveness and ambition in international affairs, the prospect of a high level of hostility between China and the United States and China's upsetting Pax Americana will be significantly reduced by China's national characteristics in dealing with the outside world which is routed in its history and culture, unless it is provoked from outside. Thus, as long as the United States handles the situation properly, the likelihood of China becoming a threat to the United States will not be as high as many Americans tend to believe. It is up to the current hegemonic power, the United States, to decide what kind of relationship it wants to have with the rising power and what attitude the rising power is to have toward the existing hegemony and its world order.

China: The Next Superpower?

A state's national strength is pivotal to its international behavior and its relations with other states. That is why people in the United States often link China's phenomenal growth in economic strength to their fear of China posing threat to the United States. To be sure, lesser states or even substate organizations can also be a security threat to a great power, as is shown in the case of 9/11. Yet, history often demonstrates that it is much harder to eliminate a threat posed by another great power. Furthermore, rapidly rising powers are often seen as possessing the capacity to challenge a hegemon.

Everyone is talking about China's rise to a great power as if it were a fait accompli, or an assured prospect. In fact, nothing can be further away from reality. Those who are overzealous about "China's rise," be they taking it positively or negatively, often see oversimplified and sensational numbers—such as the average annual growth rate of GDP (Gross

Domestic Product) at close to 10 percent for nearly three decades or the size of its economy reaching second place in the world, trailing only behind the United States, and so forth. But numbers can be fallible or misleading. A telling example is that the "International Comparison Program" of the World Bank, in its new calculations based on more accurate and comprehensive statistics, lowered China's GDP by 40 percent from US$8.8 trillion to US$5.3 trillion for the year of 2005, reducing its share of world GDP from 15 percent to 10 percent. And yet, even this recalculation may be somewhat misleading because it is based on PPP (Purchasing Power Parity) measurements. If one were to use the traditional exchange rate measurement, China's share of global GDP is only 5 percent—well behind that of the United States (28 percent), and trailing Japan (10 percent) and Germany (6 percent) (World Bank 2005).

First World or Fourth World?

When impressed with the stunning numbers of China's growth, people tend to forget or ignore some important facts about China's economy. First the size of China's population remains a serious constraint on future economic development. There is a saying in China depicting the nation's plight: Any achievement divided by 1.3 billion is nothing; any problem multiplied by 1.3 billion is overwhelming. Therefore, if we look at the global comparison of GDP per capita, China's place (US$5,300, purchasing power parity 2007 estimation) nosedives to 131 out of 230 economies (CIA 2008).

Second, China began its economic development from an extremely low baseline. Only three decades ago, the poverty and backwardness of the country was stunning. Back in 1978, 250 million people, or one-third of rural population lived in the "absolute poverty" (Chinese standard equal to under US$0.25 per day). Thanks to the economic development and the tremendous efforts by the Chinese government, impressive progress has been made in reducing poverty in China. Yet, by 2006 statistics, there were still 21 million people living in horrible misery. If measured by international poverty standards (under US$1 per day), then in 1990, even 12 years after China's initial reforms, 490 million or 40 percent of the total Chinese population fell below the poverty line. Today, this figure has been reduced to 130 million, and China still has the second largest population in poverty in the world, only next to India.

The third challenge for China is the extreme imbalance in development between China's coastal/urban and interior/rural areas. Most foreign visitors tour Beijing, Shanghai, and Guangzhou in China and return home with the impression that China has elevated itself into the First World—a developed country already. Yet, one does not have to go far from these major cities, only a hundred miles into the countryside, to see stunning poverty often found in the least developed countries in the world. According to the latest Chinese official statistics, the GDP of three Eastern coastal areas (the Zhujiang Delta centered in Canton, the Yangtse Delta centered in Shanghai, and the Beijing-Tianjin-Hebei economic circle) counts for half of the national total, leaving the rest of the country to share the other half (*Xinhua Dispatch* 2005). Provincially speaking, Canton's GDP in 2003 was 3 times of Hunan, 10 times of Guizhou, 35 times of Qinghai, and 74 times of Tibet.[1] Economist Hu Angang divides China into "four worlds" according to the World Bank grouping of countries by income per capita: only 5 percent of Chinese population in the East Coast live in the First World (above the higher mid-income line of US$8,320 ppp), 20 percent in the Second World (above the lower mid-income line of US$3,960 ppp), 25 percent in the Third World (above the low income line of US$1,790), and the rest 50 percent, or 630 million people, live in the Fourth World (below the low income line) (Hu 2007).

Growth Sustainable?

In addition to these difficulties, there are even deeper structural problems that may turn out to be fatal to the sustainability of China's economic growth. First, China's development has mainly been quantitative expansion so far, or increase in the size of the economy, rather than qualitative growth, or advancement in technology and productivity. Despite fast growth in total output, China's industrial productivity remains low. In 2004, China's overall productivity was only 1/9 of the United States, 1/6 of Japan and 1/4 of South Korea, and was ranked 57 out of 60 or 70 out of 78 economies, according to two authoritative statistics respectively (IMD World Competitiveness Yearbook 2004, as cited in Duan and Liu 2005). While China is making great progress to catch up, the gap is just too wide to fill any time soon. Major reasons for this low productivity are the labor-intensive and low technology features of Chinese economy, as well as the lack of technological innovation. Of all the patents granted by Chinese authority, three-quarters are those owned by foreign business. In the past five years, the total patents granted to the top 10 Chinese electronic information enterprises equaled the number of patents IBM received in one year alone (*Xinhua Dispatch* 2005).

Second, the overconsumption of energy and excessive environment pollution are two chokepoints that imperil the sustainability of China's economic growth. With particularly low energy efficiency, China's industries consume much more energy for the same output than most other countries (ranked 51 in the world)—for instance, 3 times more than the United States and 6.6 times more than Japan. To fuel this inefficient industrial production, China has been rapidly increasing its dependence on imported oil, putting pressure on the already stressed world market. In the meanwhile, China also has been developing at the expense of its environment. China's carbon dioxide emission for each million dollar GDP was 12 times higher than Japan, 5 times higher than the United States, and was ranked 57 out of 60 economies (Duan and Liu 2005, statistics for 1999). In 2007, China surpassed the United States to be the number one emitter in the world (Science Daily 2008). The severe air pollution causes up to 750,000 premature deaths each year (McGregor 2007).

Third, China's economic development also has been seriously distorted in terms of its fast growing and extremely high dependency on foreign trade. The dependency rate shot up from 9.8 percent in 1978 to 50 percent in 2002, and then went on to 76 percent in 2005, reaching a level higher than most major trading powers, such as the United States (28 percent), Japan (31 percent), India (40 percent), Russia (56 percent), Britain (64 percent), only lower than Germany (85 percent) (World Bank 2008). Not only does foreign trade account for such a big portion of its GDP, but China has also maintained huge trade surplus year after year. Such a high foreign trade dependency exposes China to volatile foreign markets full of uncertainties influenced by economic factors and by political and diplomatic relations. A healthy and sustainable economy must be based on solid domestic demand, which has historically been relatively small. The problem has been minimized by domestic demand for house construction and automobile manufacturing. Yet the market for these durable goods will be saturated before long, and then the problem of weak domestic demand will emerge as a major bottleneck for further growth.

Due to all of these factors and in spite of its impressive economic growth, China's international position of competitiveness among about 120 economies ranked by the World Economic Forum (Davos) has slipped year after year, from thirty-third (2002) to forty-fourth (2003) to fifty-fourth (2006). This is not very encouraging for a superpower candidate (International Herald Leader 2005, *Xinhua Dispatch* 2006).

Another problem critical to the sustainability of China's economic growth is that of social stability. In the past three decades, China's national wealth and average personal income has increased by 12 times. Unfortunately, instead of making everyone better off and happy, a significant portion of the populace has been left out and become increasingly resentful against the current social-economic system. According to various sources, China's Gini coefficient rose from 0.16 in 1978 to 0.496 in 2006, exceeding the international alarm line of 0.4 as early as 2000. It is now higher than most countries in the world except in Latin America. In 1985, the ratio of urban/rural income per capita was 1.85:1, and rose to 3.24:1 in 2005 while the East/West ratio of income per capita was 2:22:1 in 1978 but 3:01:1 in 2001. The richest 0.4 percent families own 70 percent of national wealth (He 2007, Wang 2006, Ding 2006). Tens of millions of workers lost their jobs from public-turned-private enterprises, and one hundred and fifty million peasants left their village to become migrant workers chasing any odd jobs they can find across the country. These two portions of the population, plus the poorest peasants in the rural areas, form the bottom layer of the society. They do not have stable jobs, they do not have social security, and they do not have medical insurance—in short, they received very little benefit from China's economic prosperity and they are the most vulnerable to any economic downturn. This huge reserve of unemployed labor does help the economy greatly by keeping down labor costs, yet it does suggest that China's economy is sitting on a powder keg waiting to explode.

The foregoing account of China's economic situation has been deliberately one-sided, focusing almost exclusively on its negative aspects. My intent has been to present the complexities of China's rise and to challenge the over optimism of so many who glue their eyes to the sensational achievements by China. The facts and data presented above are nevertheless meant to serve as a reminder that there is still a long way to go with many obstacles to overcome before China would become a superpower.

To be a superpower, a state requires not only hard power but soft power as well. Hard power consists of economic and military strength that is often drawn from its national endowment such as population, territory, and natural recourses. Among all these variables, economy is the most dynamic and critical one, and that's why this chapter limits its discussion of hard power to economic factors. The military aspect was left out for two reasons: first, more often than not, military strength is a function of the economy: when the later grows the former follows (Japan and Germany are all exceptions owing to the extraordinary postwar arrangement); second, the value of assessing Chinese military power by amateurs/outsiders is dubious due to the lack of reliable data, which is in turn due to the lack of transparency of the Chinese military. Aside from the hard power, however, there is a different kind of power, the soft power that is indispensable for being a great power. In the following paragraphs I will consider some major deficiencies in China's soft power that remain a roadblock for China's march toward superpower status.

Soft Power

If China is still far from becoming a superpower in terms of its hard power, then it is even further away in terms of soft power. First of all, China does not have a transcendent ideology. As French President Nicolas Sarkozy poignantly noted, a country without an ideology to export cannot be a great power. China not only lacks an ideology for export, it does not even have one for domestic consumption.

Marxism has long been abandoned not only by the people but also by the Communist Party itself, which keeps its name only for the sake of legitimacy. While in reality the Chinese Communist Party (CCP) has ironically made Chinese society more capitalist than most Western nations (in terms of capital/management being more powerful than workers, and the lack of social welfare, etc.), the ruling party is not ready to openly and wholeheartedly embrace Western ideology—capitalism, democracy, and human rights. Thus in the past several decades, 1.3 billion Chinese should have been living in a spiritual vacuum with neither the guidance of any national ideology nor a value system based on mainstream consensus. Today in China, people in general live only by the popular motto "get rich fast." The traditional values have been destroyed under the Communist rule, especially by the so-called Cultural Revolution, new values have not been widely accepted. This is why Chinese society is also in the status of "moral and ethical vacuum," as the subtitle in a major article from a recent issue of *Chinese Newsweek* suggests (2008). Today's China looks like the "wild, wild West" where anything goes.

The lack of appealing ideology or value system not only inhibits China from emerging as a superpower but, more problematic, it poses a real danger to its national unity—an index of national strength. In a country like China, so vast in territory and so diverse in ethnicity and cultural background, it is paramount for the nation to have something in common to hold the country together—such as the belief system known as the American Creed serving as a spiritual bind for the American Nation. Without such a bind, the national unity and hence the national survival is in peril, let alone its attempt to become stronger and more powerful. Without an appealing ideology, a superpower would-be will not be able to justify its dominance, to make its influence acceptable to the rest of the world, and to find followers for its leadership.

In addition, China also lacks a coherent international strategy. Since early 1990s, the Chinese government has put forward a platform called "Peace and Development—Theme of Contemporary World" that after years of modification has now taken the form of "Harmonious World

Thesis." A mixture of foreign policy philosophy and strategic overview, it argues that peace, development, and cooperation have become the main theme of our era, and holds that in order to promote a "harmonious world" featuring political multipolarization and economic globalization, China should strive for the realization of equality, democracy, and legality in the political arena; mutual trust, dialogue, and cooperation in the security arena; mutual benefit and win-win situation in the economic arena; and diversity and tolerance in the cultural arena. It is obvious that such a program is little more than rhetoric spiced with Wilsonian idealism. It also has little relevance to the real world today and hence little value for a global strategy of a big power. Recently, a major Chinese scholar/official called for formulating a compehensive and systematic China grand strategy that he argued China has not had since Mao's Theory of Three Worlds (Wang 2007).

As "Harmonious World" is too lofty and too far from reality to guide China's foreign relations, China has in the past decades actually followed Deng Xiaoping's teaching of two "never's" ("Never be the head" [of any group] and "Never uphold the red banner") and his famous axiom "hide capacity and bide time." As a consequence, China has abandoned almost all the principles it once upheld under Mao's highly ideological foreign policies, surrendered almost all the causes it once fought in the name of anti-imperialism and anti-hegemonism, given up the leadership as well as its followers of the Third World. China has become so eager to avoid trouble and conflict in which its national interests are not directly involved that as a permanent member of the UN Security Council it has cast the most abstention votes and the least veto votes among the big five in the past three decades. Thus, China's pursuit of a foreign policy with no principle, no vision, no cause, and no friends plus its relentless pursuit of economic ties and benefits around the world leaves an impression in the eyes of the rest of the world that China is simply a mercantilist nouveau riche. Such image works right against the prospect that China is to be accepted by the international community as a new comer of world power.

To sum up, even China has stunned the world with its marvelous economic achievements. Nonetheless, the inherent weakness in its social-economic structure makes slim the likelihood of China becoming a superpower in the near future. Moreover, the deficiency in its soft power makes the prospect even dimmer.

However, while I argue that China's rise is neither foreordained nor likely, what if I were wrong? Let's assume, for the sake of argument, that somehow China manages to confront the challenges it faces and that it does emerge a new giant to rival the United States: Then what?

China the Superpower: A Threat to the United States?

Many good-intentioned people who want to see U.S.-China relations improve rather than deteriorate have argued fiercely against the claim that China will become a threat to the United States when it grows into a superpower. And one argument they hold is that China would never engage the United States in a rivalry for dominance, regional or global, even when it gained strategic parity with the latter. Starting from Mao Zedong, generation after generation of Chinese top leaders have repeatedly vowed "China will never pursue hegemony—not even when we become strong and powerful," signaling the United States that China will never challenge the U.S. hegemony. Like all the people closely associated with both countries, this author does not like to see tension rising in between China and the United States either. Yet, goodwill aside, we should never substitute wishful thinking for reality.

Security Dilemma

Realist theory of international politics posits that a nation's external behavior and its relations to other nations (including whether posing a threat or not) is mainly determined by its capacity, that is, its international power position, and not by its intensions. Because no state can fully trust others, it must always be on guard. This is what the security dilemma is all about. If China becomes a superpower, it will inevitably pose a threat to the United States. Professor John Mearsheimer, a noted realist scholar from the University of Chicago, has argued that in the self-help system of international anarchy—which in his figurative words is like making a 911 call with no one on the other end of the line—the narrower the capability gap between the leading power and the secondary power, the less secure the leading power.[2] The possibility that nations like Canada or Mexico may harm the United States, he speculates, is close to nonexistence whereas the likelihood of powers such as former Soviet Union or future China if it can keep its growth to inflict harm on the United States is not only real but also high. And the reason is simple: for the latter, the capability to do harm is there ready to be employed, all you need is the intention.

Mearsheimer argues, there is no way to discern what China's intentions vis-à-vis the United States or the global order might be in 10 years or 30 years down the road, but if one looks at what the United States has done since it became a superpower, it would not be hard to figure out what the Chinese will be up to in the future (Rosenkranz Foundation 2007). As this author pointed out in the criticism of China's official foreign policy philosophy (Zhang 2007), Chinese leaders' repeated pledge not to pursue hegemony even when China gets powerful is worthless. It runs right against the grain of historical materialism (still part of the official dogma in China) that holds that material basis determines the superstructure (ideology, political and legal institutions, and policies, etc.) and against the essence of realism of international relations that holds that the power position of a nation constrains its external behavior. Hegemony (behavior or policies) is but an expression of the unmatched power the hegemon possesses. China's decisions to date to shun hegemonic behavior is only because it does not currently possess the sufficient capabilities to behave in such a manner. Once the strength is there, so will follow the behavior. A superpower may pursue hegemony wittingly or unwittingly, which may take the form of "Manifest Destiny" or "Proletariat Internationalism," or it may as well take the form of "Harmonious World." The Chinese leaders have been too eager to show the world they have no intention whatsoever to dominate the region or the world regardless, only to arouse suspicion by other nations because this is like writing a check that is highly unlikely to be honored.

Wrong Prescription

While getting the diagnosis right, Mearsheimer wrote the wrong prescription for the United States. If China is going to be a threat to the United States anyway, what should the United States do? "(T)he best way is to make sure that you are by far the most powerful state in the international system." Or, again in his vivid language, "you want to be the biggest and baddest dude on the block, so that nobody fools around with you." OK, but how? Like reacting to all other rising powers in history up to vying for dominance with the United States, such as Imperial Germany, Imperial Japan, Nazi Germany, and the former Soviet Union, Mearsheimer declares that "We go to great lengths to stop them" (Zhang 2007). There is one problem though with this prescription. If China grows into a superpower, it will pose a threat to the United States and vice versa. Yet a threat is a *potential* harm and not a real one. To turn the potential harm into real overt conflict requires one more factor—hostility between the two powers. And here is where Mearsheimer's prescription is problematic. "To stop them"—it is one thing if the United States were to attempt and succeed in stopping China's rise. It is quite another should it try but fail. If it failed, it should be prepared to face the worst case scenario—the combination of a rising power and a hostile rival.

Mitigating Factors: Chinese Characteristics

It would be nice from the U.S. standpoint to stop China from being a threat and a rival but it would not be easy. The United States stopped Germany (twice) and Japan through world wars, but it's hard to imagine a war between two nuclear powers as a rational choice of strategy. The Soviet Union was stopped not by the United States, to the misperception of most Americans, but by a renegade from within. There was no sign indicating the Soviet state was unable to maintain its old orbit in late 1980s had it not been for Gorbachev's disintegrating political reform. To compare with the difficulties the Soviet Union had experienced from the 1920s through early 1980s, the situation of the Soviet Union in late 1980s, both domestic and international, was by no means particularly adverse. A similar collapse occurring in China is indeed possible, and even probable thanks to the Western efforts led by the United States under the banner of "Peaceful Evolution." Yet it would be too opportunistic and imprudent to put all the hope for future U.S. security completely in the self-annihilation of the anticipated danger. Does that mean, then, the prospect of the U.S. security looks quite grim?

Not necessarily. In our current case, although China's great power status would pose a threat to the United States, how "clear and present" the danger would be would depend on how good or bad the bilateral relationship would be and on how strong an ambition China would have to rival with the United States for domination. These two variables leave much room for the United States to maneuver which may make quite a difference.

Best Time for Sino-U.S. Relations?

In general bilateral relations depend on both sides—their interactive attitudes and policies. In Sino-U.S. relations, however, the United States has been more responsible for the direction of the relationship. Looking back at the recent history of Sino-U.S. relations since the 1970s, a pattern based on two observations can be easily discerned: Number one, the United States has been the more active party that takes the initiative to set agenda, raise issues, and put forth demands, whereas China usually takes the passive role of following, responding, and accommodating; number two, the United States has mostly if not always been the aggressive party that uses high-handed tactics to pressure the Chinese government into concession, whereas China usually takes the defensive role to compromise and appease. Among disputes the two countries have had in the past decades, a significant part focuses on human rights and trade issues (including intellectual property rights) with a pattern in which the United States made accusations and demands while Chinese officials scrambled for explanations and self-defenses before finally going at least halfway to meet American requirements to save the relationship. Another major part of the disputes involves Taiwan where the pattern goes as follows: the United States usually takes initiative in action (arms sales in most cases, or allowing Taiwan leaders into the United States) to which the Chinese government would protest and react with diplomatic or military postures (against Taiwan) only to no avail.

It is not unfair to say, therefore, that from China's perspective, most tensions in Sino-U.S. relations in the past decades were provoked by the United States. The political support and military protection as well as the numerous arms sales rendered to Taiwan not only violate the sovereignty of China but also infringe the treaty-like communiqués between the two countries. The United States not only imposes strict embargos of high tech and military products on China but also goes to extra length to prevent other nations from selling arms to China. It went as far as forcing Israel to cancel a signed contract to sell AWACS airborne prewarning system to China, and to detain the Falcon surveillance planes China had already bought and used but sent back for maintenance. The United States has provided shelter and support for all kinds of anti-Chinese government forces ranging from democratic movement organizations, to separatist groups from Taiwan, Tibet, Xinjiang, and other parts of China, to Falungong and even terrorist group such as the East Turkestan Islamic Movement. In several instances, U.S. authorities have prevented Chinese businesses from acquiring American companies or their interests by invoking U.S. national security concerns. Despite all of this, in recent years China has joined some high ranking American officials to depict U.S.-China relations as having "the best time in three decades," showing satisfaction rather than resentment.

To be sure, China's "softness" toward the United States may well be explained by its lack of "position of strength" the United States nevertheless enjoys. Yet if one looks at the way China handled the territorial disputes in the South China Sea in recent decades in which Chinese fishing boats were often bombarded and/or detained by the navy of neighboring nations, one may find, curiously, that the pattern is not China the big guy bullying over the smaller ones but just the opposite. This phenomenon should lead people to think about factors not on the surface related to national power but deep down at the philosophical level that may help configure China's external behavior.

Ever since Confucius, mainstream Chinese philosophies have emphasized the ideas of *he*(1) and *he*(2), two different characters with the same pronunciation, and that's why the Chinese culture is sometimes called "*he-he*" culture. The first "*he*" means peace, kind, together, and harmony, whereas the second "*he*" means join, combine, unite, and inclusion. As the two concepts suggest, Chinese philosophies cherish the values that are very different from what the prevailing Western philosophies do. For instance, while competition is taken a good thing for social/economic progress and "survival of the fittest" a natural law in Western cultures and social norms, the "*he-he*" culture instead teaches "peace/cooperation is the most precious in the world" and preaches egalitarianism. While the American "tough-guy" culture admires heroes who are strong and tough, the Chinese "he-he" culture sympathizes with people who are weak and soft. While the former champions the virtues of power, struggle, and prevalence, the latter advocates the value of endurance, reconciliation, and compromise. While the former sees conflict a normal part of social life through which one upholds one's values and interests, the latter deems it an evil that should be avoided at any price. Therefore in Chinese classical literature there are tons of maxims teaching people to shun conflict, such as "stoop to compromise," "take misfortune as fortune," "take humiliation and swallow anger," and so on. With everlasting indoctrination as such, the inclination of conflict-avoiding and compromise-making has become a national characteristic of the Chinese nation when confronted by other nations. Judging from Chinese history and culture, and the history of China's foreign relations in particular, it is hard to imagine that China would be the one to cause hostility in future Sino-U.S. relations unless it is deliberately provoked. Therefore, only if the United States could treat China with some more respect for its national sovereignty, and on the basis of equality instead of tutelage, Sino-U.S. relations are bound to improve as time passes. And the better relationship the United States has with China, the less threat it would feel from the great power status China is anticipated to attain, just as it doesn't feel much threatened by its Western European allies.

What's Good for Goose Is Good for Gander?

In speculating about what strategic goal China will pursue upon growing into a great power, Professor Mearsheimer used this proverb he learned from" his mother as a boy—to predict that like the United States and all other great powers in history, China would seek dominance of its own, first in Asia and then globally, and hence become a threat to the U.S. hegemony. A Chinese proverb may help strike the point home: Just like "The ditch follows where the water flows through," hegemony arises where superpower grows. This is a general rule in international politics. Having said that, though, a caveat should be mentioned right away: There may be exceptions to the rule, or at least factors that may weaken—not invalidate—the rule by mitigating the intensity with which the newly grown superpower pursues dominance.

And one such factor is the ambition to dominate. Not all nations have the same ambition to dominate the region/world. Again, it has something to do with the nation's history and culture. In Chinese history there was a mysterious anomaly that flies in the face of the general rule about human nature in pursuing dominance: At the beginning of the fifteenth century when China was the superpower of the world, a huge Chinese fleet equipped with the most advanced technology in ship-building and the most modern navigation know-how at the time launched an exploration of the world with eight expeditions into the West Pacific and the Indian Ocean in a span of three decades, reaching the land of dozens of countries today and as far as East Africa. Just at a moment when China had the best chance to expand its rule and build a huge empire in this vast area, to the surprise and puzzlement of historians, the Chinese emperor ordered the burning of all Chinese fleet and banned all ocean-going voyages from then on. China had since turned inward until its door was bombarded open by the gunboats of Western powers 300 years later. The lack of interest in domination on the part of China can also be discerned in another unique phenomenon in Chinese history—the Tributary State System where imperial China did not seek actual control of its tributaries but only nominal submission—to show respect only.

This kind of "inward" mentality and disinterest in expansion of territory or influence has to do with a stream of traditional wisdom in Chinese culture. Unlike Western norms that encourage outgoing enterprise and pioneer spirit that knows no limit, one major virtue enshrined in Chinese philosophical classics has been "complacence." For example, Lao Tzu revealed that "A contented man is never disappointed. He who knows when to stop does not find himself in trouble. He will stay forever safe"[3] whereas another Han Dynasty classic had this famous teaching "Wealth lies in complacence while nobility lies in retreat."[4] And the proverb adds: "Always happy the contended." One should stay complacent and keep a low profile because it is just too risky to seek prominence in a world full of danger, against which too many maxims warned in lines such as "the bird sticking its head out gets shot," "big tree gets more wind" (one Chinese-English Dictionary translates the idiom this way: "A person of high position is liable to be attacked" and "doomed the pig gaining weight, doomed the man gaining fame," and so on. Remember Deng Xiaoping's famous warning for Chinese foreign policy? "Never be the head (of any group)!" Does he sound just another ancient sage? The Chinese may simply not like domination so much as Americans do, or as Americans think the Chinese do. After all, what is good for the goose is not necessarily good for the gander.

It is very difficult to know today what kind of worldview the Chinese would possess if their country grew into a superpower—if they would still stay comfortably with their cultural heritage or if they would have abandoned it for the modern Western (American) philosophy of "go get it." With the philosophical genes of being modest and moderate in the nation's blood, however, the chances are that China would not choose to be a radical challenger to the status quo and to the American hegemony but rather a responsible stakeholder of the current international order, as Americans have expected it to be and as it has actually been so far, or an incremental reformer at most in the future when the time is ripe. But all this prediction has one premise and that the current hegemon the United States will maintain the relative fairness or the legitimacy of the current system. Should the U.S. stack the cards in order to stop China's rise, China might be forced into the role of a challenger rather than a stakeholder.

The United States does have the choice of trying to stop China's development, but the risk is just too high: if it failed the United States would face a hostile rival determined to challenge the status quo. The United States also has the choice of letting China's rise play itself out while keeping U.S.-China relations manageable if not friendly and keeping U.S. hegemony legitimate and fair, so if and when China does grow into a superpower, the threat it poses would be minimized.

Notes

I want to thank the College of Liberal Arts (Political Science Department and Institute of Global Studies) at University of Minnesota for my appointment as Visiting Professor during the 2007–2008 academic year that supported my writing this chapter. I also want to thank the Mount Holyoke College for sponsoring the conference where I got the chance to present the paper and got feedback. I appreciate the help I have got for this paper from Steven Rosenstone,

Raymond Duvall, Peter Katzenstein, Susan Shirk, and the editors of this volume who have aided in different ways. All errors and responsibilities remain my own.

1. "Analysis of Regional Disparity in Economic Development". http://zhidao. baidu.com/question/41595945.html?fr=qrl, (accessed June 11, 2008).
2. Intelligence Squared U.S. Debate Results: China Not a Threat to America. http://news.findlaw.com/prnewswire/20070518/18may20071115.html (accessed February 3, 2008).
3. Lao Tsu, "zhizu buru, zhizhi budai, keyi changjiu," (Tao Te Ching [Ethics]), Chapter 44. http://elyxr.com/tao/index.cfm?fuseaction=chapter&ch=44 (accessed June 15, 2008).
4. Liu Xiang (Han Dynasty), "fuzai zhizu, guizai qiutui." (shuoyuan-tancong [Forum/Discourse]), http://www.dfg.cn/big5/zhhy/jdcy/jdcy-01.htm, (accessed June 15, 2008).

References

Chinese Newsweek. 2008. Extramarital Affairs Become Number One Killer of Marriage. January 18. http://gb.cri.cn/18824/2008/01/18/2185@1917725.htm (accessed February 3, 2008).

CIA (Central Intelligence Agency). 2008. The World Factbook. https://www.cia. gov/library/publications/the-world-factbook/index.html.

Ding Bing. 2006. Causes and Solution of China's Polarization. *TECN* September 14. http://www.tecn.cn/data/detail.php?id=11053(accessed February 3, 2008).

Duan Xiaohua and Yulin Liu. 2005. Assessment of China's International Competitiveness 2004. http://www.sts.org.cn/fxyj/zcfx/documents/20050822. htm (accessed June 11, 2008).

He Ya. 2007. Gini Coefficient: De-structing Historical Urban-Rural Policy in China. *China's State of Nation* April 11. http://www.stats.gov.cn/tjshujia/ zggqgl/t20070411_402398097.htm (accessed February 3, 2008).

Hu Angang. 2007. China: Toward Coordinated Regional Development. *DRCnet* October 29. http://www.drcnet.com.cn/DRCNet.Channel.Web/expert/ showdoc.asp?doc_id=199234 (accessed June 11, 2008).

International Herald Leader. 2005. Why China's International Competitiveness Ranking Slips? September 25. http://news.xinhuanet.com/herald/2005-09/29/ content_3561488.htm (accessed February 3, 2008).

McGregor, Richard. 2007. 750,000 a Year Killed by Chinese Pollution. Financial Times July 2. http://www.ft.com/cms/s/0/8f40e248-28c7-11dc-af78-000b5df10621.html (accessed August 26, 2008).

Rosenkranz Foundation. 2007. Beware the Dragon: A Booming China Spells Trouble for America. Intelligence Squared US Transcript of the Debate. http:// www.intelligencesquaredus.org/TranscriptContainer/China.pdf.

Science Daily. 2008. Alarming Growth in Expected Carbon Dioxide Emissions in China, Analysis Finds. March 11. http://www.sciencedaily.com/releases/2008/03/080310155857.htm (accessed August 26, 2008).

Xinhua Dispatch. 2005. Five Major Challenges during the 11th Five Year Plan. October 22. http://news.xinhuanet.com/politics/2005–10/22/content_3667933. htm (accessed June 11, 2008).

———. 2006. 2006 Global Competitiveness Ranking, Swiss on Top, China 54th. September 27. http://news.xinhuanet.com/fortune/2006–09/27/content_5141643.htm (accessed February 3, 2008).

Wang Jisi. 2007. A Few Points on the Making of China's International Strategy. International Political Studies. Peking University Press. http://www.chinaelections. com/NewsInfo.asp?NewsID=120695 (accessed February 3, 2008).

Wang Yuanhong. 2006. Chinese Gini Approaches 0.47. *Xinhua Dispatch* March 13. http://news.xinhuanet.com/fortune/2006–03/13/content_4298060.htm (accessed February 3, 2008).

World Bank. 2005. International Comparison Program Preliminary Results. Washington, DC: World Bank.

———. 2008. World Trade Indicators. http://go.worldbank.org/3Q2ER38J50.

Zhang Ruizhuang. 2007. Zhongguo waijiao zhexue de lixiangzhuyi qingxiang (The Idealistic Predisposition of China's Foreign Policy Philosophy), 21st Century. Hong Kong: Chinese University, February.

Chapter 12

Is China Rising?

Sheena Chestnut and Alastair Iain Johnston

Introduction

Is China rising? How do we know? The vast majority of today's commentary—in the United States and China, across the policy, pundit, and academic worlds—assumes that China is rising. But the vast majority also does not provide a clear definition of "rising," or consistent indicators of what a rising state looks like. This chapter makes a simple but often overlooked point: whether China is rising—and at what speed—depends on one's definition and indicators. Some suggest that China is rising rapidly, while others suggest that it is not—yet. While it may seem facile to contest the rise of China—few would argue that China is not somehow "bigger" today than yesterday—we believe that injecting a note of caution into the debate is worthwhile. The reason is that different perceptions and judgments about whether, how, and how fast China is rising have profound real-world implications.

We begin by outlining some of the conceptual and empirical "pluralism" that characterizes the rising China discourse. We then show that China is currently situated in relation to the hegemon (the United States) in material power terms such that it is not yet closing the gap. But if China continues to grow at a faster rate than the United States, then the mathematics of differential growth rates mean that China will begin to close the gap—and one will legitimately be able to claim that it is rising. We next comment on the question of China's soft power—a popular term of late—and conclude that there are reasons to be skeptical of its utility. We finish with a discussion of the implications of different measurements of China's "rise." The point of all this is an obvious one—we need to be very careful about how we use the term "rising China" because it has consequences for potential Sino-U.S. conflict.

The Rising China Discourse

The term "rising China" is seen everywhere these days. For instance, articles referencing "rising China" in LexisNexis (General News) increased almost 10 times from around 65 in 1995 to over 600 in 2006. Similarly in the same period, the frequency of articles on international relations and politics in Chinese academic journal that mention either "China's rise" (*zhongguo de jueqi*) and/or "rising China" (*jueqi zhongguo*) increased about 27 times from 35 to 940.

Despite this increasingly common description, there is little consensus in academic discourse or political rhetoric about where it leaves China vis-à-vis the United States. Hillary Clinton recently called China a "global superpower."[1] Bates Gill refers to China as "a rising star in the constellation of great powers" (2007:1). One pundit claims, "China is already a rival of the United States in many important areas" (Ramo 2004). Others are more restrained. One group of scholars wrote recently, "it will be a decade, if not two, before China has a world-class economy and military establishment" (Kupchan et al. 2001:4), while others place China's surpassing of the United States, "sometime before the middle of this century" (Lemke 2003:270). Avery Goldstein refers to China as a "rising but not yet risen power" (Goldstein 2005:29), while David Kang calls it a "major regional power" (Kang 2007:3, 12).

Chinese characterizations of the country's status or position also vary, within narrower bounds. Chinese analysts have referred to China as everything from a not-yet superpower second only to the United States (Yan 2006:10, 18; Hu and Men:23); to a "cross-regional major power" (*kuadiqu de daguo*);[2] to a "regional-type major power with global influence" (*you shijie yingxiang de diyu xing daguo*) (Renwei 2006:22); to a "developing major power starting to have an impact on Asian regional affairs" (*zai Yahzou diqu shiwu zhong kaishi fahui zuoyong de fazhanzhong daguo*) (22). One PLA Air Force analyst argued that due partly to a lack of land and sea space for potential expansion, the People's Republic of China's (PRC) only choice is to be a regional great power (*diquxing daguo*).[3] Others suggest that China's rise is severely constrained by lagging "informatization," low Gross Domestic Product (GDP) per capita, a large and inefficient agricultural sector, income inequality, and rising social welfare costs.[4]

Each claim is based on a particular implicit or explicit conceptualization of "rising." There is, however, little agreement over valid and reliable indicators of a rising state. Different conceptualizations and indicators lead to different conclusions about whether China is rising. Below we discuss several conceptualizations and assess in a heuristic fashion the empirical validity of each.

Historical (vis-à-vis a state's past). The terms *fuxing* (revival), *zhuanxing* (transformation), or *zhenxing* ([re]vitalization) have all been used to describe China's recent growth. These terms reference China's past role as a powerful state as their baseline, focusing on the country's recovery from dramatic weakness from external threats and internal chaos in the nineteenth and early twentieth century (Deng and Wang 2005:56, Khong in Kupchan et al. 2001:54). It seems self-evident that China is wealthier and more powerful today than in the last century of the Qing dynasty.

Visibility. The state is economically and politically present in more places around the globe (e.g., China's activities in Africa and Latin America). Increased visibility is perhaps best captured in a passage by Ted Fishman beginning, "China is everywhere these days" (2005:1–7). Here, too, few would deny that China is more visible to more people than ever before, certainly in the post-Mao period.

Influence. The state is more proactive and has more impact on outcomes in global political, military, and economic affairs. Bates Gill writes, "A day does not go by when events and decisions in China do not resonate in capital markets and political capitals" (2007:xvii, Shambaugh 2005). Its actions affect ordinary people's lives in more issues and at higher levels ("[China] is influencing our lives as consumers, employees, and citizens").[5] Hyperbole aside, by this definition it is probably correct to say that China is rising (though one could say the same thing, to a lesser degree, of other large, rapidly developing countries such as India).

Threat to the Hegemon's Interests. Rather than capabilities, rising states might challenge the hegemon's security *interests*.[6] For example, some analysts observe that China is developing anti-access capabilities with which it could limit the U.S. Pacific naval presence (Cliff et al. 2007, Rapkin and Thompson 2003:335).[7] Others remain confident that ongoing modernization of U.S. capabilities and deployment make it likely that the United States will prevail in any conventional military conflict (Blair 2008).

Innovation. A rising state could be one whose "radical technological innovation" enables it to challenge the hegemon's economic leadership or military potential (Rapkin and Thompson 2003:315–342). While some scholars believe that China is vastly technologically inferior and will "have to scramble to compete in the information age" (Copeland 2000), others wonder if informationalization could enable China to catch the United States faster than under past metrics. Put differently, how far are the PRC and the United States from harnessing the transformational effects of the next Revolution in Military Affairs?[8] Here the lack of consensus on what these technologies and organizational innovations might be makes measuring China's progress relative to the United States problematic.

Threat to Hegemonic Order. Rather than challenging the hegemon's interests, a rising state might contest dominant norms of "international order" itself. Some scholars argue that China's authoritarian governance challenges the prevailing Western liberal order (Barma and Ratner 2006). Others suggest that compared to the Maoist period, China has become much more involved in and supportive of international institutions, and acceptant of international norms—to the extent these exist—than ever before (Jacobson and Oksenberg 1990, Johnston 2003, Gill 2007).

Size. Often "rising" denotes a state getting bigger or obtaining more resources. A "rising" state could expand geography and capabilities through conquest (Liebman 2008:7, Gilpin 1981:187), or by allying with others (Liebman 2008:7, Woosang 1989).[9] In international relations, power is often measured by material capabilities, such as GDP, military spending, or Correlates of War National Capabilities data.

Current work on the changing "size" of Chinese power encounters three problems. First, though China is clearly searching for resources, the expansion of its resource base has thus far not been through conquest (Taylor Fravel 2005). And China has acquired no new formal alliance relationships since the start of its alleged rise. (Some see the Shanghai Cooperation Organization [SCO] has having anti-American elements, but the SCO currently lacks sufficient military coordination to constitute anything close to a formal alliance.)

Second, different indicators produce different conclusions. The Correlates of War Composite Index of National Capability data, for instance, exaggerate China's power by counting total population as an asset. The data also conclude that China essentially caught the United States in the early 1980s.[10] If one uses iron/steel production—core elements of the COW-CINC data—China began catching up in the mid-1960s and surpassed the United States in the early 1990s.[11] The "largest drop-off" rule—a rising/contending power i is the state where the difference between the hegemon's power and state i's power is smaller than the difference between state i and the next-largest state j's power—shows that Japan was the only contender to the United States from the early 1980s to the mid-1990s, after which there has been none.[12]

A third problem is whether one should use relative or absolute comparisons. That is, a rising state could be one whose capabilities constitute an increasing *proportion* of a more powerful state's (e.g., China's capabilities as a percentage of U.S. capabilities). Or the rising state is one whose *absolute* capabilities are closing in on those of a more powerful state (e.g., the absolute gap between China's capabilities and U.S. capabilities is shrinking). The difference between the two will be explored further in subsequent sections, but to telegraph our argument: China is rising in relative terms, but not yet in absolute terms.

Intersubjective Expectations. Finally, a rising state may be one whose economic and military development is *expected* to be so rapid that it moves quickly into the ranks of the system's most powerful states (Kennedy 2007:1, Liebman 2008:7–8). By this conceptualization, it may not matter what the indicators show; as long as everyone believes China is rising, actors in the international system will behave accordingly. As our earlier discussion shows, there is little doubt that Chinese and American leaders believe China is rising.

In sum, even granted some legitimate debate over operationalization of definitions, it is clear that different definitions lead to different conclusions about whether China is rising:

Table 12.1 Definitions of "rising"

Definition of "rising"	Is China "rising"?
Historical	Yes
Visibility	Yes
Influence	Yes
Threat to hegemon's core security interests	Unclear
Innovation	Unclear
Threat to hegemonic order	No
Size	
getting more of some key resource	Yes
alliance construction	No
territorial expansion	No
as a proportion of hegemon's power	Yes
closing the absolute gap in the hegemon's power advantage	No (not yet)
Intersubjective expectation	Yes

Note: These answers are for heuristic purposes, as some are based on less rigorous empirical testing than others.

While most of these definitions and indicators provide insight into the changing nature of Chinese power, we believe that the most important are size and intersubjective expectations. This is due to their interactive effects on how decision makers react to China's evolution. Specifically, real-world policy implications can arise from mismatches between intersubjective expectations of China's rise (often based on observations of increased visibility and influence), and the more nuanced picture drawn from data on relative and absolute differences between Chinese and American power. Below we explore the latter distinction in greater depth.

Rising Power: Relative and Absolute Calculations

As noted above, a wide range of conceptualizations exist in recent discourse about China's growth. But we believe that intuitively, "rising" is a question of how China's changes compare to the capabilities of the system hegemon, the United States, and that a commonsense way of thinking about rising is "catching up." What does that mean?

In international relations, there are typically two ways of measuring relative power between two actors—capabilities as a percentage of the dominant state's, and the absolute difference between the dominant state's capabilities and those of weaker challengers. In terms of the former, catching up means that state B's capabilities as a percent of A's are increasing. In terms of the latter, catching up means that the absolute gap between A's and B's capabilities is getting smaller.

For many people, both of these examples suggest that state B is rising. Yet the simple mathematics of differential growth rates show that, under certain common conditions, B can be increasing its capabilities as a share of state A while simultaneously falling behind in absolute capabilities. Suppose A and B start out with the following distribution of power and differential growth rates. A has 100 units of power and grows at 5 percent per year. State B has 10 units of power, but grows at 10 percent per year. If one projects out (see figure 12.1), state A's absolute advantage in power capabilities expands until year 36, even as B's capabilities as a percent of A's increase. Why? Because state A starts with such a large lead.

At some point (here, year 37), differential growth rates may have a tipping effect: the absolute gap favoring A begins to decline and B begins to catch up: that is, it begins to rise. This tipping point can happen sooner or later, depending on the difference in growth rates, but will inevitably occur as long as B's growth rate is higher.

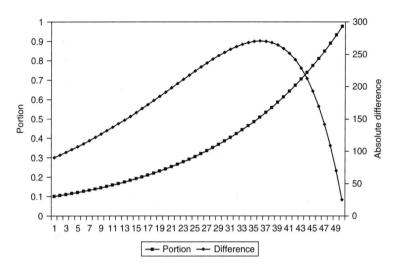

Figure 12.1 The difference between relative and absolute indicators of power: B's power as a portion of A versus the absolute difference between A and B's power

The absolute difference indicates that, at base, state A has a growing cache of resources relative to B with which to create military capabilities, distribute aid, or cement alliances—in other words, resources for internally or externally balancing against B. The growth in B's relative power indicates that the states are on a trajectory whereby at some point—assuming roughly constant differential in growth rates and linearity—a tipping point is reached. It means that B has more resources at time $t+n$ than at time t, some of which can be devoted to military capabilities. But it also means B's gain in resources is, for a time, overwhelmed by the resources A gains between time t and time $t+n$. We often think that if B is rising relative to A, it gets more and more of its will/way compared to A due to increased resources. But how is this possible during the period when A's absolute advantage in resources—carrots and sticks—is increasing?

Figure 12.2 shows (using iron/steel production) that the United States did not begin to "rise" vis-à-vis the most powerful state in the system—Great Britain—until the early 1870s. After the Civil War, U.S. power as a portion of Great Britain's grew, even as the absolute gap in capabilities favored Great Britain by wider margins. A similar pattern shows up in the case of Germany in the nineteenth century—though its power as a proportion of Great Britain's increased from the 1850s onward, Germany didn't start to rise vis-à-vis Britain until later in the 1870s.

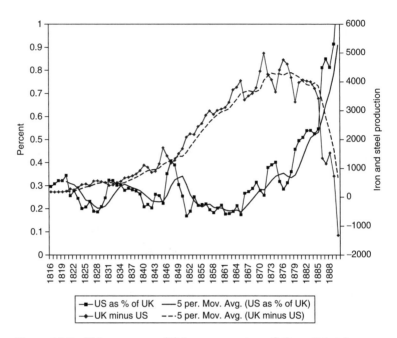

Figure 12.2 U.S. power capabilities as a portion of Great Britain's power capabilities; the absolute difference in U.S. and UK power capabilities

It strains the concept to suggest that the United States and Germany were rising when Great Britain's absolute advantage in capabilities was actually increasing. If we did so, we would also have to characterize *any* state with a faster growth rate than the United States (and a good chance of sustaining it over the long term) as a rising power. This does not fit a commonsensical notion of rising power.

Relative and Absolute Change in the Sino-U.S. Power Relationship

Today, the China-U.S. case appears to be following the theoretical and historical examples outlined above: China's power as a proportion of U.S. power is increasing, but the absolute advantage in capabilities favoring America continues to widen. China and the United States have not yet reached the tipping point indicating the beginning of rising Chinese power. This pattern holds for a wide range of standard indicators that one might use to measure power capabilities—economic (GDP), military (military spending), and scientific-technological metrics (Gilpin 1981).

GDP

According to the World Bank, in current U.S. dollars China's GDP as a percent of U.S. GDP has gone from about 13 percent in 2001 to almost 20 percent in 2006.[13] The absolute difference in GDP, however, has increased in the U.S. favor from US$8.8 trillion to US$10.5 trillion over this same period, a 20 percent increase (see figure 12.3). Figure 12.4 projects out China's GDP as a percent of the U.S. GDP and the absolute difference in GDPs using a very optimistic unchanging estimate for PRC GDP growth of 10 percent year.[14] Even using the most optimistic projections, China falls further behind in absolute terms until around 2014. If one assumes a slightly slower Chinese growth rate (8 percent), then the tipping point is delayed another eight or so years.

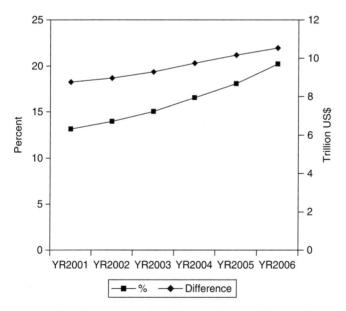

Figure 12.3 The relative and absolute difference between U.S. and China GDP

Source: World Bank Development Indicators.

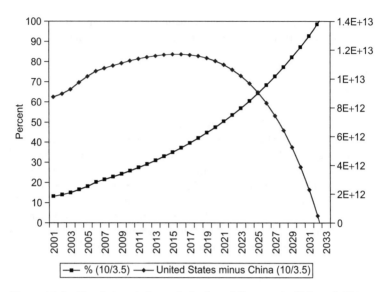

Figure 12.4   Trends in relative and absolute differences in U.S. and Chinese GDP

Source: World Bank Development Indicators to 2006; thereafter assumes 10% growth in Chinese GDP and 3.5% growth in American GDP.

Military Spending

A similar pattern appears in U.S. and Chinese military spending. As figure 12.5 shows, China's spending as a percentage of U.S. spending has increased steadily, especially since the mid-1990s. In 1997 China stood at about 5 percent of U.S. military spending, but in 2006 it approached 10 percent. Yet at the same time, due to its enormous head start, the U.S. advantage in military spending went from around US$320 billion to almost US$480 billion; the American absolute advantage in military spending increased by about 50 percent.

Science, Technology, and Information Integration

Science and technology (S&T) development and "informationalizaton" are often seen as central to power production in the postindustrial age. Here, too, the pattern of China's development is one of increasing as a proportion of U.S. capabilities while falling behind in absolute terms. Figure 12.6 shows this pattern using Chinese and U.S. patent data; polynomial trend

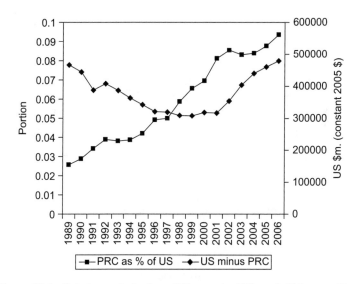

Figure 12.5 Relative and absolute difference in U.S. and Chinese military spending
Source: SIPRI Yearbook (2007).

lines illustrate an increase in both China's proportion and the U.S. absolute advantage.

China's contribution to science patents around the globe is not impressive. In key areas such as nanotechnology and biotechnology, for instance, Chinese patents constitute a miniscule portion of those from the United States,[15] even though China's average annual growth rate in patents is the world's highest. In wind-energy, fuel cell, space-related, and nuclear power technology, China simply does not register as a source of patents (OECD 2007:21–28; Lampton 2008:132).

Measures of China's engagement with global information systems confirm the familiar pattern. According to the International Communication and Technology Opportunity Index (ICT-OI)—which measures information density and use—China's figure as a portion of the United States is mostly increasing, while the absolute difference continues to favor the United States (ITU 2007:120).

Various other organizations have tried to develop globalization indices to measure the degree of economic, political, social, and technological connectivity to the rest of the world. Typically China tends not to rank very high (limited, undoubtedly, by its large, relatively poor rural population). In A.T. Kearney's globalization index, China fell from 2006 (fifty-first

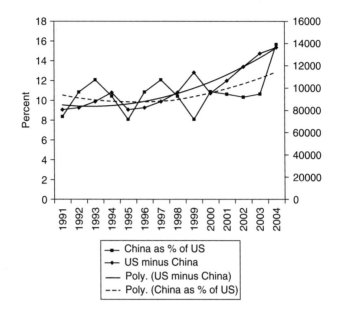

Figure 12.6   Chinese and U.S. patent applications (by residents)

Source: World Bank Development Indicators.

Note: China's 2005 patent applications to the European, U.S., and Japanese patent offices constituted 0.5%, 1.1%, and < 0.1% of total applications, respectively (OECD 2007).

place) to 2007 (sixty-sixth).[16] In an index developed by the Swiss Federal Institute of Technology, China was ranked forty-third in 2005—up from sixty-second in 1990, but still only around the level for Bulgaria, Ukraine, and Romania.[17]

At least three conclusions flow from this discussion. First, China has more material capabilities compared to its past; relative to its own history, China is clearly rising. Second, in comparison to the U.S. hegemon, it is not clear that China is yet rising. Although its power as a proportion of the United States is increasing, in absolute terms one might fairly conclude that China is less powerful vis-à-vis the United States than in the past, and will continue to decline through to at least 2015 (possibly further, depending on GDP growth rates). Third, however, China is on a trajectory to begin closing the absolute gap sometime after the next eight years: it is not yet a rising power, but a potential one.

A decline in the absolute difference in capabilities between the hegemon and the rising power may not be the best definition for all purposes. But we find it useful to illustrate that a weaker state having an increased percentage of a hegemon's capabilities is not equivalent to catching up.

The Question of Soft Power

Ever since Joseph Nye popularized the term, Western and Chinese analysts have tried to decide how "soft power" (*ruan shili*) relates to China's so-called rise. Like material power, soft power is discussed in different ways by different people. The concept is not new to Chinese discourse (Wuthnow 2008). Since the 1980s, Chinese analysts have tried to calculate the country's comprehensive national power (CNP) using a range of hard metrics and soft indicators (e.g., diplomatic influence, domestic cohesion) (Hu and Men:23), occasionally attempting to compare China's soft power to that of others (Yan and Xu 2008).

Today, soft power refers to Nye's conceptualization: the "ability to get what you want through attraction rather than coercion or payments" (2006). This definition differs from popular usage, which often incorporates material threats and incentives; several recent studies of Chinese soft power redefine the term as everything except hard military capability, thus almost guaranteeing that China is a rising soft power (Kurlantzick 2007:6, Whitney and Shambaugh 2008, CRS 2008:3).[18] Furthermore, at its most parsimonious, soft power also excludes social threats and promises; it rules out diplomatic pressure based on praising or shaming other states. What remains is pure persuasion, whereby attractiveness of values and ideas leads actors to change policy preferences.

Discussions of soft power often refer to factors such as popular cultural and ideological flows as examples. Questions remain, however, as to how precisely these flows change the preferences of relevant actors in other countries. How does popular culture translate into political influence? How does consumption of American fast food or movies lead to changes in state leaders' foreign policy preferences? Through an electoral process where voters are influenced by values embodied in American cultural products? Through indirect public opinion constraints on authoritarian leaders? One scholar suggests that the malleability of global culture means that "democracy could be short-lived if for any reason (such as the 'rise of China') authoritarianism should again become an attractive and exalted model" (Lynch 2006:27). But how would China's model foster authoritarianism elsewhere? By leading voters to favor leaders who will subsequently revoke their political privileges? By emboldening coups?

In the Chinese case, how precisely will Confucius Institutes influence the society and politics of host countries? One common perception is that these institutions—as well as educational exchanges such as the Fulbright program—cultivate elite familiarity and hopefully sympathy with Chinese positions (Wuthnow:11, Zhang 2006, Liu 2007).[19] Though

Confucian Institutes are a recent development, evidence suggests that their influence in fostering understanding of Chinese culture has thus far been limited.[20] Even if successful, however, cultural familiarity does not necessarily increase political influence. How much influence have Germany and France accrued from the Goethe Institutes or Alliance Francaise offices? The detailed causal micro-processes about how cultural flows foster political influence are very unclear.[21]

Ideological influence seems close to what Nye thinks constitutes genuine soft power. In the past century, four ideational waves or ideologies promoted by states have attracted sufficient adherents to lead to demands for change in other states' policy preferences: Fascism and Communism in early twentieth century, Nationalism in the developing world, and classical market ideology from the 1980s on. At least for a time, the attractiveness of these ideologies increased the influence of their main proponents in other countries as well as their own. But even if ideological attractiveness is a form of soft power not epiphenomenal to hard power considerations, the question remains: what ideology, exactly, does China have to market that might translate into political or strategic influence?[22] How would one know if it did? Is it rising? Is there a tipping point or power transition in soft power relationships? How would we recognize it?

Some argue that attractive elements of China's ideological or value system include prioritization of order, family, community, and social harmony. But these are not uniquely Chinese. Essentially these are "social conservative" values, already shared by certain conservative parts of the Christian and Muslim traditions. And thus far, the Chinese government has not been a particularly efficient or enthusiastic proselytizer. In contrast to the implied universalism of liberal democratic models, Chinese social conservatism is often articulated in context-dependent terms: what is appropriate for the West is not necessarily appropriate for less developed countries or ones with different cultural values (Sullivan 1999). As with the "Beijing Consensus," this particularism renders the "China model" less exportable.

Others argue that the so-called Beijing Consensus development model is prime example of China's soft power. Sometimes touted as the answer to the failed Washington Consensus, the Beijing Consensus (or China model) rejects the former's emphasis on fiscal discipline, public spending on primary education and health care infrastructure, an increasing tax base, market-based interest rates, exchange rate and trade liberalization, privatization of state enterprises, deregulation, and protection of property rights (Williamson 2002). The Beijing Consensus, then, can be seen as another element of China's challenge to U.S. hegemony, this time to American-style capitalism and free market economic liberalism—a soft power challenge.

But what is the Beijing Consensus? The person who coined the term, Joshua Cooper Ramos, claims it is a pragmatic rejection of one-size-fits-all development strategies, seeking to temper marketization with state-directed efforts to protect equality and social welfare. Others call it authoritarianism plus socialized capitalism. A Shanghai academic suggests that it is an alternative to Westernization for a developing world wishing "to grasp the opportunities of globalization," thereby diversifying international politics (Wang 2008). The normative claim underlying some Beijing Consensus rhetoric is that Western-style liberalization was inappropriately forced upon developing states by more economically powerful Western countries; absent that pressure, countries will be more likely to follow a development path closer to China's own.

As an expression of soft power, however, the Beijing Consensus is problematic. First, it is not clear that the term has much content or effect. Ramos himself noted that the core of the Beijing Consensus model is that there is no model—each country chooses its own development route.[23] Yet, it is hard to see how another state choosing its own development path translates into greater political influence for the PRC specifically. How precisely does the Beijing Consensus lead others to change foreign policy preferences to favor China or undermine U.S. hegemony? Does following some elements of the so-called China model make authoritarian leaders more likely to adopt anti-American foreign policy positions, or is it an expression of preexisting anti-U.S. sentiments? The Beijing Consensus' attractiveness may be an effect, not a cause, of dissatisfaction with the Washington Consensus and U.S.-dominated international order.

Second, given that China's economic development is not yet complete, any exacerbation of problems associated with the "Chinese model"—such as massive environmental and health problems, widening income inequality, and potential social instability—may yet weaken the attractiveness of the model, insofar as one exists (Wuthnow 2008:14, Men 2007, Zheng and Zhang 2007).

Third, and more fundamentally, the Beijing Consensus appears to be an intriguing example of the invention, reification, branding, and selling of an idea for which there may not be much evidence. Although developed by a foreigner, the Beijing Consensus term serves a useful purpose for Chinese nationalists to claim a difference between U.S. hegemony and China's rise—one reactionary, one progressive—without seriously examining the precise degree of this alleged difference. The Beijing Consensus discourse, along with the general focus on Chinese soft power, adds, however, to the outside impression of a China on the march, challenging U.S. hegemony not only materially but ideationally.[24]

Conclusion: Why It Matters

Noting that according to a moderately rigorous definition China is not yet rising does not mean that its economic growth or military modernization have little consequence. We are not resurrecting Gerald Segal's argument that China does not matter, that it is a "second-rank middle power that has mastered the art of diplomatic theater" (Segal 1999). Indeed, as Steve Chan notes, "China's sheer physical size and the rapid rate of its recent growth can be an obvious cause of concern by other states regardless of the extent of its relative power gain" (Chan 2008:25). China is increasingly capable of "posing problems without catching up" (Christensen 2001). China may not yet be closing the gap between it and the hegemon, but its effect on environmental degradation and primary product prices, to name just two examples, are already obvious.[25] China doesn't have to catch the United States—to "rise" in strict material power terms—to have a profound impact on nontraditional security and welfare issues—transnational crime, disease, and pollution. Even in security terms, it can confront the United States as a regional military contender well before it reaches parity.[26]

But behind Segal's contrarian claim was an important pedagogical point: be careful about discursive bandwagons. We would add a different word of caution (actually three words)—test, test, and test.[27] What should we expect to see empirically if China is indeed rising? Do we see it? How does one measure growing influence—the obvious consequence of rising power? How will we know whether the hype over China's "rise" is justified, or whether it will go the way of the 1980s discourse on "rising Japan"? Indeed, Japan once seemed poised to exploit large economic and technological advantages to catch the United States even faster than China today (Samuels 1992), though the economic trajectories of the two countries during the 1990s put a quick end to that debate. Concerns over China's internal stability and burgeoning social welfare costs may prove it more similar to Japan than current discourse suggests.

Why worry about the gap between the discourse and reality of China's rise? What may matter instead are people's *expectations* about China's trajectory—which are a product of rough rules of thumb and measurement heuristics. Past examples of these heuristics include the Soviet notion of "correlation of forces" or Mao's estimates of which superpower was on the "offensive." Clearly there is a shared *perception* that China is rising, and some analytic ground for the claim—why not leave it at that?

The risk—and therefore the need for greater conceptual care in policy and academic worlds—comes from the interactive effects of discursive choices on Sino-U.S. relations. There are at least four logical possibilities.

- If neither American nor Chinese leaders believe China is rising, then presumably the effect will be to dampen security dilemma dynamics in the relationship. As this chapter has demonstrated, however, this scenario is unlikely. The predominant view in America and much of China is that China's "hard power" and to some extent its "soft power" is rising, even if the two sides differ in their assessments of the extent and speed (see below).

- If American leaders do not think China is rising, while Chinese leaders believe it is, the U.S. response may seem insufficiently respectful, ignoring what Chinese leaders and citizens believe are legitimate claims to higher status. Events such as the 2005 anti-Japan protests and the 2008 demonstrations against Western criticism of China's Tibet policy underscore the power of Chinese nationalism (Shirk 2008:225–256; Gries 2005:112). Public opinion polling suggests that Chinese citizens isomorphize Chinese as a country and the Chinese people, attributing positive characteristics to both and treating an insult to one as an insult to the other (Johnston and Stockmann 2006:170).[28] This apparent sensitivity to external slights would thus be expected to exacerbate the effects of American discounting of China's power and status. Moreover, if American leaders do not believe China is rising, while Chinese leaders believe it is and act to ensure it does, then the United States may respond badly to a power transition for which it is unprepared.

- If American leaders think China is rising, while Chinese leaders do not, then the U.S. response—presumably an attempt to constrain or mold this rise—will seem to the latter an unjustified overreaction, a challenge to China's legitimate interests. In attempting to forestall China's rise, the United States may foster revisionist sentiments; classical power transition theory argues that powerful states must be *dissatisfied* to pose a threat to the hegemon (Organski and Kugler 1980, DiCicco and Levy 1999). But dissatisfaction does not inhere in subordinate power per se. It is a response to perceived treatment that is inconsistent with self-perceived status. This is, in essence, the concern behind Nye's comment that if one treats China as an enemy, it will become one. As above, the point to note is the risk posed by the mismatch between U.S. and Chinese beliefs.

- If both American and Chinese leaders believe China is rising, their beliefs may stoke current fears as to how the phenomenon poses threats or creates windows of opportunity on both sides. It may accentuate security dilemma dynamics, with all their attendant effects—arms racing, competition for politico-military influence, the dominance of decision making by hardliners, and socialization into perceptions of strategic rivalry, all conditions that tend to increase the probability of war (Copeland 2000:243–244, Lemke 2003, Vasquez 1993).

We believe this last possibility may characterize contemporary U.S.-China relations. Talk about "rising power" is not cheap if this talk is part of a power transition-type analysis based on faulty or lazy empirical claims. If we are correct about the implications of these four possibilities, it behooves scholars, pundits, and policymakers on both sides to be much more conceptually careful and rigorous in how they understand and talk about "rising" Chinese power.

Notes

Our thanks to Steve Chan, Michael Horowitz, Alex Liebman, Vipin Narang, and Richard Samuels for their careful readings of this chapter, and to Erin Baggott for excellent research assistance. All URLs in the footnotes were last accessed on July 30, 2008.

1. http://www.hillaryclinton.com/news/speech/view/?id=6196.
2. Su Hao, Foreign Affairs University, conversation with Alastair Iain Johnston (Beijing, June 2007).
3. Dai Xu. 2007. *Zhongguo shangwei dianding daguo jichu.* (China has not yet established the basis of being a great power). *Global Times.* June 28, p. 11.
4. Johnston gave presentations in Beijing and Hangzhou in summer 2007 on whether China is rising. Audience members often argued that severe economic inequities, endemic corruption, and environmental degradation all constrained China's rise.
5. Fishman (2005:1).
6. We thank Vipin Narang for this definition.
7. Rapkin and Thompson imply that China is rising if it can push the intersection between its "loss of strength gradient" and the U.S. "loss of strength gradient" further from Chinese territory.
8. We benefited from conversations with Michael Horowitz on RMAs as indicators of power.
9. Extant U.S.-centered alliances vastly outpower any foreseeable China-centered alliance.
10. On problems with using COW-CINC scores, see Chan (2008:11–25). For an earlier discussion of metrics, see Organski and Kugler (1980).

11. However, in an era of computerization, composite materials, and systems integration it would appear that iron and steel production may not be appropriate indicators of power.

12. Calculated using World Bank GDP data (2007). On the largest drop-off rule, see Chan (2008:21–22).

13. We use market exchange rate (MER) rather than PPP estimates of the size of the Chinese economy for two reasons. First, it avoids potential confusion caused by the 2008 World Bank revaluation of China's economy in PPP terms. Second, many economists believe that PPP estimates are appropriate for measuring standards of living, but not potential military or economic power. (Cooper 2005, Keidel 2008, World Bank 2008).

14. These projections do not address variation in quality and longevity of GDP components, environmental degradation and long-term costs of GDP growth, or resource strain from a rapidly aging population. All favor U.S. power.

15. In 2004, the United States held 40.3 percent of nanotech patents; China held 1 percent. (OECD 2007:Figure 3.2.1, p. 21).

16. Globalization Index Rankings. *Foreign Policy Online.* http://www.foreignpolicy.com/story/cms.php?story_id=4030#rankings.

17. 2008 KOF Index of Globalization. http://globalization.kof.ethz.ch/static/pdf/rankings_2008.pdf; KOF Index of Globalization.http://globalization.kof.ethz.ch/query/.

18. David Lampton uses "ideational power," which includes "leadership, human resources, innovation, and culture" (118).

19. See also Consul-General, PRC. 2004. "More Foreign Students Coming to China." March 19. http://www.nyconsulate.prchina.org/eng/xw/t80128.htm.

20. Their main market is high school students, business people, and Chinese descendants interested in improving language. Classes are small, and their impact relative to university programs is likely limited (Begin 2007, Xiaolin 2008).

21. Participants at a Berkeley conference on transnational cultural flows presented interesting preliminary evidence of these flows and their effects. For instance, the "Korean wave" of popular culture appears to have led to some improvement in Korea's image in Taiwan (Sang-yeon 2007).

22. Shambaugh (2005:2) is blunt: China has no values, models, or ideologies to export.

23. Ramos, Joshua Cooper. 2005. Interview at CCTV. March 23. http://www.cctv.com/program/e_dialogue/20050323/100736.shtml. See also Cui (2008).

24. With more careful comparative research, we may well find that the peak of China's ideological attractiveness was the 1960s, when the Maoist model of revolution and revolutionary development inspired movements and countries in many parts of the developing world out of reach of traditional tools of Chinese state power, and helped convince the United States to commit to a long and costly war in Vietnam.

25. An effect magnified by earlier industrialized economies' rates of global resource consumption.

26. We thank Steve Chan for this point.

27. For a possible testable framework in using power transition theory, see DiCicco and Levy (1999).
28. Respondents in the Beijing Area Study, for instance, have consistently evaluated both the Chinese state and people as peaceloving, sincere, civilized, and modest.

References

Barma, Naazneen and Ely Ratner. 2006. China's Illiberal Challenge. *Democracy: A Journal of Ideas* 2 (Fall): 56–68.

Begin, Priscilla. 2007. *The Power of Appeal of the People's Republic of China: Soft Power with Chinese Characteristics.* Master's thesis. George Washington University.

Blair, Dennis. 2008. *China's Military Modernization on Land and Sea and in the Air and Space.* Paper presented at Aspen Institute's Tenth Conference on U.S.-China Relations. March 24–30.

Chan, Steve. 2008. *China, the U.S., and the Power Transition Theory.* London and New York: Routledge.

Christensen, Thomas J. 2001. Posing Problems without Catching Up: China's Rise and Challenges for U.S. Security Policy. *International Security* 25(4): 5–40.

Cliff, Roger, Mark Burles, Michael S. Chase, Derek Eaton, and Kevin L. Pollpeter. 2007. *Entering the Dragon's Lair: Chinese Antiaccess Strategies and Their Implications for the United States.* Santa Monica: RAND Corporation.

Cooper, Richard N. 2005. "Whither China?" *Japan Center for Economic Research Bulletin* September.

Copeland, Dale C. 2000. *The Origins of Major War: Hegemonic Rivalry and the Fear of Decline.* New York: Cornell University Press.

CRS (Congressional Research Service). 2008. *China's Foreign Policy and "Soft Power" in South America, Asia, and Africa.* Study for the Committee on Foreign Relations, U.S. Senate.

Cui Liru. 2008. The Absence of a Model. *China Security* 4(2): 9.

Deng, Yong and Fei-Ling Wang, eds. 2005. *China Rising: Power and Motivation in Chinese Foreign Policy.* Lanham, MD: Rowman & Littlefield.

DiCicco, Jonathan M. and Jack S. Levy. 1999. Power Shifts and Problem Shifts: The Evolution of the Power Transition Research Program. *Journal of Conflict Resolution* 43(6): 675–704.

Fishman, Ted C. 2005. *China, Inc.: How the Rise of the Next Superpower Challenges America and the World.* New York: Scribner.

Gill, Bates. 2007. *Rising Star: China's New Security Diplomacy.* Washington, DC: Brookings Institution Press.

Gilpin, Robert. 1981. *War and Change in World Politics.* Cambridge and New York: Cambridge University Press.

Goldstein, Avery. 2005. *Rising to the Challenge: China's Grand Strategy and International Security*. Palo Alto, CA: Stanford University Press.

Gries, Peter Hays. 2005. Nationalism and Chinese Foreign Policy. In *China Rising: Power and Motivation in Chinese Foreign Policy*, ed. Yong Deng and Fei-ling Wang. Lanham, MD: Rowman & Littlefield.

Hu Angang and Men Honghua. 2006. The Rising of Modern China: Comprehensive National Power and Grand Strategy. Tsinghua University: Center for China Studies. http://irchina.org/en/xueren/china/pdf/mhh3.pdf.

ITU (International Telecommunication Union). 2007. *World Information Society Report 2007*. Geneva: ITU. http://www.itu.int/osg/spu/publications/worldinformationsociety/2007/WISR07-chapter7.pdf.

Jacobson, Harold and Michael Oksenberg. 1990. *China's Participation in the IMF, World Bank, and GATT: Toward a Global Economic Order*. Ann Arbor, MI: University of Michigan Press.

Johnston, Alastair Iain. 2003. Is China a Status Quo Power. *International Security* 27(4): 5–56.

Johnston, Alastair Iain and Daniela Stockmann. 2006. Chinese Attitudes toward the United States and Americans. In *Anti-Americanisms in World Politic*, ed. Peter J. Katzenstein and Robert O. Keohane. Ithaca: Cornell University Press.

Kang, David C. 2007. *China Rising: Peace, Power, and Order in East Asia*. New York: Columbia University Press.

Keidel, Albert. 2008. *China's Economic Rise: Fact and Fiction*. Washington, DC: Carnegie Endowment for International Peace, Policy Brief No. 61.

Kennedy, Andrew. 2007. Dreams Undeferred: Mao, Nehru, and the Strategic Choices of Rising Powers. PhD diss. Harvard University.

Kupchan, Charles A., Emanuel Adler, Jean-Marc Coicaud, and Yuen Foong Khong. 2001. *Power in Transition: The Peaceful Change of International Order*. Tokyo: United Nations University Press.

Kurlantzick, Joshua. 2007. *Charm Offensive: How China's Soft Power Is Transforming the World*. New Haven: Yale University Press.

Lampton, David M. 2008. *The Three Faces of Chinese Power: Might, Money and Minds*. Berkeley: University of California Press.

Lemke, Douglas. 2003. Power Transition Theory and the Rise of China. *International Interactions* 29(4): 269–271.

Liebman, Alex. 2008. Rising Power and Expanding Interests: A Theory of Power Transition Wars. PhD diss., draft chapter. Harvard University.

Liu Yumei. 2007. Ruanshili yu zhongfei guanxi de fazhan (Soft Power and the Development of Chinese-African Relations). *Guoji Wenti Yanjiu* 3: 16–21.

Lynch, Daniel. 2006. *Rising China and Asian Democratization: Socialization to Global Culture in the Political Transformations of Thailand, China, & Taiwan*. Palo Alto, CA: Stanford University Press.

Men Honghua. 2007. Zhongguo ruanshili pinggu baogao (Report on the Analysis of China's Soft Power). *Guoji Guancha* 2–3.

Nye, Joseph S. Jr. 2006. Soft Power and European-American Affairs. In *Hard Power, Soft Power and the Future of Transatlantic Relations*, ed Thomas Ilgen. Hampshire, UK: Ashgate.

OECD (Organisation for Economic Cooperation and Development). 2007. *Compendium of Patent Statistics 2007.* Paris: OECD.

Organski, A.F.K. and Jacek Kugler. 1980. *The War Ledger.* Chicago: University of Chicago Press.

Ramos, Joshua Cooper. 2004. *The Beijing Consensus.* London: Foreign Policy Centre.

Rapkin, David and William R. Thompson. 2003. Power Transition, Challenge, and the (Re)Emergence of China. *International Interactions* 29(4): 315–342.

Huang Renwei. 2006. Daolun: Guoji tixi: quanqiu geju tiaozheng chongjian zhanlue dingwei (Introduction: Adjustments in the International Structure, Reconstruction Strategic Status). In *Zhongguo guoji diwei baogao* (2006 China's International Status Report), ed. Huang Renwei and Zhang Youwen. Beijing: Peoples.

Samuels, Richard J. 1992. The Myth of the Independent Intellectual. In *The Political Culture of Foreign Area Studies: Essays in Honor of Lucian W. Pye,* ed. Richard J. Samuels and Myron Weiner. Washington, DC: Pergammon-Brassey's.

Sang-yeon Sung. 2007. Constructing a New Image: Korean Popular Culture in Taiwan. Paper presented to the workshop on Catching the Wave: Connecting East Asia through Soft Power. UC Berkeley: Institute of East Asian Studies. October 5–6. http://ieas.berkeley.edu/events/pdf/2007.10.05_Sung.pdf.

Segal, Gerald. 1999. Does China Matter? *Foreign Affairs* 78(5): 24–36.

Shambaugh, David, ed. 2005. *Power Shift: China and Asia's New Dynamics.* Berkeley: University of California Press.

Shirk, Susan L. 2008. *Fragile Superpower.* New York and Oxford: Oxford University Press.

Sullivan, Michael J. 1999. Developmentalism and China's Human Rights Policy. In *Debating Human Rights: Critical Essays from the United States and Asia,* ed. Peter Van Ness. London: Routledge.

Taylor Fravel, M. 2005. Regime Insecurity and International Cooperation: Explaining China's Compromises in Territorial Disputes. *International Security* 30(2): 46–83.

Vasquez, John. 1993. *The War Puzzle.* Cambridge and New York: Cambridge University Press.

Wang Yiwei. 2008. Zhongguo chenggong bushi yu bie guo zheng gao di (China's Successes Are Not a Struggle with Other States for Who Is on Top and Who Is Below). *Huanqiu Shibao* (Global Times), February 28. http://column.huanqiu.com/wangyiwei/2008-02/66452.html.

Whitney, Christopher and David Shambaugh. 2008. *Soft Power in Asia: Results of a Multinational Survey of Public Opinion.* Chicago Council on Global Affairs and East Asia Institute.

Williamson, John. 2002. *Did the Washington Consensus Fail.* Speech at the Center for Strategic and International Studies, Washington, DC. November 6.

Woosang Kim. 1989. Power, Alliance, and Major Power War, 1816–1975. *Journal of Conflict Resolution* 33(2): 255–273.

World Bank. 2008. *China Quarterly Update.* Beijing: World Bank. February.

Wuthnow, Joel. 2008. The Concept of Soft Power in China's Strategic Discourse. *Issues and Studies* 44: 2.

Xiaolin Guo. 2008. *Repackaging Confucius: PRC Diplomacy and the Rise of Soft Power*. Stockholm: Institute for Security and Development Policy.

Yan Xuetong. 2006. The Rise of China and Its Power Status. Tsinghua University: Institute of International Studies. http://www.irchina.org/en/pdf/yxt06.pdf.

Yan Xuetong and Xu Jin. 2008. Zhongmei ruanshili bijiao (A Comparison of Chinese and American Soft Power). *Xiandai Guoji Guanxi* 1: 24–29.

Zhang Yiping. 2006. Ruanshili de neihan yu waiyan (Soft Power's Connotations and Denotations). *Xiandai Guoji Guanxi* 11: 56–61.

Zhang Youwen and Huang Renwei, eds. 2006. *2006 Zhongguo Guoji Diwei Baogao* (China International Status Report 2006). Beijing: Peoples.

Zheng Yongnian and Zhang Chi. 2007. Guoji zhengzhi zhong de ruanliliang yiji dui Zhongguo ruanliliang de guancha (Soft Power in International Politics and Observations on China's Soft Power). *Shijie jingji yu zhengzhi yanjiu* 7: 6–12.

Index